Anti-Bias Curriculum

Tools for EMPOWERING Young Children

Louise Derman-Sparks and the A.B.C. Task Force

National Association for the Education of Young Children
Washington, D.C.

To BRAD CHAMBERS
whose lifework inspired and guided

Bradford Chambers, the founder and long-time head of the Council on Interracial Books for Children in New York City, was the spark that ignited the process that culminated in this book.

Photo Credits: Cover (from top to bottom and left to right)—Candice Logue, Nancy P. Alexander, © 1989 Jim Bradshaw, Rose C. Engel, © 1989 Robert Hill, © 1989 Hildegard Adler, © Harvey R. Phillips, Marilyn Nolt, and Barbara Brockmann; p. 1—Marilyn Nolt; p. 10—© 1989 Jeffrey High; p. 14—Subjects & Predicates; p. 20—Nancy P. Alexander; p. 30—David S. Strickler; p. 39—Nancy P. Alexander; p. 49—Subjects & Predicates; p. 52—Subjects & Predicates; p. 56—© 1989 Jim Bradshaw; p. 68—Subjects & Predicates; p. 75—Subjects & Predicates; p. 77—© 1988 Cheryl Namkung; p. 85—© 1988 Esther Mugar; p. 96—Francis Wardle; p. 111—Monica Paterson.

The segment of Chapter 2 entitled "Using Old Materials in New Ways: Storytelling With Persona Dolls" and the appendix "Sample Persona Doll Story" are by Kay Taus. Chapter Three, "Beginnings: Working With 2-Year-Olds," is by María Gutiérrez and Louise Derman-Sparks.

National Association for the Education of Young Children
1509 16th Street, NW
Washington, DC 20036-1426
202-232-8777 or 800-424-2460
Website: www.naeyc.org
e-mail: naeyc@naeyc.org

Through its publications program the National Association for the Education of Young Children (NAEYC) provides a forum for discussion of major issues and ideas in the early childhood field, with the hope of provoking thought and promoting professional growth. The views expressed or implied are not necessarily those of the Association. NAEYC thanks the editor and authors, who donated much time and effort to develop this book as a contribution to the profession.

Library of Congress Catalog Number: 88–63731

ISBN: 0–935989–20–X

NAEYC #242

Editor: Polly Greenberg
Book design and production: Jack Zibulsky

Printed in the United States of America

Louise Derman-Sparks, a faculty member of Pacific Oaks College, has worked for 25 years with the many-faceted issues of diversity and social justice as a teacher of children and adults, child care center director, researcher, parent, and activist. Her experience includes the Ypsilanti Perry Preschool Project and the Piagetian-based Early Childhood Program. At Pacific Oaks, Louise teaches about the social-political contexts of human development and the impact of biases on education. She conducts in-services and workshops with early childhood educators across the country.

This book represents the work of a task force of early childhood educators—Black, Latina, White; female and male; teachers of children 2 through 5 with a variety of racial/ethnic and class backgrounds and physical abilities—from Pasadena and Los Angeles, California. Dissatisfied with current curricula for helping children learn about diversity, the task force worked together for two years to conceptualize and implement the anti-bias curriculum written and shaped into book form by Louise Derman-Sparks and presented here.

ReGena Booze, an activist and teacher in the African-American community for 15 years and a member of a strong family of liberators, is currently a Master Teacher in the preschool at Pacific Oaks. She has taught children 2 through 5 years old, and works with parents and adults in workshops and college courses.

Cory Gann has most recently been teaching in a bilingual kindergarten in the Los Angeles Unified School District. As a Master Teacher in Pacific Oaks Preschool, Cory's work with children, parents, and college students specialized in socialization and social issues. He has long pursued an interest in how men develop as nurturers and in nurturing professions.

Cheryl Greer, M.A., is on the faculty of Pacific Oaks College and a Master Teacher in the Children's School. She has presented at state and national conferences, including NAEYC's Annual Conference.

María Gutiérrez is the Master Teacher for 2-year-olds at Pacific Oaks College, where she has worked for 10 years. She has taught classes on parenting and anti-bias issues for Head Start and other private agencies. She has a master's degree in Human Development from Pacific Oaks.

Francois Polifroni is a kindergarten teacher in the San Gabriel School District, California. Previously, he was Head Teacher at the Pacific Oaks Child Care Center. "The hardest aspect of an anti-bias curriculum is being open with others about my own bias. When I can do that, I open the door for my children to do the same."

Lissa Peterson Samuel is Director of Child Care at California Pediatric Center and was Assistant Director of Child Care at Pacific Oaks College. Her national and local conference presentations have specifically focused on anti-bias attitudes in working with families and curriculum planning.

Mary (Molly) E.D. Scudder was a Master Teacher at Pacific Oaks Children's School from 1965 to 1985. She currently is curriculum resource person for special needs children there. A frequent presenter for NAEYC, Molly has addressed anti-bias issues with children for over 25 years.

Marjorie Shore expanded child and adult awareness through books while serving as Head Librarian of Pacific Oaks College and Children's School; at University Elementary School at UCLA; and at schools in Beverly Hills, California, Oregon, and Hawaii.

Bill Sparks is a Mentor Teacher in Los Angeles, where he teaches children with learning disabilities at 36th Street School. Experience includes day care, preschool children with physical disabilities, inservice teacher training, and college teaching at Pacific Oaks, CSULA, and UCLA.

Sharon R. Stine, Dean of Children's Programs at Pacific Oaks College from 1980–1986, received her doctorate in Human Development in 1979, and currently consults in the area of environmental design.

Kay Taus teaches at Seeds University Elementary School (UCLA) and directs the Extended Day Program. An activist with parents and children for 20 years, she previously taught in Head Start and, with parents, organized a community-based child care center. Kay is fluent in American Sign Language.

Mae Varon taught early childhood education for 35 years. In her work with children, parents, and college students, she sought to teach ways of treating all people with respect and dignity. She is mother of four daughters, all teachers, and grandmother of two.

CONTENTS

ACKNOWLEDGMENTS

I am indebted to the members of the Anti-Bias Curriculum Task Force, who collectively made this book possible, and to the children of Pacific Oaks Children's School, Sophia Salvin Special Education Center, and Corrine Seeds Elementary School who taught the grown-ups and gave life to our ideas. Special thanks to David Rover, former Director of Burgess House, Pacific Oaks child care center. I am also grateful to Susan Freeman, Mary Beth Lakin, Rachel Moore, Susie North, Kathy Rinden, Carol Standel, Tamara Trotten, Cindy Kulberg, and Mohammed Dezgaran, who gathered data and contributed curriculum ideas, to Kim Sakamoto for her support, to Jacki Breger for her music curriculum and insights, and to Susanne Dame, who made a significant contribution to the curriculum about Native Americans.

To the colleagues who generously read and critiqued early drafts of the manuscript, heartfelt thanks. Rayko Hasimoto and Lyla Hoffman carefully went through every page with a fine-toothed comb and offered invaluable content and organizational feedback. Elizabeth Prescott's incisive questions helped transform the manuscript into a coherent book. Betty Jones, Dale Weiss, John Nimmo, Susan Freeman, Noreen Winkler, Witt Hayslip, and Carol Cole made important suggestions. Randy Fishfader provided advice and a nurturing haven in which to work at a crucial editing stage. Shelly Stratton did the exacting work of putting together the bibliography of children's and adult books and resources, with assistance from Dottie Granger, Pacific Oaks Librarian.

Over the years, many people have made significant contributions to the evolution of my thinking about anti-bias education and I am beholden to them all. The pioneering work of the Council on Interracial Books for Children sharpened my consciousness. The extraordinary tutelage of Brad Chambers and Lyla Hoffman, founders and long-time staff members of the Council, gave me the tools and confidence to develop new practice. Past and present colleagues at Pacific Oaks College have stimulated, challenged, and stretched my perspective and practice. Special thanks go to Carol Brunson Phillips with whom this all began, and with whom I learned the essential lessons about antiracism work. Deep appreciation goes to Antonia Darder, who continues my education through struggle and love. Many thanks also go to Edward Greene, Ruth Pearce, Barbara Richardson, Karen Fite, Nikola Trumbo, and Yolanda Torres, and to Ruth Beaglehole and the late Geraldine Wilson, colleagues in early childhood education. Finally, the numerous early childhood people who extended invitations to talk about the anti-bias curriculum at conferences and in-services provided the opportunities for feedback that enriched my awareness of issues in various parts of the country.

I am grateful to the California Community Fund for their financial support of the anti-bias curriculum project and to Barbara Martin, who obtained the grant and gave gentle encouragement throughout the project. Laila Aaen, Dean of Pacific Oaks College, helped keep me on track during the writing. The Mattel Company provided funding to cover the costs of preparing various drafts of the manuscript.

My deep appreciation goes to Julie DeKoning, who cheerfully and patiently deciphered illegible handwriting and countless letter reversals to type the manuscript drafts, and to Shelagh Mullings, who not only elegantly typed the final draft, but was also always there to meet deadlines and shore up lagging spirits.

Polly Greenberg, publications director at NAEYC, provided just the right blend of challenge and support, criticism and assistance to enable me to persist in the task of pruning and fine-tuning a final version of the manuscript.

Finally, I am thankful to the special people in my personal life who contributed in great measure to making this book possible: To Al and Ann Robbins for first teaching me to care about injustice and work for a more humane world; to Crickett Potash, Bob Gottlieb, and Marge Pearson for their unstinting friendship and understanding; to Ruth Kupers for always believing in me; to Douglass and Holly Sparks for their generous and loving willingness to share my time and attention with this book. Last, but definitely not least, boundless appreciation to Bill Sparks, who was always there to listen and whose love, steadfastness, and willingness to take on more than his share of household duties gave me the freedom to write.

INTRODUCTION

Children are aware very young that color, language, gender, and physical ability differences are connected with privilege and power. They learn by observing the differences and similarities among people and by absorbing the spoken and unspoken messages about those differences. Racism, sexism, and handicappism have a profound influence on their developing sense of self and others.

A 4-year-old boy, wanting to take over the wheel of a pretend bus, tells the child already there, "Girls can't be bus drivers."

"Ann can't play with us. She's a baby," a 3-year-old tells her teacher. Ann, 4 years old, uses a wheelchair.

A 2½-year-old Asian child refuses to hold the hand of a Black classmate. "It's dirty," he insists. At home, after bathing, he tells his mother, "Now my hair is white because it is clean."

Two 5-year-old White boys are playing in the sandbox. A Vietnamese boy asks to join them. "Nah, nah, you can't play with us, you Chinese," they chorus, pulling their eyes into a slant.

All children are harmed. On the one hand, struggling against bias that declares a person inferior because of gender, race, ethnicity, or disability sucks energy from and undercuts a child's full development. On the other hand, learning to believe they are superior because they are White, or male, or able-bodied, dehumanizes and distorts reality for growing children, even while they may be receiving the benefits of institutional privilege.

Although there is a great deal more to know about how children "go about forming the intricate maze of knowledge and values" (Phillips, 1987, p. 5) that result in self-identity and attitudes, we know enough not to underestimate the power of children to perceive the negative messages in their world or the power of those messages to harm them. It is too dangerous for early childhood educators to take an "ostrich-in-the-sand" stance. As Carol Brunson Phillips (1987) points out,

> It has been said that actions more often than not speak louder than words. And if this is so in the case of child-rearing, then we must be especially vigilant in our actions to shape the values children will attach as they learn about the people in their world. If we don't, they will learn by default the messages that are already prevalent out there and both we and they will contribute to perpetuating past ideas which we do not want to replicate in our children's future. (pp. 5–6)

Young children **can** begin the journey toward anti-bias identity and attitudes. Listen to the voices of four children who are participating in anti-bias curriculum:

A kindergarten teacher shows the children a magazine picture entitled "Brides of America." All of the women pictured are White. She asks, "What do you think of this picture?" Sophia responds, "That's a silly picture. My mom was a bride, and she's Mexican."

One morning 4½-year-old April arrives at the child care center hiding a stereotypic "Indian Warrior" figure. Kiyoshi, another 4½-year-old, says to her, "Don't let Suzanne see that. It will hurt her feelings." Suzanne, a staff member, is Cherokee-Cree.

Donald, 4½, playing at home with his Lego™ set, says to his mother, "You know, all of the Lego people in this set are White people. Why?"

After hearing the story of Rosa Parks and the Montgomery bus boycott and role playing the bus sequence, 5-year-old Karen turns to her friend Tiffany and exclaims, her voice expressing both indignation and wonderment, "Tiffany, you wouldn't be able to sit next to me. I don't like that at all!"

Tiffany, whose skin is light brown, ponders whether she would have had to sit in the back of the bus. Is her skin dark enough? Finally, Tiffany firmly asserts, "I'm Black, and anyway all this is stupid. Everyone should sit wherever they want to. I would just get off the bus and tell them to keep their old bus."

Sophia, Kiyoshi, Donald, Karen, and Tiffany are learning to think critically and to speak up when they believe something is unfair. They are becoming empowered. They are participating in "the practice of freedom; the means by which men and women deal critically and creatively with reality and discover how to participate in the transformation of their world" (Freire, 1970, p. 15).

The "practice of freedom" is fundamental to anti-bias education. Curriculum goals are to enable every child: to construct a knowledgeable, confident self-identity; to develop comfortable, empathetic, and just interaction with diversity; and to develop critical thinking and the skills for standing up for oneself and others in the face of injustice.

The specific tasks for achieving these goals vary

according to how each child is affected by the prevailing bias in U.S. society. Empowerment for children of color requires that they develop both a strong self-identity and a proud and knowledgeable group identity to withstand the attacks of racism. In contrast, White children's task is to develop a positive identity without White ethnocentricism and superiority. Girls need to learn that they can be competent in all areas and can make choices about their lives. Boys need to learn competence without also learning to feel and act superior to girls. The developmental tasks of children with disabilities include learning to use alternative abilities and to gain skills for countering societal practices that sabotage their opportunities for growth. Able-bodied children's tasks include learning ease with differently abled people and how to resist stereotyping.

Anti-bias curriculum embraces an educational philosophy as well as specific techniques and content. It is value based: Differences are good; oppressive ideas and behaviors are not. It sets up a creative tension between respecting differences and not accepting unfair beliefs and acts. It asks teachers and children to confront troublesome issues rather than covering them up. An anti-bias perspective is integral to all aspects of daily classroom life.

Anti-Bias Curriculum: Tools For Empowering Young Children is not a recipe book. Using its principles and methodology, teachers (and parents who choose to use the book) must recreate anti-bias curriculum in their setting in relation to specific groups of children and families. Therefore, developmental information about children, illustrated by their comments, questions, and behavior, supplements suggested activities so that the teacher can understand the "why" as well as the "what" and "how" of the activities.

It is not always easy to implement anti-bias curriculum on a regular basis, whenever the appropriate moment pops up. Few early childhood educators have been prepared to talk with children about race, ethnicity, and disabilities. The situation is similar to the discomfort adults felt in the past when responding to the question "Where do babies come from?" Now many more early childhood teachers know how to address that question.

Like children, grown-ups must learn by doing: by making mistakes, and thinking about it, and trying again. Anti-bias teaching requires critical thinking and problem solving by both children and adults. And, because at heart anti-bias curriculum is about social change, it may meet with resistance —from other teachers, from parents, from administrators—and from one's own ambivalences and discomforts. Nevertheless, it is worth the hard work. Through anti-bias curriculum, teachers enable every child to achieve the ultimate goal of early childhood education: the development of each child to her or his fullest potential.

References

Freire, P. (1970). *Pedagogy of the oppressed.* New York: The Seabury Press.

Phillips, C. B. (1987). Foreword. In B. Neugebauer (Ed.), *Alike and different: Exploring our humanity with young children* (pp. 5–6). Redmond, WA: Exchange Press.

WHY AN ANTI-BIAS CURRICULUM?

Children's Identity and Attitudes

"Why can't we just let children be? Children don't know anything about prejudice or stereotypes. They don't notice what color a person is. If we just leave them alone and let them play with each other, then everything will be fine," argue many parents and early childhood teachers. Many adults assume that children are unaffected by the biases in U.S. society. Nevertheless, what we know about children's identity and attitude development challenges this comfortable assumption.

Research data reveal that

- children begin to notice differences and construct classificatory and evaluative categories very early;
- there are overlapping but distinguishable developmental tasks and steps in the construction of identity and attitudes; and
- societal stereotyping and bias influence children's self-concept and attitudes toward others.

Data about how young children first develop awareness about different physical abilities are still sparse, but do suggest that the same three points apply. Awareness of other types of disabilities seems to appear later than the preschool years (Levitt & Cohen, 1976).

Children construct their identity and attitudes through the interaction of three factors:

- experience with their bodies,
- experience with their social environments, and
- their cognitive developmental stage.

Thus, their growing ideas and feelings are not simply direct reflections either of cultural patterns or of innate, biological structures.

Phyllis Katz, writing about racial awareness, suggests that from 2 through 5 or 6, children (1) make early observations of racial cues; (2) form rudimentary concepts; (3) engage in conceptual differentiation; (4) recognize the irrevocability of cues (cues remain constant—skin color will not change); (5) consolidate group concepts; and (6) elaborate group concepts. Evaluative judgments begin to influence this process at step 2 (Katz, 1982). Kohlberg's (1966) stages of gender identity development suggest a similar developmental sequence to Katz. Alejandro-Wright (1985) also finds that racial awareness begins in the preschool years, but cautions that full understanding occurs much later (age 10 or 11). She states that "knowledge of racial classification evolves from a vague, undifferentiated awareness of skin color differences to knowledge of the cluster of physical-biological attributes associated with racial membership and eventually to a social understanding of racial categorization" (p. 186).

Even toddlers are aware . . .

Let's look briefly at what these developmental patterns mean. During their third year of life, children begin to notice gender and racial differences. They may also begin noticing physical disabilities, although so far indications are that this may begin a year or two later. By 2 years of age, children are learning the appropriate use of gender labels (girl, boy) and learning color names, which they begin to apply to skin color.

By 3 years of age (and sometimes even earlier), children show signs of being influenced by societal norms and biases and may exhibit "pre-prejudice" toward others on the basis of gender or race or being differently abled.

Between 3 and 5 years of age, children try to figure out what are the essential attributes of their selfhood, what aspects of self remain constant. They wonder:

Will I always be a girl or a boy?

If I like to climb trees, do I become a boy?

If I like to play with dolls, do I become a girl?

What gives me my skin color?

Can I change it?

If I interact with a child who has a physical disability, will I get it?

Will I always need a prosthesis in place of my arm?

During this time, children need a lot of help sorting through the many experiences and variables of identity as they journey the path to self-awareness.

By 4 or 5 years of age, children not only engage in gender-appropriate behavior defined by socially prevailing norms, they also reinforce it among themselves without adult intervention (Honig, 1983; Roopnarine, 1984). They use racial reasons for refusing to interact with children different from themselves and exhibit discomfort and rejection of differently abled people. The degree to which 4-year-olds have already internalized stereotypic gender roles, racial bias, and fear of the differently abled forcefully points out the need for anti-bias education with young children.

Do we know what we are teaching?

How adults teach children to conform to societal norms and biases, sometimes without intention or awareness of how they are acting, is also documented through many ingenious studies. In one study, done in 1982, observations and teacher-directed interviews in more than a dozen mainstream and special education early childhood classrooms in California, North Carolina, Illinois, and New York revealed not a single classroom with images of differently abled people (Froschl & Sprung, 1983). In an observational study of 158 children ages 2½ to 5 years, in preschools, girls and children with disabilities were particularly likely to experience "over-help" and "over-praise" from teachers. The researcher concluded that differently abled children and girls in general are trained for dependence and passivity, not for independence:

If a three-year-old boy and girl are getting ready to go out to play and are attempting to put on jackets, the girl is more likely to receive help. If both receive help, the girl will probably have her jacket put on for her, the boy will be shown a technique for putting it on himself. If the same situation arises and one child is disabled, it is the disabled child who will have the jacket put on, whether a girl or a boy. This is the beginning of the syndrome of "learned helplessness." (Froschl & Sprung, 1983, p. 21).

Studies also reveal that teachers praise young girls mainly for appearance, cooperation, and ob-dience while praising young boys mainly for achievement. Teachers tend to describe boys as more active than girls, even in cases where research instruments showed similar levels of activity (Hoffman, 1983).

Homophobia, the fear and hatred of gay men and lesbians, is another form of gender bias adults teach young children. As Letty Cottin Pogrebin, author of *Growing Up Free: Raising Your Child in the 80's*, points out:

Before children have the vaguest ideas about who or what is a homosexual, they learn that homosex-

Some Definitions of Terms

Anti-bias: An active/activist approach to challenging prejudice, stereotyping, bias, and the "isms." In a society in which institutional structures create and maintain sexism, racism, and handicappism, it is not sufficient to be non-biased (and also highly unlikely), nor is it sufficient to be an observer. It is necessary for each individual to actively intervene, to challenge and counter the personal and institutional behaviors that perpetuate oppression.

Bias: Any attitude, belief, or feeling that results in, and helps to justify, unfair treatment of an individual because of his or her identity.

Handicappism: Any attitude, action, or institutional practice that subordinates people due to their disability. Handicappist institutional practices prevent the integration of disabled people into the mainstream of society and keep them socially and economically oppressed.**

Homophobia: A fear and hatred of gay men and lesbians backed up by institutional policies and power that discriminate against them.**

People of color: All the different national or ethnic groups that are targets of racism in the U.S. This includes: Asian-Pacific Americans, Black Americans, Latino and Puerto Rican Americans, Native Americans. Use of the inclusive term is not intended to deny the significant cultural and historical differences among these groups.

Prejudice: An attitude, opinion, or feeling formed without adequate prior knowledge, thought, or reason. Prejudice can be prejudgment for or against any person, group, or sex.*

Pre-prejudice: Beginning ideas and feelings in very young children that may develop into real prejudice through reinforcement by prevailing societal biases. Pre-prejudice may be misconceptions based on young children's limited experience and developmental level, or it may consist of imitations of adult behavior. More serious forms are behaviors that indicate discomfort, fear, or rejection of differences.

Racism: Any attitude, action, or institutional practice backed up by institutional power that subordinates people because of their color. This includes the imposition of one ethnic group's culture in such a way as to withhold respect for, to demean, or to destroy the cultures of other races.*

Sexism: Any attitude, action, or institutional practice backed up by institutional power that subordinates people because of their sex.*

Stereotype: An oversimplified generalization about a particular group, race, or sex, which usually carries derogatory implication.

Whites: All the different national ethnic groups of European origin who as a group are disproportionately represented in the control of the economic, political, and cultural institutions in the United States.

* From *Guidelines for Selecting Bias-Free Textbooks and Storybooks* (CIBC, 1980).
** From *Homophobia and Education* (CIBC, 1983).

uality is something frightening, horrid and nasty. They become homophobic long before they understand what it is they fear. They learn that "what are you, a sissy?" is the fastest way to coerce boys into self-destructive exploits. (Pogrebin, 1980, p. 12)

Moreover, homophobic attitudes and misconceptions about homosexuality also interfere with opening up nonsexist play options for young children when teachers and parents accept the false assumption that what a child does determines his or her sexual orientation.

Lessons about the value of racial identity also occur repeatedly. Just speaking English teaches differential values for whiteness and blackness. The dictionary lists 44 positive meanings for whiteness, while blackness has 60 negative ones (Hoffman, 1983). One pervasive example is the equation of white with cleanliness and black with dirt. Think of the popular children's book *Harry the Dirty Dog* (Zion, 1956). A white dog falls into a coal bin and becomes all black, i.e., dirty. His family doesn't recognize him until he gets washed and then reemerges as the dog they love—white.

Young children are harmed by the impact of sexism, racism, and handicappism on their development. Gender stereotyping closes off whole areas of experience to children simply because of their sex. Consequently, neither boys nor girls are fully prepared to deal intellectually or emotionally with the realities and demands of present life. Handicappism severely harms differently abled children by limiting access to the educational experiences necessary for well-rounded development and by interfering with the establishment of a proud self-concept. Able-bodied children are also harmed because handicappism prevents them from understanding and comfortably interacting with the full range of human variability and teaches a false and anxiety-producing sense of superiority based on their not being "disabled."

Research exists

Research about the impact of racism on children's identity development exposes the damage it inflicts on both White children and children of color. Most of the studies about children of color have focused on Black children. After reviewing these studies, Cross (1985) argues that to understand Black children's identity development, it is necessary to distinguish between personal identity and reference group orientation. The first category includes self-concept factors such as self-esteem, self-confidence, and self-evaluation. The second category includes factors such as racial identity and awareness, race esteem, and racial ideology. Using his two categories to analyze the research results of studies on Black children's self-concept, Cross concludes that (1) most studies actually looked at reference group orientation and not personal identity; (2) Black children's personal identity is equal to or surpasses White children's; (3) Black children's reference group orientation comes out low in many of the studies; and (4) low reference group orientation impedes Black children's ability to withstand and challenge the damaging impact of racism on their life experiences (Cross, 1985).

Low reference group orientation is a product of young Black children's (and other children of color's) experiences in the dominant culture, in which schooling plays a major role. In addition, Black and other children of color are disproportionately faced from an early age with the risks of poor housing, inadequate health care, poverty, and family unemployment. Given these realities, a number of Black writers conclude that Black children need to develop an extended self-identity (Semaj, 1985) that includes a strong group identity as well as an individual identity. Race consciousness and pride, or, in Cross's words, high reference group orientation, provide a foundation for the resilience and coping strategies necessary for resisting racism (Cross, 1985). Studies on children of color from other groups are fewer in number; however, some also suggest that all children in a political and cultural "minority" status in our society need to construct a strong group identity for healthy development (Beuf, 1977; Gutierrez, 1982; Levine & Ruiz, 1978; Milner, 1983).

Only a handful of studies have been done about White children. Those that do exist agree that racism damages White children intellectually and psychologically. Bernard Kutner (1985) found that racial prejudice in young children affects their ability to reason and distorts their judgment and perception of reality. Kenneth Clark (1955) identified the disturbing moral hypocrisy and double messages White children are taught about racial equality. Alice Miel (1976) also found that White children "learn to be hypocritical about differences at a very early age. The prejudices of their society were still very much with them, but they had it drilled into them that it was 'not nice' to *express* such feelings" (p. 13).

What is our responsibility?

Early childhood educators have a serious responsibility to find ways to prevent and counter the damage before it becomes too deep. Selma Greenberg (1980) forcefully argues for active intervention to remedy the cognitive, social-emotional, and physical deficits brought about by constraining gender stereotypes that limit growing children's access to specific areas of experience:

> When they enter an early childhood environment, children are more open to friendships with members of the other sex, and more open to non-stereotypic play experiences than they are when they leave. Clearly, while the early childhood environment cannot be held solely responsible for this biased development, it cannot be held totally guiltless either. (p. 5)

Greenberg suggests that early childhood teachers reevaluate existing early childhood curriculum and develop ways to prevent and remediate the developmental deficiencies created by gender stereotyping.

Other researchers also conclude that active intervention by teachers is necessary if children are to develop positive attitudes about people of different races and physical abilities. Contact with children of various backgrounds is *not* enough. For example, Cohen (1977) states that "in the absence of a variety of supports, direct contact can exacerbate mildly negative reactions" (p. 8). Moreover, Sapon-Shevin (1983) finds that "interventions not handling the direct confrontation of difference seem doomed, or do little more than bring temporary changes in the patterns of social interaction and acceptance within integrated groups." Consequently, "mainstreaming should not be viewed as an effort to teach children to minimize or ignore difference, but as an effort to teach them *positive, appropriate* response to these differences" (p. 24).

Goodman's (1964) research about young children's racial attitudes adds further substantiation to the position that direct contact is not enough. She documented numerous examples of biased behavior and feelings as she watched children play "freely" with each other in interracial, "nonbiased" preschool programs. Emihovich (1980), looking at children's social relationships in two integrated kindergartens, found that structure and teaching methodology significantly affected the amount and quality of children's interracial peer interaction. Even though both teachers espoused pro-integration attitudes, interracial interaction was high and positive in one classroom but low and negative in the other.

In sum, if children are to grow up with the attitudes, knowledge, and skills necessary for effective living in a complex, diverse world, early childhood programs must actively challenge the impact of bias on children's development.

Empowerment

Along with the data about children's identity and attitude development, the notion of empowerment —of people having the intellectual and emotional ability to confront oppression and work together to create a more just society— had a strong influence on conceptualizing anti-bias curriculum goals and methodology. Many educators and activists in the United States and elsewhere have devoted their lives to developing forms of education for empowerment and self-determination. In the United States there is a long, continuing tradition, although often unknown to many early childhood educators, of freedom and community schools organized by educator/activists of color and a few antiracist Whites, with the goal of empowerment for children of color. These schools are run, wholly or in large part, by people of color, preferably by the children's parents and others in their community. Curriculum stresses a reclaiming of the history, culture, and identity stolen by racism, and pushed aside by academic skills.

One of the largest and best known examples of this approach in the United States was the Child Development Group of Mississippi, 1965–67, in which 1,100 poor Blacks provided full-day, year-round Head Start for 18,000 four- to 6-year-olds. In

The Devil Has Slippery Shoes (1969), Polly Greenberg describes the work of this project. Other well-known examples include the work of Sylvia Ashton-Warner (1963) in New Zealand, and of Paulo Freire, the author of *Pedagogy of the Oppressed* (1970) and *Education for Critical Consciousness* (1981).

A second direction taken by researchers and educators within the empowerment tradition is biculturalism. A new and growing body of research, based on the assumption that cultural differences are real but do not constitute deficits, has opened up whole new vistas for understanding how development and learning occur within sociocultural contexts (Baratz & Baratz, 1970; Cohen, 1969; Hale-Benson, 1986; Hilliard, 1977; Labov, 1975; Ramirez & Castaneda,

1974). The work of these pioneers paved the way for fostering bicultural, bicognitive development in early childhood programs.

Bicultural, bicognitive education means children (1) learn the beliefs, values, rules, and language of their own culture in the learning/teaching style appropriate to their culture and also (2) learn the beliefs, values, rules, language, and learning style of the dominant culture.

The ideal early childhood program would incorporate both an anti-bias approach as described in this book and, where appropriate, bicultural, bicognitive curriculum. (See Resources, pp. 137–140 for readings.)

Common Questions and Answers About Anti-Bias Curriculum

Won't an anti-bias curriculum make things worse? "If you point out differences, won't children start seeing differences they haven't been noticing?" "If you talk about stereotypes, won't you be teaching them things they would otherwise not learn?" "Isn't it better to emphasize the positive than the negative (how we are different)?"

Concern about addressing differences arises from a mistaken notion of the sources of bias. *It is not differences in themselves that cause the problems, but how people respond to differences.* It is the *response* to difference that anti-bias curriculum addresses. If teachers and parents don't talk about differences, as well as similarities, then they can't talk about cultural heritages, or about the struggles of groups and individuals to gain equality and justice. For example, if teachers don't talk about differences in physical ability, children can't figure out ways to modify the environment so that the differently abled child can be as independent as possible. Similarly, celebrating Martin Luther King, Jr.'s birthday means little unless teachers talk about his role in organizing millions of people to challenge racism.

The question "Won't an anti-bias curriculum make things worse?" comes out of a "colorblind" or "color-denial" philosophy of how to deal with racial differences. This attitude assumes that differences are insignificant and is exemplified in statements such as "We are all the same" and "A child is

a child. I don't notice if they are brown, purple, or green." Child development research is frequently based on a colorblind position and therefore makes the serious error of assuming that the issues of development are the same for all children and that they all share similar contexts for growth.

Colorblindness arose as a progressive argument against racial bigotry, which ranks racial differences, putting "White" on top. However well-intentioned, this is not an adequate response to children's development realities. It has been a soothing view for Whites, while blatantly ignoring the daily experience of people of color. It establishes the White experience as the norm, and the differences in others' experience become unimportant. It promotes tokenism and a denial of the identity of persons outside the mainstream. Within it, curriculum need not address the fact of diversity nor the specifics of a child's identity. Paradoxically, however, people espousing a colorblind position do often recognize the need to bring children of diverse backgrounds together so that, by playing with each other, they can discover that "we are all the same."

"I don't like Indians. They shoot bows and arrows at people and burn their houses," a 4-year-old informs his class after a visit to Disneyland. "Oh, those aren't real Indians," explains his White teacher. "Real Indians are nice people. They live in houses and wear clothes just like us."

The teacher obviously means well. But, does the "colorblind" teacher's explanation mean that Native Americans who don't live "just like us" (i.e., "just like Whites") are *not* nice people?

Ultimately, the colorblind position results in denial of young children's awareness of differences and to nonconfrontation of children's misconceptions, stereotypes, and discriminatory behaviors, be they about race, culture, gender, or different physical abilities. Many caring parents and early childhood teachers make mistakes of this kind. In contrast, an anti-bias approach teaches children to understand and comfortably interact with differences, to appreciate all people's similarities through the different ways they are human, and to recognize and confront ideas and behaviors that are biased.

In an environment in which children feel free to ask questions and make comments about disabilities, gender, and race, there will be an increase in adults' and children's interactions over issues of bias. Sometimes children will test the limits set by teachers or parents on unacceptable biased behavior. This does not mean that directly addressing bias is a mistake; it means that children understand that bias is an important issue and are testing to find out how clear and how firm the rules/limits are, as they do when adults set other types of behavioral boundaries.

How does anti-bias curriculum differ from multicultural curriculum? The approach of choice among early childhood professionals today is multiculturalism. Its intent is positive: Let's teach children about each other's cultures, so they will learn to respect each other and not develop prejudice. However, deterioration into *tourist curriculum* often keeps this approach from accomplishing its intent.

Tourist curriculum is likely to teach about cultures through celebrations and through such "artifacts" of the culture as food, traditional clothing, and household implements. Multicultural activities are special events in the children's week, separate from the ongoing daily curriculum. Thus, Chinese New Year is the activity that teaches about Chinese-Americans; a dragon is constructed, and parents are asked to come to school wearing "Chinese" clothing to cook a "Chinese" dish with the children, who have the opportunity on this one day to try eating with chopsticks. Mexican-American life is introduced through Cinco de Mayo, another celebration. Indeed, some multicultural curricula are written in the form of calendars, suggesting foods, crafts, and perhaps a dance to do on specific days. Paradoxically, the dominant, Anglo-European culture is not studied as such. Christmas is not perceived as an "ethnic" holiday coming from specific cultural perspectives, but is treated as a universal holiday.

Tourist curriculum is both patronizing, emphasizing the "exotic" differences between cultures, and trivializing, dealing not with the real-life daily problems and experiences of different peoples, but with surface aspects of their celebrations and modes of entertainment. Children "visit" non-White cultures and then "go home" to the daily classroom, which reflects only the dominant culture. The focus on holidays, although it provides drama and delight for both children and adults, gives the impression that that is all "other" people —usually people of color—do. What it fails to communicate is real understanding.

Ramsey (1982) highlights other problems that may characterize multicultural curriculum:

1. It frequently focuses on information about other countries—learning about Japan or Mexico—rather than learning about Japanese-Americans or exploring the diversity of culture among Mexican-Americans.

2. It may be standardized, with the assumption that there should or can be one set of goals and activities for all settings, ignoring the importance of taking into account the backgrounds of the children, their experience or lack of experience with people from other groups, and their attitudes toward their own and other groups.

3. Teachers may assume that children only need multicultural curriculum if there is diversity in the classroom. This seems to be an issue particularly for teachers in all-White classrooms, when, in fact, White children may be the most in need of learning about the differences that exist in American society.

Anti-bias curriculum incorporates the positive intent of multicultural curriculum and uses some similar activities, while seeking to avoid the dangers of a tourist approach. At the same time, anti-bias curriculum provides a more inclusive education: (a) It addresses more than cultural diversity by including gender and differences in physical abilities; (b) it is based on children's developmental tasks as they construct identity and attitudes; and (c) it directly addresses the impact of stereotyping, bias, and discriminatory behavior in young children's development and interactions.

Isn't an anti-bias approach really an adult issue? Why bring children into it? In one sense, anti-bias or bias is an adult issue: It is adults who have the power to create, to teach, to maintain bias. On the other hand, children are involved whether adults like it or not. Failure to address and challenge bias allows children to adopt the socially prevailing attitudes.

It is important, however, to be clear about what aspects of anti-bias work are appropriate for children, and what aspects are the appropriate arena for adults. Adults have a twofold responsibility: to provide children with anti-bias education and to try to eliminate bias in the institutions of our society. Sometimes individuals confuse the two tasks, assuming that working with young children is sufficient, thereby abdicating their responsibility as adult citizens to participate in their own chosen way in creating a more just society. Adults often use the valid issue of what are developmentally appropriate methods as an excuse—an excuse to mask their own discomfort about addressing anti-bias issues with children. In this sense, too, it is important to be very clear about adult problems and children's needs.

Is it developmentally appropriate to openly raise these anti-bias issues of injustice with young children? Certainly, they have lots of experience with the day-to-day problems and conflicts generated by their own differences. They have lots of experience with problem solving "fair" or "not fair." They have the capacity for expressing hurt and for enjoying empathy and fairness. Adults often want to defer children's exposure to the unpleasant realities of bias, to create a protected world of childhood. By so doing, however, they leave children to solve troublesome problems by themselves.

Anti-bias curriculum should be grounded in a developmental approach. In order to develop activities that respond effectively to children's specific interests and concerns, it is first necessary to understand what it is a child is asking, wants to know, or means by a question or comment. Moreover, unless curriculum consistently takes into account children's perspectives, it may become oppressive to them. They must be free to ask questions about any subject, to use their own ideas in problem solving, to engage in real dialogue with adults, to make choices, and to have some say in their daily school life. If we are to facilitate children's sense of self-esteem, critical thinking, and ability to stand up for themselves and others, then our methodology must allow them to experience their intelligence and power as having a constructive effect on their world.

I already have so much to do, how am I going to find time to learn the necessary skills and add anti-bias activities to my curriculum? A teacher has no choice if she or he wants to enable children to develop fully. The point to remember is that an anti-bias approach is *integrated into* rather than *added onto* existing curriculum. Looking at curriculum through an anti-bias lens affects everything a teacher does. Much classroom work will continue; some activities will be modified, some eliminated, some new ones created. Beginning *is* hard, not because of new activities, but because teachers have to re-evaluate what they have been doing. This means being self-conscious and learning by trial and error. After a while—six months, a year—it becomes impossible to teach without an anti-bias perspective.

Implementing anti-bias curriculum requires the same skills and sensitivity and respect for individuality as any other aspect of teaching young children. It also requires additional areas of knowledge and insight. Chapter 12, "Getting Started," suggests activities for teacher self-education in these areas.

Willingness to risk controversy is another important requirement. Although controversy is not unique to anti-bias work, it is an unavoidable part of it. Teachers must be prepared to explain and discuss their anti-bias work with other teachers, parents, and administrators.

References

Alejandro-Wright, M. N. (1985). The child's conception of racial classification. In M.B. Spencer, G.K. Brookins, & W.R. Allen (Eds.), *Beginnings: The social and affective development of Black children* (pp. 185–200). Hillsdale, NJ: Erlbaum.

Ashton-Warner, S. (1963). *Teacher.* New York: Simon & Schuster.

Baratz, S., & Baratz, J. (1970). Early childhood intervention: The social science base of institutional racism. *Harvard Educational Review, 40*(1), 29–50.

Beuf, A. (1977). *Red children in White America.* Philadelphia: University of Pennsylvania Press.

Citron, A. (1969). *The "rightness of Whiteness": The world of the White child in a segregated world.* Office of Urban Education, College of Education, Wayne State University, Detroit, MI 48202.

Clark, K. (1955). *Prejudice and your child.* Boston: Beacon Press.

Cohen, R. (1969). Conceptual styles, culture, conflict and non-verbal tests of intelligence. *American Anthropologist, 71,* 828–856.

Cohen, S. (1977). Fostering positive attitudes toward the handicapped: New curriculum. *Children Today, 6*(6), 7–12.

Council on Interracial Books for Children. (1980). *Guidelines for selecting bias-free textbooks and storybooks.* New York: Author.

Council on Interracial Books for Children. (1983). Homophobia and education [Special issue]. *Interracial Books for Children Bulletin, 14* (3&4).

Cross, W.E. (1985). Black identity: Rediscovering the distinctions between personal identity and reference group orientations. In M.B. Spencer, G.K. Brookins, & W.R. Allen (Eds.), *Beginnings: The social and affective development of Black children* (pp.155–172). Hillsdale, NJ: Erlbaum.

Emihovich, C.A. (1980). Social interaction in two integrated kindergartens. *Integrated Education, 19*(3–6), 72–78.

Freire, P. (1970). *Pedagogy of the oppressed.* New York: The Seabury Press.

Freire, P. (1981). *Education for critical consciousness.* New York: The Continuum Publishing Corp.

Froschl, M., & Sprung, B. (1983). Providing an anti-handicappist early childhood environment. *Interracial Books for Children Bulletin, 14*(7–8), 21–23.

Goodman, M.E. (1964). *Race awareness in young children.* New York: Collier.

Greenberg, P. (1969). *The devil has slippery shoes: A biased biography of the Child Development Group of Mississippi.* London: Macmillan.

Greenberg, S. (1980). Eliminating sex bias in early childhood. *Equal Play, 1*(4), 5.

Gutierrez, M.E. (1982). *Chicano parents' perceptions of their children's racial/cultural awareness.* Unpublished master's thesis, Pacific Oaks College, Pasadena, CA.

Hale-Benson, J. (1986). *Black children: Their roots, culture and learning styles.* Baltimore: John Hopkins University Press.

Hilliard, A. (1977). Intellectual strengths of minority children. In D.E. Cross, G.C. Baker, & L.J. Stiles (Eds.) *Teaching in a multicultural society* (pp. 97–120). New York: Free Press.

Hoffman, L. (1983). Sexism: Related problems, research and strategies. *Interracial Books for Children Bulletin, 14*(7–8), 7, 15–17.

Honig, A.S. (1983). Sex role socialization in early childhood. *Young Children, 38*(6), 57–70.

Katz, P. (1982). Development of children's racial awareness and intergroup attitudes. In L. G. Katz (Ed.), *Current topics in early childhood education* (Vol. 4, pp. 17–54). Norwood, NJ: Ablex.

Kohlberg, L. (1966). A cognitive-developmental analysis of children's sex-role concepts and attitudes. In E.E. Maccoby (Ed.), *The development of sex differences* (pp. 82–172). Stanford, CA: Stanford University Press.

Kutner, B. (1985). Patterns of mental functioning associated with prejudice in children. *Psychological Monographs, 72*(406), 1–48.

Labov, W. (1975). The logic of nonstandard English. In P. Stoller (Ed.), *Black American English.* New York: Dell.

Levine, E., & Ruiz, R. (1978). An exploration of multi-correlates of ethnic group choice. *Journal of Cross-Cultural Psychology, 9,* 179–187.

Levitt, E., & Cohen, S. (1976). Attitudes of children toward their handicapped peers. *Childhood Education, 52,* 171–173.

Miel, A. (1976). *The short-changed children of suburbia.* New York: Institute of Human Relations Press.

Milner D. (1983). *Children and race.* London: Ward Lock Educational.

Pogrebin, L. (1980). *Growing up free: Raising your child in the 80's.* New York: McGraw-Hill.

Pogrebin, L. (1983). The secret fear that keeps us from raising free children. *Interracial Books for Children Bulletin, 14*(3–4), 10–12.

Ramirez, M., & Castaneda, A. (1974). *Cultural democracy, bicognitive development and education.* New York: Academic Press.

Ramsey, P. (1982). Multicultural education in early childhood. *Young Children, 37*(2), 13–24.

Roopnarine, J. (1984). Sex-typed socialization in mixed age preschool children. *Child Development, 55,* 1078–1084.

Sapon-Shevin, M. (1983). Teaching young children about differences: Resources for teaching. *Young Children, 38*(2), 24–32.

Semaj, L.T. (1985). Africanity, cognition and extended self. In M.B. Spencer, G.K. Brookins, & W.R. Allen (Eds.), *Beginnings: The social and affective development of Black children* (pp. 173–184). Hillsdale, NJ: Erlbaum.

Zion, G. (1956). *Harry the dirty dog.* New York: Harper & Row.

CREATING AN ANTI-BIAS ENVIRONMENT

2

An environment that is rich in possibilities for exploring gender, race/ethnicity, and different-abledness sets the scene for practicing anti-bias curriculum. The material and people resources in the classroom provide children with important data. What is in the environment also alerts children to what the teacher considers important or not important. Children are as vulnerable to omissions as they are to inaccuracies and stereotypes: What isn't seen can be as powerful a contributor to attitudes as what is seen. Creating a diverse environment is the first step in implementing new curriculum. Then the classroom has the materials and conditions which serve as a basis for children's initiating conversations and for teachers introducing activities (Neugebauer, 1987).

In most early childhood programs there is an abundance of materials reflecting White, able-bodied children in traditional gender roles. This is often as true in classrooms for children of color and children with nonstandard bodies or senses (vision, hearing, etc.) as it is in classrooms of White children. In addition, materials depicting people of color are frequently biased: They may be stereotypic, or reflect only images of the past, or only token images of people of color (one or two in a sea of White). So the challenge is

- to increase materials that reflect children and adults who are of color, who are differently abled, and who are engaged in nonstereotypic gender activities; and

- to eliminate stereotypic and inaccurate materials from daily use. (They do have a use as teaching tools in specific activities.)

The Visual/Aesthetic Environment

There should be:

1. Images in abundance of *all* the children, families, and staff in your program. Photos and other pictures reflecting the various backgrounds of the children and staff should be attractively displayed.

2. If the classroom population is racially/ethnically homogeneous, images of children and adults from the major racial/ethnic groups in your community and in U.S. society.

3. Images that accurately reflect people's current daily lives in the United States working and with their families during recreational activities.

4. A numerical balance among different groups. Make sure people of color are not represented as "tokens"—only one or two.

5. A fair balance of images of women and men, shown doing "jobs in the home" and "jobs outside the home." Show women and men doing blue-collar work (e.g., factory worker, repair person) and pink-collar work (e.g., beautician, salesperson), as well as white-collar work (e.g., teacher, doctor).

6. Images of elderly people of various backgrounds doing different activities.

7. Images of differently abled people of various backgrounds shown doing work and with their families in recreational activities. Be careful not to use images that depict differently abled people as dependent and passive.

8. Images of diversity in family styles: single mothers or fathers, extended families, gay or lesbian families (families with two mothers or fathers), families in which one parent and a grandmother are the parents, interracial and multiethnic families, adopted families, differently abled families (the atypical person may be either a child or a parent).

9. Images of important individuals—past and present. They should reflect racial/ethnic, gender, and abledness diversity and they should include people who participated in important struggles for social justice.

10. Artwork—prints, sculpture, textiles by artists of various backgrounds that reflect the aesthetic environment and the culture of the families represented in your classroom, and of groups in your community and in the United States (Neugebauer, 1987).

Toys and Materials

Every center should contain regularly available materials representing the backgrounds of the families in your classroom and then extending beyond to the major groups in your community and in the nation.

Books

All children's books reflect social values and attitudes, some more obviously than others. Many, including books that are considered classics, reflect bias of some kind. Since books are a significant part of young children's lives in school and child care, much care must be given to their selection and use. Books should:

- Reflect diversity of gender roles, racial and cultural backgrounds, special needs and abilities; a range of occupations; a range of ages.
- Present accurate images and information (watch out for the "I is for Indian" stereotypic image in many alphabet books).
- Show people from all groups living their daily lives—working, being with family, solving issues relevant to young children, as well as having celebrations. Most books should be about contemporary life in the United States.
- Depict a variety of children and families within a group. This means having at least a few books about a culture.
- Depict various family lifestyles and incomes (beware of using only the large number of children's books picturing only families with two parents, and always with one parent of each sex; beware of using the large number of books that assume readers are Christian).
- Reflect different languages: alphabet books and stories in Braille, sign, different spoken languages.

When choosing books to read to children, consciously pay attention to fostering their awareness of diversity. Choose books that depict different ways of living and books that show various groups solving similar problems (e.g., having a new baby).

Dramatic play

The equipment, objects, and spatial organization of the dramatic play area should include and encourage:

- Diversity of gender play: tools and spaces for working in and out of the house, rooms in the home other than the kitchen, male and female work and play clothes.
- Cultural diversity: cooking, eating, objects, work tools and clothes, personal objects like different kinds of combs and brushes, objects used for holiday celebrations all reflecting a variety of cultures. Begin with the variation in your children's homes, then add other groups.
- Accessibility and exploration of the tools used by people with various special needs: wheelchairs, crutches, braces, canes, heavy glasses, hearing aids.
- Child-size mirrors.

Language

The environment should provide numerous opportunities for children to see and hear various languages, including sign and Braille. Opportunities include labeling materials (e.g., blocks, puzzles), alphabet and number posters, books, story tapes, songs, finger games.

Music

Regularly heard music should reflect the various cultural styles of the children and staff as well as other groups in the United States. Opportunities include singing, background music, music for movement and dancing, lullabies at naptime.

Art materials

- Tan, brown, and black paint, paper, collage materials and play dough, and skin-tone crayons, along with other colors
- Mirrors for children to check out their physical features
- Artwork (paintings, drawings, sculpture) by artists of diverse backgrounds depicting women and men from various racial and ethnic backgrounds

Dolls

- Bought and homemade dolls that represent a fair balance of all the major groups in the United States—Black, Latino, Asian-Pacific, Native American, as well as White. Black and Latino dolls should reflect the range of skin tones within these groups, by supplementing commercial dolls with homemade dolls. (See "Making New Materials," p. 15.) All dolls should be reasonably authentic-looking.
- A fair balance of male and female dolls with a variety of clothes. Girl dolls need dresses and pants. Some of the dolls should be anatomically correct.
- A selection of bought and homemade dolls with different kinds of disabilities. They should reflect various racial and ethnic backgrounds and include both boys and girls.
- Persona dolls. (See "Using Old Materials In New Ways," p. 16.)

Manipulatives

Regularly available manipulative materials should depict diversity in race, ethnicity, gender, physical abilities, and occupations. These include puzzles, Playmate™ and Playskool™ sets of people, family and community helper figures, lotto games, and card games. Avoid stereotypic images such as the Playmate's "Cowboys and Indians" set.

Cameras

A Polaroid™ and regular color camera are invaluable tools for creating anti-bias materials of your own.

ADAPTATION

If the population of the class is predominately

- **children of color,** more than half, although not all, of the images and materials in the environment should reflect their backgrounds in order to counter the predominance of White, dominant cultural images in the general society.
- **poor children** (White and children of color), a large number of images and materials should depict working-class life in all its variety in order to counter the dominant cultural image of middle- and upper-class life.
- **White children,** at least one-half of the images should introduce diversity in order to counter the White-centered images of the dominant culture.
- **differently abled children,** they deserve learning about gender and cultural diversity as well as about the capabilities of people with special needs. A large number of images should depict children and adults with disabilities doing a range of activities.

If there are a few children who are different from the rest of the group, then take care to ensure that those children's background is amply represented along with representations of the majority groups in the class.

Interactions

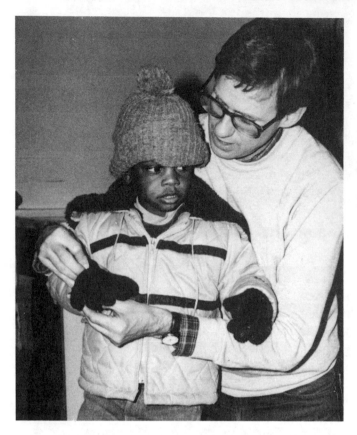

Interactions between teachers or caregivers and children may teach gender, racial, and handicappism biases even without deliberate intent. Find a way to observe your interactions objectively and pinpoint behaviors you wish to change. A video is great; if you don't have access to video equipment, make an agreement with other staff to take turns observing each other.

1. Do teacher/caregivers pick up on nonverbal and verbal expression of interest as quickly with girls as they do with boys? With differently abled children? With children of color?

2. Do teachers/caregivers offer girls as much physical freedom and use of large-motor equipment as they offer boys? Do they allow boys freedom to express feelings? Do they help more often or do more for girls than boys?

3. Do teachers and caregivers provide adapted opportunities for children with certain limitations to interact actively and independently with materials and other children? Do they overhelp or overprotect children who are different in some way from "the average child"?

4. Are similar behaviors interpreted and responded to differently with boys than girls? White children than children of color? Lighter skinned than darker skinned children of color? Able-bodied than differently abled children? For example, do teachers and caregivers respond differently to an aggressive act of a boy or a Black child or a mentally retarded child?

5. Are girls complimented on appearance and boys on achievement?

6. When children touch an adult or child's hair or skin, or make comments about skin color or hair texture, do teachers and caregivers support and facilitate their explorations, or do they ignore or redirect them?

7. When children ask or make comment about genitals, do teachers or caregivers give them matter-of-fact, accurate feedback?

8. When children ask or make comments about disabilities, do teachers and caregivers give them direct, accurate feedback?

9. Are children's cultural learning styles respected? Are provisions made

(a) for children who prefer to play and work with other children or who prefer to work alone?

(b) for children who prefer a personal relationship with a teacher to get started, or to try a new or hard activity? Or who prefer the teacher to intervene when the child requests help?

(c) for children who prefer learning with action- or people-oriented activities (e.g., dramatic play) or who prefer working by themselves with objects?

Are all children supported in their preferred learning styles and also encouraged to try new ways of interacting with people and materials?

(Some of the foregoing ideas are taken from Judy Leipzig's "Questioning Our Behavior When Working With Young Children" (1982) and Melanie Booth-Butterfield's "The Cues We Don't Question" (1981).)

Selecting Anti-Bias Materials

Decisions about eliminating current materials

Images displayed on the walls of the classroom and in books and other materials should never be inaccurate or stereotypic. There are uses for stereotypic images—as tools for helping children learn to identify and critique unfair pictures—but these should be used only for specific teaching purposes; they should not be available for daily use. For help in deciding which materials are stereotypic, consult "Guidelines for Selecting Bias-Free Textbooks and Storybooks" (CIBC, 1980).

Sometimes it is possible to alter stereotypic material. Many alphabet books have the stereotypic "I is for Indian" illustration; paste a different picture over the stereotypic image. Many commercial posters and charts used for teaching about health, the seasons, or numbers show only White, able-bodied children in traditional gender roles. Create diversity by pasting new pictures over some of the old ones. Coloring in is not a good idea because the features still have White characteristics.

Decisions about purchasing new materials

Depending on your budget, there are some good anti-bias materials to purchase. A resource guide is in the appendix. Flexible, open-ended materials that can be used in many ways are more economical in the long run. For example, purchasing a few Polaroid™ cameras will enable you to make many kinds of materials relevant to your children. Another excellent purchase is a set of dolls of diverse backgrounds and physical abilities.

Making new materials

Finding sufficient anti-bias materials can be difficult, and sometimes impossible, even in large cities with more access to educational materials. Making one's own anti-bias materials is essential. With ingenuity, patience, resourcefulness, and a little help from parents and friends, wonderful things can happen.

Picture files: Finding accurate, nonstereotypic pictures of people of color; of people with hearing or vision impairments, orthopedic conditions, and so on; and of men and women in nontraditional roles takes persistence and patience. If you keep at it, you will eventually have a valuable collection. Possible sources include:

Magazines such as *Young Children, Ms., Ebony, Life, Faces* (See Resources, p. 135). It may be more economical for your program to subscribe to these magazines than to purchase commercially made pictures. Sometimes *National Geographic* is useful, but be careful about selecting only exotic images of non-European cultures that depict people at special celebrations, not daily life. Special calendars made by organizations such as the National Black Child Development Institute, Syracuse Peace Workers, or feminist groups, and sold in women's book stores or by mail order, often have excellent anti-bias pictures.

Photographs of your children, their families, people in the community, and people you meet on travels throughout the country. Take your own; ask parents for duplicates or negatives or extra copies.

CAUTION

When selecting materials:
- Don't do token diversity—having only one picture, or doll, or object, or book about a particular group.
- Don't substitute images and information about people in other countries for life in the U.S.—e.g., Japanese-American children do not live the same culture as do children in Japan.
- Don't show only images of a group from the past, even though they may be easier to find than contemporary images. (This happens frequently with images of Native Americans.)

UNICEF greeting cards.

Posters. Organizations concerned with rights for children, women, people of color, and the disabled often have good posters and photos. NAEYC has some suitable posters. (See Resources, pp. 134–136.) Educational supply companies make posters of well-known men and women, although these may not be interesting to young children.

Good photo books like *Children of Many Lands* (Reich, 1984), *Children and Their Mothers* (Reich, 1964), and *Children and Their Fathers* (Reich, 1966).

Dolls: Using patterns found in sewing books, or with help from someone you know who makes dolls, make cloth dolls of different skin colors and shades, hair texture, and eye color, and dolls with different physical abilities: a doll in a wheelchair, with braces, with a hearing aid, with a seeing-eye dog. Make sure your special needs dolls reflect various racial and ethnic backgrounds.

Puzzles: If you have access to someone who does woodworking and knows how to use a jigsaw, you can make your own puzzles with enlarged

(8 × 10) photos mounted on wood and then cut into as many pieces as you wish.

Card games: Mount playing-card-size magazine pictures and photos of children and adults of diverse backgrounds, physical abilities, and occupations, two of each picture, on cardboard. Children can play an anti-bias "Go Fish" game with these cards.

Books: Make small books with magazine pictures and photos placed in "autograph"-size picture albums. Use your imagination. Books could be about "All the things girls and boys can do" (including children of various races, ethnicity, and abilities), "Babies come in many different colors," "All kinds of families," and an "Anti-Bias Alphabet Book."

*   *   *   *   *

We have discussed decisions about eliminating from our programs inaccurate or stereotypic materials. We have also discussed decisions about purchasing new materials. Next, we will see what Kay Taus, a teacher who does it, has to say about using old materials in new ways.

Using Old Materials in New Ways: Storytelling With "Persona" Dolls*

Good stories capture the heart, mind, and imagination and are an important way to transmit values. However, too few children's books depict people from diverse backgrounds respecting one another and living in a mutually beneficial way. Moreover, even good books do not always deal with the specific events that occur in chidren's daily lives. So I began to write and tell my own stories. I found that using dolls enhanced young children's connection to the stories and their participation in solving the problems that arose in the dolls' "lives."

The "persona" dolls

Each doll has his or her own life story. Stories reflect the composition of the class and offer a vehicle for introducing differences that do not exist within one classroom. Here are the persona dolls that are part of my classroom.

David (6) is White. When he was born, his legs weren't strong because of a birth defect in his spine. He can't walk so he has a wheelchair instead. He lives with his daddy and mommy.

Eric (6) is White. A few years ago, he had a serious sickness (cancer) and part of his leg had to be removed because it was unhealthy and was causing the rest of his body to get sick too. Now he has crutches. As he grows older, he will be able to get a prosthesis to wear on his leg, which will allow him to walk without crutches. He lives with his mother. He doesn't see his father.

Jennifer (5) is White and lives with her mother and her mother's roommate or friend whom she also considers to be her mommy. She is profoundly deaf. Her primary language is sign language. She is learning to read lips and to talk, but it will take time to learn really well.

---

* A sample of the stories Kay invents about the dolls is in the Appendix, p. 146. For a fuller discussion of this method, see Taus (1987).

Jerry (6) is Jewish. He lives with his father and mother. He is blind and is learning Braille. He knows some sign language by touch because he goes to a summer camp for deaf and blind children.

Joe (6) is Black. He lives with his mother, father, two brothers, and a sister. (One year Joe was a Jehovah's Witness because I had two Black children whose families were of that faith.)

Joshua (5) is Jewish. He is adopted. Joshua's parents are divorced. He spends one week living with his father and one week living with his mother. He has a younger brother who is 3 and is also adopted.

Laura (5) is deaf. Sign language is her first language. Her parents and three of her four grandparents are also deaf. Her older brother is hard of hearing, but can hear voices with his hearing aids. Laura cannot hear voices even with her hearing aids. Laura is Jewish and attends a special temple for deaf people. She lives with her immediate family but has a large extended family of deaf relatives and friends.

Marisela (6) is from Mexico. She and her mother came to Los Angeles when she was 4. Her father and mother are divorced. Her father lives in Mexico and she doesn't see him. She has aunts and uncles in Mexico and in Los Angeles. She speaks English and Spanish.

Mary (6) is Navajo. She lives with her mother and father. Her grandmother and grandfather still live in Arizona on the reservation. She knows a little of the Navajo or Dine language because she visits her grandparents.

May (5) is Chinese. Her family is from Hong Kong. She lives with her father and sister. Her mother died when she was very little. She speaks Cantonese very well because that is her first language, and she is learning English.

Molly (5) is White. Because she has cerebral palsy, she walks with braces on her legs and she uses crutches. She lives with her mother and sees her father every other weekend and on special occasions.

Rachel (6) lives with her father in Los Angeles and visits her mother, who lives in San Diego, fairly often. She speaks English and a little Spanish because her grandmother (her father's mother) speaks only Spanish. Her father's family is from Mexico; her mother's family is Anglo-Saxon.

Suzanne (5) is Black. She lives with her mother and father and her younger sister. She is blind. Like Joe, she is learning Braille.

Tekkai (5) is Japanese-American. He and his mother and father speak Japanese and English. His grandmother still lives in Japan.

Teresa (6) is Salvadorian. She lives with her mother. They came from El Salvador when Teresa was 3 years old. She speaks Spanish and English. The rest of her family, including her father and her grandmother, are still in El Salvador.

Zoreisha (5) is Black. She lives with her mother and her grandmother.

With a general idea of family life, ethnic background, language, and differing abilities, I can begin to create stories about each doll. Their "lives" gradually unfold in the same way that children's lives unfold and open to each other as they become friends. Stories build upon each other and become more complex. It is usually a good idea first to introduce each doll to the children in a simple story that includes information about the doll's family and other specifics relevant to the particular doll. Some of the introductory stories have little plot and focus primarily on opening up children's questions.

Each time I've introduced a doll with an obvious physical difference, there were children who were afraid. "Why does he have that wheelchair?" asked Jason in a quavering voice about David. And the most dramatic—"I don't want to touch him!"—was Diana's first response to Eric, the doll with half of one leg missing. "That leg must scare you, Diana. I'll come and sit with you. Emily, will you hold Eric very gently for me while I help Diana?" I said. "Yes," said Emily, "I think he's feeling kind of sad that Diana doesn't want to touch him." "I think so too," added Todd. "I think it's hurting his feelings." "I want to touch him," said Anne. "Me too," said Colin. "Well, I think that Diana has never met a person whose body is very different and I think it scares her. Is that right, Diana?" "Yes," she said as she leaned her head into my lap. "We will all help you get to know Eric. He has feelings and ideas just like all of us, even if his leg is different."

Sometimes it is effective to introduce dolls together. If I want to talk about what might be exciting, or scary, on the first day of school, I use three dolls and share how they met each other, how it was hard to say good-bye to their parents, how confusing it is to understand new rules, and who had a hard time finding the bathroom. I might include Jennifer or Laura in that group and begin talking about sign language.

I first introduce the dolls that are most like the children in the classroom. This year I introduced Zoreisha, Rachel, and Tekkai to share their first-day-at-school stories. Kira (who is Black) wanted to know if Zoreisha missed her mommy. Ryan (who is Japanese) asked me if Tekkai brought Japanese food to school in his lunch box. Ryan had previous experience with other children saying "yuk" when he had Japanese food for lunch. Kira sat holding Zoreisha. "She's sad," she told me.

"She misses her mommy." Rachel was glad to be back at school, I told the children. "She likes to play on the yard; she likes to paint; she likes everything!" "That's just like me," said Emily. "All summer, all I did was ask my mother when would school start, when would school start!" "Rachel is a good person to ask for help . . . like if you didn't know where the bathroom was or you needed the teacher. She knows a lot about this school." "Just like me," said Todd. "If there's any new kids here, you can ask me for help. I'm really good about that." Jason, who was completely new to the school, asked, "Where do the dolls sleep?" "They sleep in my office," I answered. "Do they have beds?" "No, they sit in a special place." "Do they have other clothes?" asked Matthew. "Where are their parents?" asked Anne. The process of connecting had begun. Many children wanted to play with the dolls on the rug after story time was finished.

During the first few weeks, I bring in at least one doll every day so that the children can continue to "make friends" with them and begin to raise anti-bias issues. Joe comes in to talk about how it is OK for boys and girls to cry. Joshua comes in to talk about how he loves to cook in the housekeeping corner. Teresa comes to introduce some Spanish songs and talk about how she doesn't like to be teased. Within a few months, all of the dolls have made an appearance.

There are rules for the persona dolls. I do not leave them out in the housekeeping corner for "regular" play. I do want them to be close at hand for my use and the use of children, but I want it to be clear that these dolls are very special. I keep many of the dolls on top of the piano. Everyone knows where they are and that they are available for play, but only if you ask first. For example, after a story about Molly going into the hospital to have an operation, the children decided to build a hospital with the big blocks. They got out all the doctor and nurse equipment and began to act out Molly's surgery. At one point, Michael came over to me and said, "Can I get down Laura and David and Joshua? I think Molly's going to be scared without some of her friends." "Of course," I replied, and together we gathered up her friends who joined her in the block hospital.

Recently when I was using three dolls to tell a story, Emily said, "That's an artificial story, isn't it, Kay? Because it's about dolls." The children accept the doll stories as "real" but also remember that they are "only dolls." They do become quite at-

tached to them. James asked me to be sure and take them home over winter break so they wouldn't get lonely all by themselves at school.

Creating stories

Anti-bias stories emerge from four sources: *(1)* issues that emerge from children's daily lives; *(2)* events that are currently happening in the world; *(3)* information that I, as the teacher, want children to have; and *(4)* history.

Ideas for stories arise spontaneously from children's everyday interactions, emotions, and family relationships. The breakup of Diana's family, several children using "Chinese" as an insult, and the boys saying that no girls are allowed on the boat are examples of classroom issues that resulted in stories this year. I always ask children first if it is alright with them for me to tell a story that is very much like their own. It is important to respect their privacy and not surprise them. I've never had a child say "no."

I wrote one story to open up the problem of a group of boys who were being extremely aggressive. They played "war," shot each other, used karate kicks, talked constantly about weapons, and even physically hurt one another when their play went too far. I took six of my boy dolls onto the rug and began a story about how much fighting they were doing with each other. I talked about all of the things that the real boys were doing. Then I said I knew something about each of the dolls. I knew that they all acted very tough, but that really they were afraid of things just like everyone else. Joshua, for example, was afraid of the fights that his mom and dad have. He hides under his bed at night because he is so scared. Joe is afraid of robbers. He's afraid they will get into his room at night when he's asleep. Jerry is afraid of bigger kids at school. He thinks they are so tough, they might really hurt him. Tekkai is afraid of the dark, and David is afraid of being kidnapped. Tom is afraid that something will happen to his dad who drives a Greyhound bus and takes long trips.

Immediately Todd, one of the real-life boys involved, said, "That sounds like me and David." "Oh, really?" I said. "What is like you?" "I fight a lot with David and I'm afraid of robbers." Jason, another of the group, said, "Well, I'm not afraid of robbers or anything." "I am," said Aaron. "I'm afraid of kidnappers, like that doll David." "Do you think the teachers here or your parents at home can protect you from kidnappers, Aaron?" I asked. "Do you have guns?" he asked me. "No, we don't have guns. We have other ways of taking care of you, just like your mommy and daddy do." "Yeah, like you would call the police," said Todd. "Or you'd hide us in the closet," added Emily. "Or I'd call all the teachers together and the principal. We have a lot of grown-ups here to help keep you all safe." We had a long discussion about fears; I believe the story and the dolls opened up a safe way to explore new ways of acting.

A second source of stories are current "hot" world events that appear on the news or are talked about by parents. For example, right after the Mexico City earthquake, Carlos, whose family is from Mexico and whose grandparents still live there, asked me if he could say something very important on the rug. "Of course," I said, and Carlos began to talk. "Who here does not want to die?" he asked, as I fell over with surprise. "Because," he continued, "there's going to be a big earthquake in California, just like in Mexico City, and everyone is going to fall into the ocean." I gasped, but quickly grabbed Marisela, the doll, and told how her grandmother, too, was in Mexico City and how scared she was about the earthquake. Carlos said that he was also very frightened. Through the story and some reassurances on my part, he worked out some of his fear and other children were able to see that his words had come from being afraid.

I also tell stories about peace. One of the dolls brings a new "war" toy to school and we talk about what to do. Since there has been a campaign against war toys, I've told a story about one or two dolls going to a meeting with other children and burying their G.I. Joes™, Rambos™, guns, and tanks. It turned out that one of my children had really been to a rally and buried his G.I. Joe.

I have stories to go with most holidays, like "Jerry's Chanukah" or "Marisela's Posada." I use them to discuss various cultural practices and issues of children in my class and to introduce new information. For example, in the "Dias de los Muertos" story, which Marisela's family celebrates, I deal with the Mexican idea of death.

A third source of stories is issues the teacher believes are important for children to think about. For example, even if children have not actually played "cowboys and Indians" in our school yard, I tell a doll story about how Mary, the Navajo doll, feels when she sees children playing that game because it is a theme that has run through non-Indian childhood games in this country. Tell-

ing Mary's story is also an effective way to find out how children feel about "Indians."

Stories based on history are the fourth source. Just as adults have always passed on historical stories (religious, patriotic, family) to children, I also choose to tell stories from the past. I don't expect 5-year-olds to remember all the details, but I do want to give them a sense of the great many people like themselves who have reflected a spirit of justice and freedom. I use historical stories about the Montgomery Bus Boycott, Harriet Tubman, Frederick Douglass, Helen Keller, the Great Flint Strike, Jane Addams, Chief Joseph, and the United Farmworkers. These stories are full of adventures, and children often request them. Recently, when I asked the children what story they would like to read or hear, Emily quickly spoke up and said, "Kay, tell the one about the slaves escaping! That's so exciting!" "Yeah," said Matthew. "I like that one." "It's sad," said Kira, "but I like it."

When I tell stories about the Montgomery Bus Boycott, I share my involvement in the Civil Rights Movement. Darren asked if I knew Rosa Parks and Danielle asked me if I sat in the front or the back of the bus. Todd wanted to know if I got put in jail too. Kira wanted to be reassured that we did not have those rules anymore. I also tell my story about saving seven baby skunks and about my friendship with Karen, a blind girl whom I met in high school. I like sharing my own history in this form. It helps establish an intimate connection with children. Just as their lives are the sources of many stories, so is mine. Person to person, we are exchanging our experience of the world.

References

Booth-Butterfield, M. (1981). The cues we don't question: Unintentional gender socialization in the day care. *Day Care and Early Education, 8*(4), 20–22.

Council on Interracial Books for Children. (1980). *Guidelines for selecting bias-free textbooks and storybooks.* New York: Author.

Leipzig, J. (1982). Questioning our behavior when working with young children. *Equal Play, 3*(3 &4), 7–9.

Neugebauer, B. (Ed.). (1987). *Alike and different: Exploring our humanity with young children.* Redmond, WA: Exchange Press.

Reich, H. (1964). *Children and their mothers.* New York: Hill & Wang.

Reich, H. (1966). *Children and their fathers.* New York: Hill & Wang.

Reich, H. (1984). *Children of many lands.* New York: Hill & Wang.

Taus, K. (1987). *Teachers as storytellers for justice.* Unpublished master's thesis, Pacific Oaks College, Pasadena, CA.

BEGINNINGS: WORKING WITH 2-YEAR-OLDS

3

Two-year-olds are just beginning the journey that leads to self-identity and understanding of others. This is a rich and busy period of life. As 2s construct their sense of self as an individual both separate from and interconnected to others, and acquire language, early stages of autonomy, communication, empathy, and friendships further emerge. Beginning awareness of gender, race, ethnicity, and different physical abilities is part of this process.

Paradoxically, although 2-year-olds depend on adults for providing the necessary *materials, support,* and *safety* for physical, intellectual, emotional, and social development, they must *do their own learning* as they interact with the physical world and with each other. Formal lessons by adults just don't work! Consequently, planning primarily consists of thoughtfully integrating anti-bias content in all aspects of the classroom environment. Children's play, comments, and questions then become the basis for interactions between child and teacher that address anti-bias issues. Planned group activities such as reading children's books, singing, and finger games should take up only a small percentage of the daily program for 2-year-olds.

GOALS

1. To provide a rich, accurate, nonstereotypic "data base" about gender, race, culture, and physical abilities
2. To enable children to become familiar with differences in gender roles, racial characteristics, language, and physical abilities
3. To encourage and support 2-year-olds' budding curiosity about their physical and social selves and about others

---

Developmental Tasks and Guidelines for Child-Teacher Interactions

Two-year-olds primarily notice physical aspects of identity

Awareness of gender usually appears first, as a reflection of 2-year-olds' more general curiosity about their anatomy. As they learn the names and purposes of the various parts of their bodies, they also notice and comment about their genitals. Interest in gender also reflects the great importance in our society put on knowing the newborn's (and sometimes the fetus's) sex. From the moment of birth, differential behaviors toward girls and boys begin to teach the cultural attributes of gender.

Diaper changing and toilet learning are two activities in the daily schedule where learning about sex identity spontaneously arises. A lot of looking occurs; all the teacher has to do occasionally is casually say, "Cindy has a vagina; Malcolm has a penis." As children acquire more language in general, they also begin making comments of their own: "My mom doesn't have a penis, she has hair"; "I have a penis; my sister has a bagina." To these and similar comments, the teacher responds, "You're right. That is what makes you (your mom, your sister, your dad, your brother) a girl/a boy."

Brief, simple, matter-of-fact feedback helps 2-year-olds begin to gain the information and emotional acceptance they need to construct an accurate and healthy sex identity. Knowing that it is anatomy that makes a child a girl or a boy lays the necessary foundation for constructing nonsexist gender identity—for understanding that being a girl or a boy does not depend on hair length, clothing, expression of feelings, or play choices.

At first 2s may get confused about anatomy differences. They may think they have both a penis and a vagina. They may think they can change their body parts if they so wish. At this age, comments that reveal such confusion are part of normal developmental "errors" and not signs of emotional disturbance. As such, provide brief, matter-of-fact feedback: "Eddie, you don't have a vagina, only girls have a vagina. You are a boy and you have a penis." If the teacher is comfortable, then children will gain the clarification they need and feel free to continue asking questions as they sort out an essential aspect of their identity.

CAUTION

- Do not make fun of a child's comments about genitals.
- Do not reprimand the child for asking or commenting about genitals.
- Remember that by making brief responses to children's comments you are not doing "sex education"; you are responding to children's developmental task of learning about their body and about what makes them a girl or a boy.

Awareness of skin color also begins in the third year of life. Teachers and parents consider it an appropriate task for 2s to learn color names: indeed, many consider it a sign of intelligence. Yet, it often comes as a big surprise when the same 2-year-old also notices the colors of people's skin.

Sherry, a dark-skinned Mexican-American 2½-year-old, spent a large part of snack time looking at the photographs of the children in her small group, which were mounted behind the group's snack table. "Why I a color?" she asked, pointing to her chest. Her teacher replied, "We all have a color. We each get our special and beautiful color from our mommies and daddies. Different people have different colors." Then the teacher went around the table and talked about each child's skin, hair, and eye colors, emphasizing how special and beautiful each color is. After snack, Sherry gave her teacher a big hug before going off to play. Later, at circle time, her teacher read the picture book *Brown Bear, Brown Bear, What Do You See?* (Martin, 1983) and Sherry held up her hands and feet to the color brown. "Yes, your hands and feet are the same color brown," said her teacher.

The teacher's matter-of-fact recognition of Sherry's observations, her simple response, which included positive valuing of the children's identity, and the follow-up activity (reading a relevant book), all support the beginning of Sherry's positive awareness of her racial identity.

Maria, a Latino teacher, was reading the book *Ten, Nine, Eight* (Bang, 1983), which is about a young Black child's bedtime ritual with her dad. When Maria got to the "brown toes" illustration, the children, a mixed group of White, Asian, Black, and Latino children, looked at her. She responded, "Yes, I have brown toes. I also have brown hands, legs, and a brown body."

Paying attention to 2-year-olds' nonverbal cues is as important as addressing their verbal comments. Acknowledging and giving words to their observations encourages children to develop comfortable awareness of others.

Carey, a White 2½-year-old, likes the TV program "Different Strokes." He tells his mother, "That's Julie and that's Mark" (friends of his), pointing to Arnold and Willis (the two Black children on the program). Carey's mother replies, "Mark and Julie have brown skin just like Arnold and Willis, but they are not the same children. Julie is a girl and Arnold is a boy. Mark is taller and older than Willis."

Carey's "error" is typical of 2-year-olds' thinking. He identified a common characteristic among the children and then either overgeneralized or explained the connection he saw as best he could. Carey's mom's response both supported his observation of similarity while also helping him differentiate the four children.

Sandy (White), Kim (Japanese-American), and Shauna (Black) are sitting on the tire swing. They take turns touching each other's hair. Their teacher comes over, "It's fun to touch each other's hair. Each of our hair feels different. Shauna's is curly, Kim's is straight, and Sandy's hair is in long braids. They are different colors, too. Shauna and Kim's hair is black, Sandy's hair is red."

Twos are curious about hair texture. Opportunities to feel each other's hair, along with their teacher's brief and supportive feedback, is all the activity they need.

Paul announces, "Look, here's my Black mommy," as his mother comes to pick him up. His teacher responds, "Yes, your mommy is Black and you are Black too." Paul's mother is surprised. She had not planned to discuss race with him yet. His teacher tells her that when she reads books about Black children, Paul points at the picture and then points out the Black children in his group.

Paul's mother may not have been ready to talk with him about racial identity, but Paul was. Helping parents understand how soon their children begin this journey is part of anti-bias curriculum for 2-year-olds.

Awareness of disabilities tends to come later than gender and race. However, some 2-year-olds may begin noticing more obvious difference in physical abilities, such as a person using a wheelchair, a brace, or crutches to move around.

At the park, Lucia slowly walks closer to a woman who is seated in a wheelchair. She stands quietly, staring at her. Her teacher notices and walks over. "Lucia, you are looking at a person who is using a wheelchair. Sometimes a person's legs can't walk, so then she uses a wheelchair to move around. Let's go back to the other children now." The teacher says a few collegial words to the woman in the wheelchair. He is low-key about all of this. Upon returning to school, the teacher shows a few pictures of people using wheelchairs to the children at circle time. He tells them how Lucia and he had seen a woman using a wheelchair, explains briefly about why people use wheelchairs, and then helps children see the different things the people in the pictures are doing. He then reads the book *Grandma's Wheelchair* (Henriod, 1982), shortening the story a little to help keep the children's interest.

Sonia keeps staring at Benjamin's foot, which has a brace on it. When Benjamin walks, Sonia tries to imitate his leg movements. Their teacher, noticing Sonia's behavior, walks closer to her. She says, "Benjamin has a special thing called a brace on his foot. Benjamin's foot is not strong enough to move by itself. His brace helps him to walk." Sonia says, "Like this," and limps a little. "Benjamin's brace does make him walk a little differently than you do. Now let's see you walk like you do."

As with their noticing of color and anatomy differences, 2-year-olds need simple feedback that supports their observations and helps sort out what is happening. Imitation is one of the major ways 2s learn and is not meant as teasing.

As early as 2½ years, signs of "pre-prejudice" —of discomfort with physical differences—may also appear and should be addressed.

Terri's behavior, in contrast to Sonia's, indicates discomfort with Benjamin. Her teacher observes that Terri stops herself before she gets close to Benjamin and moves away if he approaches. One day at snack time, while Terri is playing with a child on one side of her, Benjamin sits down on the other side. When Terri sees him, she jumps up and runs over to the teacher and tries to sit on her lap. Her teacher lets her. After snack, the teacher talks with Terri: "How come you didn't want to sit next to Benjamin?" Terri stares at her. "I think maybe you are afraid of him." Terri nods her head yes. "Would you like to know about Benjamin's brace?" Terri nods her head yes again. "Benjamin's foot never grew strong. In order to walk, his leg needs some help. That is why Benjamin wears a brace on his leg. Let's go find the doll that has a brace so you can see how it fits on the doll's leg."

Later in the morning, the teacher asks Benjamin if Terri can touch his brace so that she can learn about it. Benjamin agrees. The teacher then asks Terri if she would like to look at and touch Benjamin's brace. Terri looks apprehensive, but agrees. She stares at the brace, gingerly touches it. Then she sits down in the sand next to Benjamin and starts playing, not with Benjamin, but alongside him. It takes Terri a while longer to be completely comfortable with Benjamin. In the next few weeks, she occasionally goes up to Benjamin, touches his brace, and then goes to play somewhere else. She frequently plays with the doll with the brace. At the end of the month, Terri begins sitting next to and playing with Benjamin comfortably.

Jeffrey, an Asian-American child, exhibited a number of behaviors indicating discomfort with dark-skinned children. As his teacher read a book showing children of different racial backgrounds, Jeffrey said, "Yucky" every time he saw a picture of a dark-skinned child. His teacher responded, "It isn't yucky, it is a different color than your skin." The next day, Jeffrey refused to hold the hand of a Black classmate, saying the child's hand was "dirty." His teacher replied, "Mark's hand isn't dirty, his hand is the color brown." Jeffrey still refused, so the teacher found another partner for Mark. The following week, Jeffrey's mother related a disturbing incident that had occurred at home the evening before: After she washed Jeffrey's hair, he said to her, "Now it's white." She responded, "Your hair is black." Jeffrey insisted, "No, it is white, only the dirt is black." The teacher decided it was time to develop a plan together with Jeffrey's parents to help Jeffrey overcome his discomfort with "blackness."

At school, the teacher did a variety of activities with Jeffrey over the next two months. She and Jeffrey put dirt on dark and light-skinned dolls and washed them many times. The teacher pointed out how the dirt came off and the skin was still dark—that brown skin was still brown when it is clean. They washed the dolls' hair and saw how it was still black. The teacher sat with Jeffrey and played with him with the brown and black play dough, finger paints, and easel paint. They mixed different shades of brown paint together with water. The teacher noticed and positively commented on black and brown colors in children's clothes. She and Jeffrey spent time looking at each other's skin, hair, and eye colors.

One day, three months from the first pre-prejudice incident, Jeffrey initiated the following with his teacher: "You're brown," he stated matter-of-factly. "Yes, I'm brown," his teacher replied. "You're my friend," Jeffrey said next. "Yes, I'm your friend," she agreed.

The activities and methods illustrated in the anecdotes about Terri and Jeffrey are all part of an anti-bias curriculum with 2-year-olds. Terri and Jeffrey needed a more intensive, one-on-one series of interactions with their teacher in order to overcome their pre-prejudice.

By 2½, children are beginning to be aware of cultural aspects of gender and ethnic identity

Young children are acute observers of gender behavior:

"Why are you wearing man's shoes?" Stacy asks her teacher, who has on loafers. "These shoes are for women and for men. Women can wear them too," her teacher explains.

In Katie's home, her dad cooks all the meals. While Katie was visiting her aunt and uncle's home, her uncle called to say he would be home late. Katie turned to the aunt and said, "Who is going to make my dinner?" Her aunt reassured Katie that she also knew how to cook!

Two-year-olds are not only acute observers, they also make generalizations based on the cognitive tools and experiences available to them.

Joshua is on the climbing structure humming to himself, "I'm going on a whale. I can go on a whale because I'm a man." Elena is standing at the foot of the ladder, getting ready to climb up the same structure. "You can't," Joshua adamantly insists. "Girls can't." Elena starts climbing. Joshua says even louder, "Girls can't," and tries to block the top of the ladder. Their teacher steps in: "Elena, can you go on this whale?" Elena says, "Yes." "Joshua, Elena says she can and I think she can too. Girls can climb just like boys. There is room for two people on the whale. You find a place for yourself and Elena will find place for herself."

Joshua already has a gender-based "reason" for getting what he wants. It is important that his teacher explicitly countered his statement, "Girls can't," and also supported Elena's sticking up for herself. As the teacher clarifies children's ideas about gender behavior, she models ways to counter stereotyping and provides words for children to eventually use themselves.

Teachers also model new behaviors:

Luis and Tim put on fire hats and announce they are "firemen." Their teacher says, "Great," and then says, "You know, girls can be firepeople too." Luis and Tim respond, "You be the girl." Their teacher joins the play.

The teacher and children are singing "The wheels on the bus go round and round." When they come to the line, "The mommy on the bus goes . . . ," the children sing "shush, shush, shush"—the traditional words. The teacher then asks, "What else could the mommy do besides say 'shush' to the baby?" One child says, "Read the newspaper," so all the children sing that line. On another day, the teacher asks, "Could the daddy on the bus say 'shush, shush, shush'?" One child says, "My daddy does" . . . so all the children sing the new line.

A student teacher is supervising children on the swings. She says to Sean, "What wonderful, big circles you are making"; to Pam she says, "Be careful, you might hurt yourself." The teacher steps in, "I think Pam is making wonderful, big circles too."

Small changes, but it is the numerous, repeated small steps that provide 2-year-olds with the data they need to begin to construct nonsexist gender identity.

Twos can also take the very first steps toward awareness of cultural diversity if appropriate experiences are part of their daily classroom life. Simple language activities work well:

Maria regularly interchanges singing the "Good Morning" song with its Spanish version. After a few months, one day, upon announcing that it was time to sing the "Good Morning" song, one of the children asked, "You mean the Buenos Dias song?" "What a good question," Maria replied. "Let's sing the song two ways—in English, the "Good Morning" way, and in Spanish, the "Buenos Dias" way.

Teaching the children "Feliz Cumpleaños" (the Mexican version of happy birthday), the teacher explains, "We are learning to sing happy birthday in Spanish because this is how Rosie's family sings to her at home. Rosie's family is Mexican." "I Mexican," Rosie repeats.

"I want to speak like Angie," Tim announces at snack time. Other kids chime in "Me too." Angie, a teaching assistant, has been using Spanish words for frequently used objects and expressions with the children as she interacts with them, but has made no attempt to teach them directly. Now, Angie and the teacher decide that she will teach the children a few words at snack time (water, juice, glass, cookie, chair, table, thank you).

Integrating Anti-Bias Content Into the Daily Environment and Schedule

Free play/Choice time

Art materials
- Regularly provide brown and black tempera and finger paints, crayons, magic markers, colored chalk, easel paper, drawing paper, paper for pasting.
- Frequently provide play dough in a spectrum of brown shades from light to dark brown.
- Frequently mix tempera paint for easel painting in different skin shades.
- Occasionally, as a child is using a color close to her or his skin, hair, or eye color, remark: "You are using a beautiful chocolate brown—it matches your skin (hair, eyes)"; "You are using a beautiful peach color, which is just like your skin," and so on.
- Occasionally, when children are washing off paint, clay, or finger paints together, suggest: "Let's look at what happens to our skin color when we wash off paint (clay, etc.). See, our skin color stays the same. It doesn't come off. Only the paint (clay, etc.) comes off."

Manipulatives
- Make sure there are no stereotypic images on any of the materials.
- Paint some of the small blocks and "shape" pieces various shades of brown and black.
- If you use simple puzzles, make sure they show diversity: You may have to make some of your own (see Chapter 2).

- Encourage, but do not force, children to use a variety of materials.

Dramatic play
- Provide hats and clothing worn by men and women; a variety of "work" props that reflect blue-collar as well as white-collar work; kitchen implements from different ethnic groups.
- Post pictures in the housekeeping area that show families from a variety of racial/ethnic backgrounds; family members who are differently abled; different kinds of family organization (single-parent, extended); women and men doing a variety of household tasks.
- Support children's exploration of nonstereotypic gender roles: Intervene when a child tells another child that she or he can't do it because the child is a girl or a boy. Help boys get involved in dramatic play.
- Place a few full-length mirrors in the housekeeping center. Occasionally, when two or three children are playing there, ask them questions about their skin, eye, and hair color as they look at each other in the mirror.

Large motor equipment
- Regularly observe which children use large motor equipment such as climbing structures, trikes, play cars, slides. Help girls and differently abled children who may be more reluctant to use these materials to develop skills and to be comfortable with them.

- Intervene if a child tells another child he can't use the material because of who he is.

Blocks, trucks, small people figures

- Make sure small people figures include men and women from a variety of racial and ethnic backgrounds.
- Regularly observe which children use the blocks and trucks. Make sure girls get to use these materials.

Sand

- Girls are often taught not to get dirty, so some may be reluctant to use sand. Help children become comfortable with this material. Use old clothes kept at school, or a man's shirt as a smock, if necessary. Find ways to make sand accessible to children with physical limitations.

Water

- Washing dirt off dolls with different skin colors and seeing what happens to their skin color is an important activity with 2s (and 3s) because they are trying to figure out what stays the same and what changes about themselves, and some lighter skinned children may equate darker skin with being dirty. This does not need to be a preplanned activity. When children are playing with dolls in water, join in. Say, "Let's look at the doll's colors. Now let's put some dirt on each doll and wash them. Let's see what happens to their color." You can also do the same "experiment" with the children's hands and arms.

Dolls

- Regularly playing with dolls that reflect different racial/ethnic identities, physical abilities, and gender, including anatomically correct dolls, enables young children to gain familiarity and ease with diversity. The teacher puts the dolls in the classroom; the children invent the activities.
- Observe if a child never chooses to play with a doll that looks different from him. Invite the child to play with you—you choose the "different-looking" doll, and the child chooses his doll. After a while, suggest a way for the two dolls to be together (riding in a carriage, or going to sleep), and for the child to play with your doll (feeding your doll while you cook dinner). Do similar doll play with the child until he seems

comfortable with the different dolls in your classroom.

Small-group snack time

- Do "learning about us" activities:

  (a) Talk about children's skin, hair, eye color, and hair texture. Have children look at themselves and other children in large mirrors so they can see themselves in relation to others. Have children put their hands into the middle of the table and talk about what is the same and different about each other's hands. Make hand- and footprint murals, using premixed paints that match children's skin colors. Have children touch each other's hair and talk about how each child's hair feels.

  (b) Make a book about each child with 4 or 5 photos of the child busy doing her favorite activities. Talk about the child's gender; skin, hair, and eye color; what the child can do; what she likes to do. Read about a different child each day.

  (c) Have a photograph of each child's caregivers (mother, father, mother or father's partners, grandparent, etc.). Talk about how they look.

- Read teacher-made picture books: "All about girls," "All about boys," "People come in all colors."

- Teach simple sign language words (see Resources, pp. 119–132, for easy sign books).

Large group/Circle time

- Regularly read appealing picture books that depict gender, racial, ethnic, and physical ability diversity. Read the same book many times so that children become familiar with it. Observe children's nonverbal responses and comment (e.g., Maria saying, "Yes, I am brown" when reading *Ten, Nine, Eight*). Simply answer any comments that children make ("My grandma has one like that"—pointing to a wheelchair in the book. "Yes, your grandma uses a wheelchair so that she can move around because her legs can't walk, just like the grandma in this story").

- Never use stereotypic or inaccurate books with 2s: they do not yet have the data base for making comparisons between "fair" and "unfair" images. (Fours and 5s can do this.)

- Interchange male and female pronouns when reading popular stories: For example, in *Runaway Bunny* (Brown, 1942), the rabbit child is written as a "he"; read "she" every other time you read the story.

- Teach simple songs in more than one language (e.g., "Mary has a red dress" can use Spanish words or sign language for certain words such as color names).

- Add skin color, hair texture and color, and eye color to songs about body parts.

- Sing frequently used songs, such as "Good Morning" or "Happy Birthday," in more than one language including sign language.

- Change words or add verses to songs and finger games to make them nonsexist (e.g., "The Noble Duke of York, he had ten thousand *friends*" instead of *men*).

Integrating Anti-Bias Issues Into Parent Discussions About 2s

The earlier parents become aware of how issues of gender, race, culture, and disabilities influence childrearing, the more chances there will be for teachers and parents working together to promote children's anti-bias development. The following seven sessions illustrate ways to integrate anti-bias issues into parent discussions about socialization tasks for 2-year-olds. The methodology can be adapted to parent discussion with preschool and kindergarten children by substituting other relevant developmental tasks. The discussion leader may be the teacher of the parents' children, the school or center's director, or a parent educator.

Each session uses a dialogue model: storytelling followed by guided discussions led by the group facilitator. Preparation for the discussion leader includes:

(1) knowledge of the developmental tasks facing 2-year-olds;

(2) self-awareness of one's own beliefs and practices with children; and

(3) sensitivity to how issues of gender, race, culture, and physical abilities affect parents' childrearing. (See the self-education activities in Chapter 12, "Getting Started.")

Session #1: Separation

Goals: As school begins for 2-year-olds, separation is a central issue for both children and parents. Help parents identify their difficulties with separation and think about how issues of gender, culture, or disabilities may influence separation.

Discussion questions and issues:

(a) *Ask:* "Tell about the first time you remember being left by your parents." Each parent takes a turn. Some may find it difficult to remember; as other parents talk, memories are stimulated.

(b) *Ask:* "Now tell about the first time you left your child. With whom? For what reason? How did it feel? If this is the first time you have left your child, share why."

GOALS

To enable parents:
1. To relate and reflect on their parenting experiences
2. To explore their similarities and differences
3. To use research about child development to increase understanding of their experiences
4. To learn from each other

The intent of the parent discussions is to *uncover* the complexities of childrearing, not to "cover" topics. None of the questions raised in the sessions have simple answers: Families must find their own solutions within their own specific contexts.

(c) *Ask:* "Now let's look at how your cultural backgrounds, and your child's gender, or disability, affects your separation attitudes and behavior." Listen for examples of this in the previous sharing of experiences, and now point them out. If no examples emerge from the parents, mention examples, from your own experience or from research articles, relevant to your particular group of parents.

Points to remember:

- Cultural discontinuity, including language, between home and school compounds the difficulties of separation. Some families may experience conflict between the dominant culture's emphasis on early independence and autonomy and their cultural belief that good mothers do not leave their 2-year-olds with anyone else. Help parents understand the conflict and facilitate their exploration of what balance between their cultural values and the dominant cultural values they want to create.

- Some parents may find it harder to separate from girls than from boys: Research does indicate that generally, from infancy, parents allow boys to move further away from them.

- Parents of a child with a disability of any variety may also experience greater difficulty in separating. Not overprotecting differently abled children is an important task for parents and teachers.

Session #2: Messiness

Goals: Programs for 2-year-olds should encourage play with "messy" materials such as sand, water, mud, paint, clay. Even with smocks, children will get dirty. Help parents identify their limits and concerns about messiness and explore ways to resolve differences between program and parent limits about messiness.

Discussion questions and issues:

(a) *Ask:* "What are your limits and concerns about your child getting dirty?" List their responses on a chalkboard or easel paper in two columns: *limits* and *concerns*.

(b) *Ask:* "What were your family's beliefs about children being messy? What are your

community's beliefs? Where do your beliefs conflict with your family and/or community?"

Points to remember:

- Sexism influences thinking that boys are allowed to get more dirty than girls.

- Racism influences thinking that a dirty White child is "cute," a dirty child of color "inferior."

- Economic considerations make it harder for low-income families if children's clothes get dirty.

(c) *Discuss:* How to resolve any differences between parents' and the school's handling of messiness.

Session # 3: Aggression

Goals: As 2s interact with each other, pushing, hitting, and biting occur; parents often are more upset by these behaviors than the children. Help parents identify what behaviors they allow and limit and why.

Discussion questions and issues:

(a) *Ask:* "What are your definitions of aggressive behavior and assertive behavior? What do you feel comfortable allowing your child to do?" Make a list on the chalkboard or easel paper. Help the group identify differences among them.

(b) *Ask:* "How do you think your racial or cultural background and your ideas about gender behavior influence the kinds of aggressive and assertive behavior you allow your child?"

Points to remember:

- Different cultures have very different standards of assertive and aggressive behavior: Some emphasize group cooperation and noncompetitiveness; others emphasize individual competitiveness and self-assertion.

- Sexism influences adults to teach girls to be both nonaggressive and nonassertive and to teach boys a double message—to be aggressive is "manly," but aggression is then often punished.

- Racism influences people to differentially perceive aggressive behavior in White children and in children of color. Members of the dominant culture frequently perceive assertive and aggressive behavior in children of color, particularly Black and Latino children, as more threatening than in White children.

(c) *Describe:* The school's definitions and limits on aggressive and assertive behavior. Discuss any differences with parents' ideas.

Session # 4: Setting Limits, Part I

Goals: As 2-year-olds construct their sense of self, they explore and test the limits their parents set. How to say "no" and enforce limits becomes a big issue for parents during this period. Help parents examine their ideas and behaviors regarding limit setting and identify where they want to make changes.

Discussion questions and issues:

(a) *Ask:* "When and how do you say 'no' to your child? When is it hard/easy to say 'no'?" List on the chalkboard or easel paper: *behaviors, hard or easy,* and *how.* Help parents identify the differences and similarities among their ideas about limit setting.

(b) *Ask:* "How do cultural background, gender, or disabilities affect when and how you set limits?" Use the list to explore this issue.

Points to remember:

• Parents often set different standards for boys and girls. Ask parents to reflect about why and if they want to continue doing so.

• Parents from "minority" cultures may experience conflicts with when and how the dominant culture sets limits and feel torn about what direction to go. Help parents explore the pros and cons of different solutions to this conflict.

• Children with special physical or mental difficulties also need limits appropriate to their developmental level. They should not be treated as if they are infants.

(c) *Ask:* "Are you comfortable with how you set limits? Are there areas you want to change?"

Session # 5: Setting Limits, Part II

Goals: Same as for Part I.

Discussion questions and issues:

(a) *Ask:* "How were you disciplined as a child? What did you like/not like?" Make a list.

(b) *Ask:* "Do you have conflicts with your spouse/partner or your own parents about limit setting for your child?" Help parents identify the sources of their differences: cultural, different ideas about gender behavior.

(c) *Ask:* "How do you deal with the differences?" Encourage parents to share their ideas.

(d) *Describe:* When, how, and why limits are set in the 2-year-olds' class. Discuss ways to resolve any differences between parents and program.

(For further ideas for parent meetings about anti-bias curriculum, see Chapter 11, "Working With Parents.")

References

Bang, M. (1983). *Ten, nine, eight.* New York: Greenwillow.
Brown, M.W. (1942). *Runaway bunny.* New York: Harper & Row.
Henriod, L. (1982). *Grandma's wheelchair.* Niles, IL: Whitman.
Martin, B., Jr. (1983). *Brown Bear, Brown Bear, what do you see?* New York: Holt, Rinehart & Winston.

LEARNING ABOUT RACIAL DIFFERENCES AND SIMILARITIES

4

Figuring out who I am and who you are and how I feel about me and you are central, absorbing tasks for 3-, 4-, and 5-year-olds. Gender, race, culture, and physical-abledness are major pieces of the puzzle. Young children are very open to developing anti-bias attitudes and behaviors if adults actively counteract the negative impact of sexism, racism, and handicappism. Empowerment starts early.

In any aspect of good early childhood education, much learning occurs spontaneously and informally, when adults respond to children's comments and behaviors. Also, in all aspects of early childhood education, good teachers plan learning encounters. Effective anti-bias teaching means listening for and using spontaneous moments. However, adult-planned activities that help children directly address their misconceptions, discomforts, and unfair behaviors are also essential.

The next five chapters lay out developmental tasks, guidelines, and activities for working with 3-, 4-, and 5-year-olds. Many 5-year-olds will continue to work on the same developmental tasks that preschoolers are involved with. As their general cognitive ability expands, kindergartners will also be able to gain from additional activities that explore the relationship between the individual and the group. Kindergarten teachers should begin with preschool activities, in order to build a foundation for the more advanced activities.

GOALS

1. To encourage children to ask about their own and others' physical characteristics
2. To provide children with accurate, developmentally appropriate information
3. To enable children to feel pride, but not superiority, about their racial identity
4. To enable children to develop ease with and respect for physical differences
5. To help children become aware of our shared physical characteristics—what makes us all human beings

---

Racial Differences and Similarities

Although race is not a scientifically valid way to categorize people, racism endows "race" with very significant social meaning. The physical characteristics all humans share are far more biologically important than the variations in skin color, hair texture, and eye shape that originally were adaptations to different environmental demands. Nonetheless, access to economic resources, political power, and cultural rights are still very much determined by a person's membership in a specific "racial" group. Stereotyping and prejudice based on race remain a powerful part of prevailing social practice. Children need guidance in sorting out their ideas and feelings about skin color, hair texture, and eye shape so that racism cannot harm their self-concept or teach them to reject others.

Developmental Tasks and Guidelines

Three- and 4-year-olds continue the study of physical characteristics begun in their second year. Their observations of differences expand, and they become interested in more than noticing and naming.

Preschoolers are aware of variations and wonder where they fit in

Skin color is a frequent focus of interest:

Coloring with brown crayon, Donald (3½) announces at large, "I'm brown too. I'm about as brown as this crayon." "Yes," appropriately responds his teacher, "your skin is a beautiful brown." Positively acknowledging a child's skin color is an important step in a child's developing concept of who he is and how he feels about himself.

Another teacher might have said, "Oh, it doesn't matter what color you are; we are all people," diverting Donald's attention from his skin color. This is an inappropriate response, based on the mistaken notion that noticing skin color causes prejudice. In fact, that response could teach Donald to think that there is something wrong with his skin color.

Cindy (4) asks her teacher matter-of-factly, "If I'm Black and White, and Tiffany is Black and White, how come her skin is darker?" "Well," her teacher explains, "each of you has a mommy who is Black and a daddy who is White, but when the colors of Black and White mix together it doesn't always look the same. Sometimes it is lighter brown and sometimes darker brown. All the colors are beautiful."

"What color blood do we all have?" the teacher casually asks a group of 3-year-olds in a child care center after having read a story about a child who hurt himself. "I have light red," says Michelle, who is White, "but I think Jannine (who is Black) has dark red." Surprised, the teacher asks the others if anyone else thinks we have different-colored blood. Some say yes, others no. The teacher is surprised because the children have certainly seen each other's blood from the times they have scraped or cut themselves. "Well," says the teacher firmly, "everyone has the same color blood, no matter what our skin color is. We all need blood to make our bodies work." Moral: Never take for granted what young children's theories are about physical characteristics!

Two 4-year-old friends, one Black, one White, are chatting. Mike: "I'm going to get new pants." Doug: "What color?" Mike: "Blue." Doug: "What about brown?" Mike: "I don't like brown." Doug: "Oh, then you don't like me."

Mike (looking surprised): "Yes, I do." At this point, the teacher steps in: "There's something important I want to help the two of you figure out. Doug, why do you think Mike doesn't like you?" Doug: "I'm brown; he said he didn't like brown." Teacher: "Mike, Doug thought when you said you didn't like brown you meant you didn't like his brown skin either. Is that how you feel?" Mike: "No, I don't like brown pants; I like brown Doug." Teacher: "Doug, is that okay?" Doug nods his head yes and the two go off together.

Preschoolers are sensitive to other children's attitudes toward their skin color because they are already becoming aware of the societal bias against darker skin.

Hair and eyes are also frequently the subject of preschoolers' comments:

Kathy, a 3-year-old Asian child whose hair is straight, loves to play with her teacher's hair. "It's bouncy and cuddly," she says. Regina, who is Black and wears her hair in an Afro, responds, "I'm glad you like it. My hair is different from yours. Mine is curly, yours is straight. I like mine and I like yours."

During story time, Hector (4) leans over and touches Jamal's hair. Jamal pushes his hand away. Their teacher intervenes: "Hector, have you ever touched hair like Jamal's before?" Hector shakes his head no. Jamal interjects, "He didn't ask me if it's OK." Teacher: "Would it be all right if Hector asked first?" Jamal: "Yes. (He turns to Hector.) Ask me and then you can touch it. Then I want to touch your hair." Teacher: "Yes, it's fun to touch and learn about each other's hair as long as we ask first. Did Jamal's/Hector's hair feel the same as or different than your hair?"

Hector and the rest of the children are having an important lesson—how to respectfully learn from each other. If Jamal had said it wasn't all right for Hector to touch his hair, then the teacher might have said, "We have to respect what Jamal says. There are other ways to learn about each other's hair." In this way, he supportingly acknowledges as OK both Hector's curiosity and Jamal's rights.

"Craig's eyes go like this," says 4-year-old Ruth, pulling her eyes up. "They look funny." Her teacher replies: "Craig's eyes are not funny; they have a different shape than yours. Craig's eyes are the same shape as his family's eyes, just as your eyes are shaped like your family's. Your eye shape is fine. Craig's eye shape is fine. Both of your eye shapes are good for seeing. It is OK to ask questions about how people look. It is not OK to say they look funny—that hurts their feelings."

If Craig were a child who had been adopted by a non-Asian family, then the teacher might substitute the sentence, "Craig's eyes are shaped like the millions of people who live in the country he came from," for "shaped like his family's eyes," and follow up with more about Craig's country of origin.

Preschoolers want to know how they got their color, hair, and eye characteristics

Sometimes preschoolers verbalize interesting theories of their own:

"How do people get their color?" asks 3-year-old Heather. "What are your ideas?" her teacher responds. "Well, I was wondering about pens. You know, the pens you can put red or blue or brown on your skin if you want to." Teacher: "I'm glad you are trying to figure things out, but that's not how people get their skin color. We get our skin color from our mommies and daddies. Your skin is the same color as mine. Marizza's skin color is like her mommy and daddy's. Denise's skin is lighter brown because she is a mixture of her mommy's white skin and her Daddy's black skin."

Respect children's ideas while also giving them accurate information.

Rebecca, who has been playing with Miyoko, a child recently arrived from Japan, asks the teacher: "Can you make my eyes like Miyoko's? If I learn to speak Japanese, will I have eyes like hers?" Her teacher explains that her eye shape cannot be changed, even if she learns to speak Japanese. "We get our eyes from how our parents look; we learn to talk the way our parents talk. Miyoko's parents talk Japanese, so she speaks Japanese. Your parents speak English, so you speak English."

A few days later, the teacher sees Rebecca trying to make her eyes look Japanese. She says, "Rebecca, it isn't polite to pull on your eyes; Miyoko might think you are making fun of her." Rebecca: "I want to talk Japanese." Teacher: "It is a good idea to learn some Japanese so you can talk with your friend in her language. Remember, we talked about how changing your eye shape won't help. Let's ask Miyoko to tell us the names of some of our toys; you can also teach her the English words for the same toys."

Aware that getting older brings physical changes, preschoolers wonder if skin color, hair, and eyes remain constant

It is not easy to learn which aspects of humanness *change* with growth and which do not.

"If I eat melon, will my skin get darker?" asks 4-year-old Ben, after hearing his teacher read a book about melanin and skin color. The teacher responds, "No, I used the word *melanin*—it sounded like *melon* to you, but it is not the same thing. Melanin is something inside our bodies that our daddies and mommies give us when they make us. Once we are born, we don't change our skin colors." The concept of melanin is hard for preschoolers to grasp, because it is an abstract concept for them.

"But," chimes in Robin, "last summer I got to be as dark as Maria. So then I was Mexican, now I'm not." Teacher: "Yes, our skin color can get darker when we play a lot in the sun, and lighter when we don't. That doesn't mean we can change our skin color any way we want. Even when your skin color looked like Maria's you still weren't Mexican. Maria is Mexican because her mom and dad and grandparents are Mexican. You are Irish because your parents and grandparents are Irish." Robin: "But I want to be just like Maria. She's my best friend." Teacher: "It's great that you and Maria are best friends. I know you have a lot of fun playing together at school and at home. You don't have to be just the same to be best friends."

"I'm going to make my eyes straight and blue," 4-year-old Kim tells her teacher. "Why do you want to change your lovely eyes?" her teacher asks wonderingly. Kim: "It's prettier." Teacher: "Kim, I don't think straight eyes are prettier than yours are. Your mommy and grandma and grandpa don't think so either. We like you just the way you are, with your beautiful, dark brown eyes shaped just as they are. Why do you think straight and blue eyes are prettier?" Kim: "Sarah said I had ugly eyes, she likes Julie's better." Teacher: "Sarah is wrong to say you have ugly eyes. It's not true and it is unfair and hurtful to say so. In this classroom we respect how everyone looks. Let's go and talk with her about it."

Children of color, more often than White children, may verbalize not liking the color, texture, or shape of their skin, hair, or eyes. This happens because racism attacks children of color's physical characteristics. Sometimes the teacher can pinpoint the incident that precipitated the remark; sometimes the child cannot verbalize why. It is very important to address the child's feelings immediately and to assure her that how she is is just right, that her family and teacher love her as she is, and that people who think her looks are not OK are wrong. Help the child understand that there are millions of people who have the same skin color or eye shape as they do, even if she is numerically a minority in the class. The goals are to facilitate children's awareness that their racial identity does not change, to help them understand that they are part of a large group with similar characteristics (they are *not* "different"), and to foster their desire to be exactly who they are.

Preschoolers get confused about racial group names and the actual color of their skin, and why two people with different skin tones are considered part of the same group

"Why am I called Black? My skin is brown." "I'm not yellow, I'm tan." "I don't look white like the piece of paper." "Is Mexican my color?" These are examples of questions that reflect children's puzzlement about "racial" labels. It is easy to understand their difficulties; it is not so easy to explain.

"My skin isn't white, it's pink," 3-year-old Jane insists. "Yes, it's true; your skin color isn't white like a piece of white paper, it does look pink. When grown-ups say 'White,' we mean people whose families once came from a place called Europe. You are part of the White group because your family once came from the continent of Europe. Let's go look at the globe and see where Europe is."

As their classification ability expands, so too will their further understanding.

"You're not Black, you're White," 4½-year-old Letticia, a Black child with dark brown skin color, tells 4½-year-old Carol, a light-skinned Black child. Carol looks confused. Their teacher steps in and explains: "Carol is Black just like you are Black, Letticia, even though the shades of your skin are different. You are both Black because you are part of a big family called Black people or Afro-Americans whose ancestors came a long time ago from the continent of Africa. Let's go look at our globe and see where Africa is and then read *Colors Around Me* (Church, 1971) again to see the different skin shades Black children have."

"I'm not Black," Tiffany, a dark-skinned Black child, kept saying during a discussion about skin color. Her teacher, worried about her self-concept, tried talking with Tiffany, but she kept insisting, "I'm not Black." Talking with her parents that evening, to figure out what to do, the teacher learned to her embarrassment that they use the term *Afro-American,* not *Black.* As soon as her teacher used the term Tiffany recognized, her self-concept was fine.

This incident highlights the importance of finding out from parents the terms they use and what and how they are teaching their child about her racial/ethnic identity. However, the teacher's concern and immediate phone call to Tiffany's parents were appropriate, even if her interpretation of the situation lacked a vital piece of information.

"Am I red?" Leroy, a 4½-year-old Navajo child, asked in a puzzled tone. "Tom (a 4½-year-old White child) said I'm a red Indian, but I don't see any red on me." "You're right, Leroy, there is no such person as a red Indian. Some people use that word and it isn't true. You are a Navajo and your skin is brown, not red. Let's go talk with Tom and explain to him so he won't make the same mistake again."

A Navajo man visits Joshua's child care center to talk about his life. He is dressed in jeans, plaid shirt, "cowboy" hat, and boots. Joshua (3½) calls out, "You're not an Indian." His teacher, much embarrassed, says, "Yes, he is. He is a Navajo Indian. Why do you think he isn't an Indian?" "He's not wearing feathers," Joshua replies. "People who are Indians wear many different kinds of clothes. Many do not wear feathers. We need to learn more about this," the teacher responds, before turning the discussion back to the visitor.

"I'm not Mexican, I'm White," Anita forcefully insists during a discussion about children's ethnic identities.

Her teacher explains, "Anita, you are Mexican because your family is Mexican-American. Do you know that Mexican is not a color? Mexican people have many different skin colors, from dark brown to very light. All those are good colors to be."

Some adults suggest not talking about racial/ethnic labels with young children. This does not work because children have already begun to ask questions about the meaning of such labels. They need adult guidance to sort out their ideas and get accurate feedback. Otherwise, their confusion and misconceptions can develop into prejudice. Though adults often feel embarrassed when children blurt out questions and comments in the presence of those they are talking about, it is very important to overcome the embarrassment and be an educator.

Activities for Learning About Racial Physical Differences

Even when if you have not heard your preschool children specifically raise any of the questions illustrated in the previous section, silence does not mean they have not wondered about the same issues other children have verbalized. It just means that the teacher must initiate activities rather than introducing them as a follow-up on a child's comment.

Creating a rich anti-bias environment in the classroom sets the stage for learning about physical differences and similarities. Review Chapter 2 for the materials that should be a part of the daily classroom experience and which will also be used for specific activities. The richer the environment, the more likely children will ask questions, even in classrooms where the staff and children come from similar racial backgrounds.

Learning about the children and staff in your classroom

1. Make a book, "We All Look Special," about the physical characteristics of each child and staff member. Take color photos of each child, paste each on its own page; ask children to describe themselves and write what they say under the photo. Include skin color, hair, and eyes among

the characteristics. With darker skinned children, be careful about having sufficient lighting when photographing them so that their features are clear. When the book is complete, read it to the children at circle time.

Note: This activity will also bring up characteristics based on gender and physical-abledness. Be sure to include any such information in what you write about each child.

2. Get paint chips from a paint store. In small groups identify the ones closest to each child's skin tone, hair color, and eye color. Make a poster with the paint chips and names of children. With 4-year-olds, you can also make a simple chart stating the range of colors and how many children have which color. Talk about how everyone has skin and the functions it serves for everyone.

3. With 3-year-olds, provide skin-colored crayons (available from Afro-Am—see Resources, p. 134). Help them choose the one closest to their skin color and then draw pictures of themselves. In addition, with 4-year-olds, mix paints so that each child has her or his individualized color for painting pictures of her or himself. Be creative in talking about the beauty of each shade.

ADAPTATION

- In an all-White class, help children see differences in skin shades, including freckles, and emphasize that skin color differences are desirable.
- In classes of children of color, emphasize the beauty of all the different skin tones and hair textures to counter the influence of racism, which makes physical characteristics closer to "white" more desirable. Be aware that within a group of color, children may exhibit bias against each other.
- In a diverse interracial/interethnic class, emphasize the theme, "Beautiful children come in all colors," and that the classroom is a wonderful mixture of differences.
- In a class where most children are of one background and a few are different, be sure to provide thoughtful support for the children who are in the minority. When learning about physical differences, do not just talk about the few who are more obviously different.
- If you have one or more children from interracial or multiethnic families, through marriage or adoption, be sure to include a variety of materials and activities reflective of their lives. Be sensitive to the particular issues of identity for such children.

    Activities should be based on all the children. However, make sure that your visual environment—pictures, posters, books, dolls—well represents the children who are in the minority. Include parents with racially nonmatching (adopted) children.

4. Make a life-size cutout of each child with butcher paper and use mirrors to help each child select the crayons and paints that most closely look like her or him to color in skin, eyes, and hair. Children can take turns at circle time telling about their cutouts. Mount the cutouts around the room.

5. Cut a tiny bunch of hair from each child, paste each one on a 3″ x 5″ index card, put them in a box, and then ask children to identify each swatch of hair. Then, take a photo of each child's face and make a collage about different hair styles. Bring in different combs and hair materials (conditioners, Afro-Sheen™, etc.) that children use and have them tell each other about how their hair is fixed. Talk about how everyone has hair and what function it serves.

6. Read books about the beauty of Black hair such as *Cornrows* (Yarbrough, 1979) and *Honey, I Love* (Greenfield, 1978). In a class with Black children, support Black children's pride in themselves. In classes without Black children, reading these books is one way to expand children's awareness of diversity.

7. Make a collage about different eye shapes and colors. Include photos of your own children and then add other pictures as part of the activities for broadening their awareness about diversity.

8. Make a bulletin board of color photos of each child and his or her mom, dad, grandparents, aunts, uncles, brothers, sisters, and cousins. Take photos of family members, and ask for extra photos from them. Talk about ways in which each child looks and doesn't look like family members. Highlight the point that we get our looks from our parents, but we never look exactly the same as them.

9. Read *Colors Around Me* (Church, 1971), which illustrates the variations of skin shades among Black children and then emphasizes that they are still all members of the same "family" of Afro-Americans. This can be used in a variety of ways to help children explore the concept that people with different skin shades are still considered members of the same group.

    If your children are Black, read the book and then have each child choose an object that looks like their skin color. Make your own *Colors Around Me* book or poster with photos and sentences about your own children.

    If you do not have Black children, first make a similar book about your children. Talk about

ADAPTATION

Interracial and multiethnic families, by marriage and by adoption of children from different racial and ethnic backgrounds, are becoming more common in our society. Parents in these families differ in how they define their children's identity, and in their choice of identity names: interracial, biracial, multiracial, multiethnic, mixed, and rainbow are all used. Some parents will need support for sorting out their ideas and feelings about what to teach their children about themselves.

Familiarize yourself with current professional thinking about the needs of interracial children (see Wardle, 1987). Be prepared to respond to children's questions and comments. If you have multiracial children in your class, find out how their parents explain identity to them before doing activities about racial similarities and differences. Be sure that your classroom environment shows interracial children and families in all aspects of the curriculum. Ask families for help in locating and making materials. Read children books such as *Black Is Brown Is Tan* (Adoff, 1973), and extend its approach to include other combinations of interracial and multiethnic families. Expose the children in your class to role models of adults who grew up in interracial and multiethnic families.

the larger "family" group to which the children belong. Then read the book as an activity about diversity beyond your classroom.

10. Encourage positive feelings about black and brown colors. This is important for darker skinned children to counter the negative attitudes toward these colors created by racism. It is also important for White children to counter their learning that brown and black are inferior. Make sure children regularly use different shades of black and brown in their play dough, paints, and paper. Collect black and brown cloth, yarn, and paper of different textures and shades, and make all-black or all-brown collages. Read *Black Is Beautiful* (McGovern, 1969) and have children make a list of beautiful black and brown objects they

know. Play songs like Paul Robeson's recording of "Curly-Headed Baby," or Oscar Brown, Jr.'s recording of "Little Brown Baby."

Expanding children's awareness of physical diversity

• Find out how your children think about racial differences not present in your classroom: Read a book about a child from a different racial background engaged in a task familiar to your children (a birthday, a visit to the doctor, a new sibling). Ask them: What did you like about the story? Does the girl/boy have the same color skin, hair, and eyes as you do? How do you think they got their different skin color? Do you know anyone or see anyone on TV who has the same

ADAPTATION

• If your class is already diverse, then learning about themselves will simultaneously provide learning about diversity.

• If your class is predominantly children of color, the primary task is building their knowledge and pride in themselves. A secondary task is learning about groups not present in the class.

• If your class is White, the goal is to counter a White-centered view by first establishing differences among the White children and then introducing activities about people of color. Begin with a group that has some visibility in the children's world because they live in the larger community or are represented on TV programs the children watch.

skin color? Are the children doing things you do? Further activities should address the children's thinking as well as issues you know are developmentally important.

- Expand children's understanding of physical diversity by adapting the activities listed above. For example, to learn about Black children: (a) Using dolls representing different skin shades among Black Americans, have children find crayons and mix paints to match their skin; (b) read books that show variations in Black children's skin color and hair texture; (c) create a poster, "Beautiful children and grown-ups come in all colors." Include photos and pictures of children with different skin shades, hair styles, and eye shapes and colors engaged in a variety of daily activities.

Developmental Tasks for Kindergarten Children

Five-year-olds' growing cognitive ability opens up two further areas of learning, in addition to those developmental tasks already discussed. Remember that before working on these additional concepts, kindergarten children need to have first had many opportunities to build the earlier concepts. Unless you are certain that your 5-year-olds have had the anti-bias curriculum outlined in these chapters, assume nothing and begin at the beginning.

1. Five-year-olds can begin to understand scientific explanations for differences in skin color, hair texture, and eye shape.

2. Five-year-olds can more fully explore the range of physical differences within racial groups and the range of similarities between racial groups.

These concepts need the cognitive structures of seriation and multiple classification (as Piagetian theory defines these cognitive abilities) in order to be understood.

Supplementary Activities for Kindergarten Children

1. After learning about each other's skin colors—using paint swatches, skin-color crayons, and paint mixed to the right shade of each child—make simple charts showing the range of skin colors ("We come in many shades of colors"). Children can each make a handprint with their skin-shade paint on individual sheets of paper. Cut out the hands and put them in order from lightest to darkest. In a classroom of all White children, also make a seriation chart of freckles—from the least to the most.

2. Do the same kind of activity with hair texture as the variable—go from curly to straight.

3. Make a graph of the differences in eye color: how many have each color.

4. Read books that provide simple scientific explanations of the biological reason for variation in skin color, hair texture, and eye shape.

5. Talk about the advantages certain physical attributes give people under certain environmental conditions: Darker skin gives more protection from the hot sun than does lighter skin; the "epicanthic fold," which determines the eye shape of people with Asian origins, provides protection against the glare of snow. "White" skin and blue eyes are predominant among peoples who originated in Northern Europe where the sun is less strong.

References

Adoff, A. (1973). *Black is brown is tan.* New York: Harper & Row.

Bunin, C. (1976). *Is that your sister?* New York: Pantheon.

Church, V. (1971). *Colors around me.* Chicago: Afro-American Publishing.

Greenfield, E. (1978). *Honey, I love and other love poems.* New York: Crowell.

McGovern, A. (1969). *Black is beautiful.* New York: Scholastic.

Rosenberg, M. (1984). *Being adopted.* New York: Lothrop, Lee & Shepard.

Wardle, F. (1987). Are you sensitive to interracial children's special identity needs? *Young Children, 42*(2), 53–59.

Yarbrough, C. (1979). *Cornrows.* New York: Putnam.

5

LEARNING ABOUT DISABILITIES

You gave us your dimes; now we want our rights.
(From a poster of a disability rights activist group)

In 1972, Congress mandated that children with physical, speech, hearing, visual, intellectual, and emotional impairments ranging from mild to severe make up at least 10% of the children enrolled in Head Start programs. In 1975, Public Law 94–142 extended educational rights to school-age children by declaring that all children with disabilities are entitled to a free, appropriate education in the "least restrictive environment." As a result of these two federal laws, children with a variety of disabilities and nondisabled children are finally having the opportunity to interact and to learn together.

However, fostering anti-bias attitudes toward disability and empowering children with disabilities requires much more than being together in the classroom. Children with disabilities need to see themselves reflected in the world around them, in pictures, in toys, in books, in role models. They need acceptance for who they are and an environment that fosters their autonomy and the development of alternative modes of interaction with the

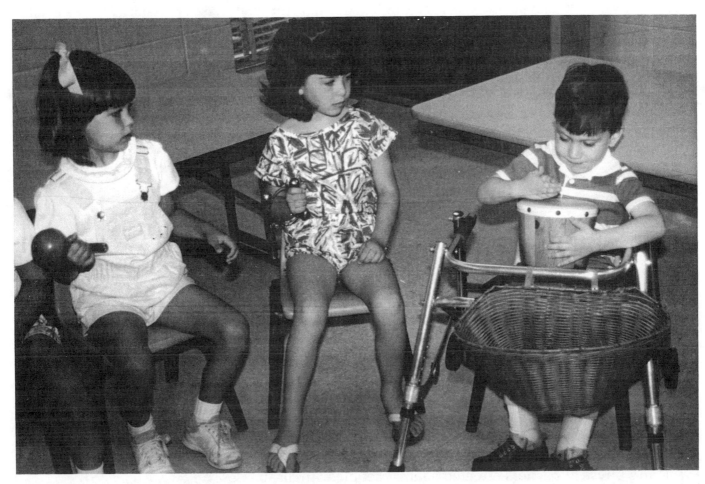

world. Nondisabled children need to gain information, ask questions, and express their feelings about disabilities. Contact by itself does not necessarily reduce nondisabled children's misconceptions or fears—it may even intensify them—unless adults take active steps to promote children's learning about each other.

Anti-bias teaching about disabilities also requires that teachers become aware of their own deep-seated attitudes.

> Most nondisabled people have been socialized not to think about disability unless it directly affects them or a close family member . . . [and] have to some degree internalized society's myths and stereotyped attitudes toward people with disabilities. (Froschl, Colon, Rubin, & Sprung, 1984, p. 18)

Dynamics such as invisibility (keeping disabled people out of sight, not "noticing" or talking about disabilities), infantilizing (treating a person with a disability as incapable and dependent), and objectifying (seeing only a person's disability rather than seeing the whole person) may interfere with teachers' and other caregivers' ability to work effectively toward anti-bias goals.

Stereotyping of people with disabilities is both reflected and reinforced by many of the terms in the English language. Words such as *cripple, idiot, crazy, retardate, feeble-minded,* and *deaf and dumb* contribute to a negative self-image and perpetuate handicapped attitudes and practices. Such words convey helplessness and dependency, evoking feelings of pity rather than respect. Expressions of speech such as "the blind leading the blind," commonly used to describe people who don't seem to know what they are doing, also reflect negative attitudes (Froschl et al., 1984).

There has been and continues to be controversy over what terms to use.* This reflects the changing awareness of professionals and advocates for the rights of people with disabilities. In this book we use the words *disability* and *disabled* since they are currently the preferred terms of the disability rights movement. It is also important to use the phrase "person with a disability" rather than "a disabled person," or "a child who is deaf" rather than "a deaf child." These preferred formulations refer to a disability (e.g., deafness) as only one of a person's characteristics rather than his or her total being. We also use the term *differently abled* because we like its connotation.

Although the term *handicapped* is still used by some professionals, by the federal government, and in the new legislation to protect disabled people against discrimination, it is rejected by many activists because of its historic connection with a "cap-in-hand" begging image. As Merle Froschl points out (personal communication, September 1988), the term *disability* refers to a person's condition, while the term *handicap* refers to the consequences of society's barriers. People with disabilities are not handicapped by their conditions but by prejudice, lack of accessibility, and discrimination.

---

* Thanks to Merle Froschl of Educational Equity, Inc., for input on the issues surrounding terminology.

GOALS

1. To provide an "inclusive" educational environment in which all children can succeed
2. To enable children with disabilities to develop autonomy, independence, competency, confidence, and pride
3. To provide all children with accurate, developmentally appropriate information about their own and others' disabilities and to foster understanding that a person with a disability is different in one respect but similar in many others
4. To enable all children to develop the ability to interact knowledgeably, comfortably, and fairly with people having various disabilities
5. To teach children with disabilities how to handle and challenge name calling, stereotypic attitudes, and physical barriers
6. To teach nondisabled children how to resist and challenge stereotyping, name calling, and physical barriers directed against people with disabilities

Developmental Tasks and Guidelines

Young children notice and ask questions about disabilities

Children need simple, brief, accurate answers:

While singing at circle time, the teacher notices that 3-year-old Mia is looking intently at Lucy, the new teacher assistant. (Lucy's arm is shorter and her hand only has two tiny fingers.) Mia reaches out and tentatively and very briefly touches Lucy's hand. After the song is over, the teacher matter-of-factly says to Mia: "I saw you looking at Lucy's hand. It doesn't look like your hand. Do you wonder why her hand and arm are like that?" Mia nods her head yes. "Lucy, will you please tell Mia and the other children about your arm and hand?" Lucy: "I was born with my arm and hand like this." Mia: "Does it hurt?" Lucy: "No." Mia: "Will my hand be like that?" Lucy: "No, because you were born with your hand just like it is." The teacher joins in: "Do you want to touch Lucy's hand, Mia? Is it OK if she does, Lucy?" Mia feels all around Lucy's arm and hand. At the end of circle time, the teacher suggests, "Mia, why don't you show Lucy where we keep the juice and you and she help each other get snack ready?" The two go off.

"Why doesn't Malcolm paint with his hands?" asks a preschool classmate. (Malcolm's arm muscles are rigid and he paints with a brush mounted on a helmet he wears for protection.)

"Malcolm paints differently because the muscles in his hand don't move. His brain sends a message to his hands to always be tight. This is because Malcolm has had cerebral palsy since he was a baby. The tiny part of his brain that tells his hands how to move does not work right. Malcolm likes to paint just like you do so we figured out a way that he could do it."

"Why does Alisha have a machine in her ear?" 4-year-old Letticia askes her teacher.

"Alisha is hearing impaired. That means that her ears aren't able to hear sounds by herself. When she uses a hearing aid, she can hear some sounds."

"Why can't she hear?"

"Because Alisha had an illness when she was a baby and it hurt her ears."

"Why doesn't she talk? I don't know what she wants," Letticia continues.

"She is learning how to talk with her hands—that is called American sign language. We can learn sign language too so we will be able to understand and talk with her."

"Benjamin acts like a baby. He doesn't talk right and he scribbles and he doesn't even know how to write his name," 5-year-old Brandon complains to his teacher.

"Benjamin isn't a baby. He is 5 years old just like you. Benjamin can do many things that you can do: He can ride a bike, run, play ball, and climb. Benjamin also can't do some things yet that many of the other children in kindergarten can do. He will be able to talk more clearly and draw and learn to write his name, but it will take him longer. Remember how long it took you to learn how to ride the two-wheel bike? You didn't like it when other children teased you. I expect you to be a good friend to Benjamin and accept that he needs a lot of time to learn."

Young children are able to see their shared abilities and similarities

Build on this awareness while providing information about specific disabilities:

Four-year-old Tim, who has Down's syndrome, is pulling the wagon around the playground, one of his favorite activities. His classmate, Elena, joins him and gets into the wagon. She announces to the nearby teacher: "He's a messy painter, but he's a good wagon puller." "Yes, he sure is—I know it's one of your favorite things to be pulled in the wagon."

Three-year-old Misha, who has had a tracheotomy, arrives at school the first day. As she comes in the door, 3-year-old Matt asks, "What's with her?" Busy with greeting the children, the teacher replies, "Her name is Misha. She is in our class. I will be telling you about her a little bit later." At circle time, after some opening songs, the teacher asks Matt, "Do you want to ask your question about Misha now?" Matt responds, "No, she sings!" Their teacher concludes, "Yes, Misha sings and talks. She gets air for singing and talking through a special tube in her throat. Do you have questions about it?" The children are silent, so the teacher moves on to finger games. On another day she will explain more.

Children need information, words, and support for handling questions about their disabilities

Misha, Malcolm, Alisha, and Benjamin, like other children with disabilities, will be asked similar questions in and out of the classroom, and, indeed, throughout their lives.

- Find out how the child's parent(s) are explaining the specific disability to the child and to others.

- Help children find the words to answer questions. Discuss with them what they wish other children to know. Some children may need or want to practice what they will say privately with the teacher at first.

- Find out what they want you to tell other children. The words and manner of your response model ways to handle questions.

- Teach children that they have the right to choose to answer another child's question, say they don't want to answer, or say they would rather the child ask the teacher.

- Show support for children's feelings about having to answer questions about their disabilities. "I know it's hard sometimes when other children ask about why you wear a brace (or paint with a brush in your helmet, etc.) and that sometimes you wish they wouldn't ask so many questions. When you feel tired or sad or angry about it let me know and I will help you feel better."

Children are curious about the equipment and devices people use for specific disabilities

It is the unknown that frightens us, not the familiar. Let children become familiar with props people with particular needs use.

"Why does Mark have a hook?" 4-year-old Laura asks (referring to Mark's prosthesis).

"Mark has a special hand called a prosthesis because he was born without his own hand. His prosthesis hand was made especially for him. Mark's prosthesis hand helps him do the things you do with your hand, like picking up a toy, or painting, or eating."

"Does it hurt him?"

"It may have hurt Mark a little as it was getting adjusted, but I don't think it hurts him now. Let's go ask Mark if you and I can talk with him about his prosthesis —to find out if it hurts him and if it is OK for you to touch his hand so that you can feel what it is like."

"Will Mark hurt me?"

"Mark's prosthesis can only hurt you if he hits you, just like you could hurt Mark with your hand if you hit him. Remember, we don't let children hit each other in our class."

Children may be confused about what a child or adult with a particular disability can and cannot do

They need accurate information and many first-hand experiences to broaden their awareness.

The child care center teacher asks her 4- and 5-year-olds what they think it means for a person to be handicapped or disabled. Heather's response is a lovely example of how young children grapple with this question: "It means that they can't do stuff but they can still do the stuff you can do but they can't do almost the stuff you can but they can almost do the stuff you can."

Further questions from the teacher about what people with a specific disability can or can't do reveal that many of the children think that an adult who uses a wheelchair cannot be a parent or a teacher or, indeed, do any work. They are not sure that a child who is hearing impaired can know what a hearing child knows. Many say that a child who is blind cannot be active because "they wouldn't know where to go and they might hurt themselves."

CAUTION

- Provide supervised opportunities for children to explore and try out equipment used by people with disabilities, including those used by children in your class, or by renting or buying equipment for the classroom.

However

- Do not let another child touch equipment used by a child with a disability without first getting permission from the child and from the child's parents/caregivers.

- Always supervise a child's touching or holding another child's equipment. It may be expensive to fix or replace.

- Teach children to respect other children's equipment.

Children's difficulty with grasping what it really means to have a specific disability is further illustrated in an anecdote from *Including All of Us: An Early Childhood Curriculum About Disability* (Froschl et al., 1984). Ellen, one of the people who helped develop and pilot test this curriculum with 3-, 4-, and 5-year-olds, is blind:

> It was difficult for the children to comprehend that . . . [Ellen] really couldn't see them. They would tell her that she was only fooling, and many children brought objects for her to identify. She continually assured them that she could not see and that she could tell who they were by the sound of their voices. By the end of the pilot testing, however, when Liang, a three-year-old girl from the class, was teaching Ellen how to say goodbye in American sign language, she realized that Ellen could not see her making the sign. Liang took Ellen's hands and helped her to place them on her body correctly. (Froschl et al., 1984, p. 55)

In addition, children with disabilities need adult role models in their daily environment so that they can learn about how adults with disabilities function in their daily home and work life.

> Without such role models, adults with disabilities report that as children they believed that 1) they would outgrow their disability, or 2) they would die and not grow up. . . . One only has to remember the limited frames of reference and the very literal learning styles of young children to understand how such conclusions could be reached. (Froschl, et al., 1984, p. 17)

Children with disabilities need support for developing autonomy and independence

Some parents, caregivers, and teachers have difficulty encouraging autonomy and independence in any child, let alone children with big problems to overcome. But we can do it.

Miriam, a 3-year-old with a hand prosthesis, is learning how to feed herself. It's still hard, and she drops a lot of her food. Samantha, a 4-year-old, picks up Miriam's cracker and starts feeding her. Miriam accepts the help. Their teacher intervenes, "This isn't the time to help Miriam. She is learning to eat her cracker by herself just like you are learning to tie your shoes by yourself. You *can* help Miriam after snack by pushing her wheelchair to the next activity. Miriam, I want you to try to eat the cracker by yourself. You can do it."

Juanita (4½) is working on a collage. Her hand muscles are spastic and she is having trouble with one of the pieces. She gets a lot of paste on herself. Linda (4½) says to her, "I'll do that for you." Juanita keeps pasting and ignores Linda. The teacher intervenes, "Juanita, do you want help now?" Juanita responds, "No. I do it myself." Their teacher explains, "Linda, I'm glad you want to help Juanita, but it is important that you give her help only when she wants it. Next time, why don't you first ask, 'Do you need help?'" To Juanita the teacher says, "I'm glad you are making the collage by yourself. You are really being independent."

Young children may have anxieties and fears about people with disabilities

They worry about being hurt themselves and of "catching" the disability through contact with another person or even with the equipment used.

The teacher has brought a child-size wheelchair to the class and the preschoolers are taking turns sitting and moving in it. Eduardo refuses to even touch the wheelchair. His teacher asks, "Eduardo, you decided not to try the wheelchair. How come?" Eduardo: "Cuz I hate it." Teacher: "Why is that?" Eduardo: "Cuz my mom says I never like it." Teacher: "Why do you think that?" Eduardo: "Cuz it's too scary for me." Teacher: "What do you think will happen to you if you sit in the wheelchair?" Eudardo: "I won't walk." Teacher: "You think that if you use a wheelchair then you really won't be able to walk?" Eduardo nods his head yes. Teacher: "When a person needs a wheelchair it is because something happened to his legs *before* he needed the wheelchair. Sitting in the wheelchair *will not* hurt your legs, Eduardo. Let's ask the other children who wheeled themselves around in the wheelchair." Eduardo and the teacher check with the other children, who each show him that they can still walk.

At this point, Eduardo gingerly sits down in the wheelchair for a few seconds. As soon as he gets up his teacher asks, "Now, you sat in the wheelchair. Let's see if you can still walk." Eduardo walks, smiles, and goes off to a new activity.

If Eduardo had still refused to try the wheelchair, the teacher would have let it go for the moment, and then asked Eduardo's parents for more information about what may be causing his fears. For example, his grandfather may have been using a wheelchair right before he died. Then his teacher would have done further work with Eduardo to help him overcome his confusion between what happened to his *grandfather* and *other* people who use wheelchairs.

Young children may reject a child with a disability because of fear, impatience, stereotyping, or lack of skills for interacting with a child who is different from them

Such rejection must be immediately handled. The child who is the target of rejection needs support and assurance that the teacher will not permit such behavior. The child doing the rejecting needs help sorting through the reasons for the rejection, as well as clear limits about the teacher's expectation that all children are accepted and respected in the classroom.

Four-year-olds Patty and Selina are playing with the blocks. Kathy (who has burn scars on her face and arms from an accident when she was 2 years old) tries to join in their play. "I hate Kathy, she's ugly," Patty declares loudly to Selina.

Their teacher intervenes: "Patty, that is a hurtful thing to say about Kathy. Why do you say it?" Patty: "Because she has those things on her face. I don't like them.

They're scary." Teacher: "I know it looks different and scary to you. Kathy has scars on her face and arms because she was in an accident when she was a baby." The teacher has one arm around Kathy and one around Patty. "Kathy, do you want to tell Patty about how you got your scars?" Kathy says, "You." (Sometimes she chooses to explain herself, and sometimes she delegates the task to the teacher.) Teacher: "When Kathy was 2 years old, some very hot fat in a frying pan spilled on her and burned her. It hurt her very badly at first, and she had to be in a hospital for a long time. Her scars are her new skin growing so that the burns won't hurt anymore." Patty: "Do they hurt?" Kathy joins in at this point: "No, they used to itch, but not now."

Teacher: "It is OK to want to know about Kathy's scars, but it is not OK to say she's ugly or not let her play with you. Kathy, how did you feel when Patty said you were ugly?" Kathy: "Sad." Teacher: "What do you want to tell her about how you felt?" Kathy: "Don't say ugly." Teacher: "Remember that in our classroom I expect us to all work and play together. Let's you and me and Kathy and Selina play with the blocks together."

CAUTION

- Do not deny differences in the physical abilities of people: Saying that a child who is hearing impaired is "just like you" to a child who can hear is confusing and doesn't give either child the information they need for interacting with each other. An anti-bias response would help the two children recognize how they are different *and* how they are the same: "You both like to play with play dough; to talk together you both need to use sign language."

- Do not criticize a child for noticing and asking questions about physical differences. Responses such as "It isn't polite to look," or "It isn't nice to ask that question," will teach children to stop asking questions but will not stop their curiosity. Such responses will leave children without the necessary information for comfortable interaction and will lead to misconceptions and to treating people with disabilities as if they are invisible— one of the major forms of "handicappism" in our society.

- Do not belabor the response to children's questions. Listen to what they want to know and answer briefly. Ask if they have more questions.

- Do not lightly dismiss children's expressions of anxieties and fears about disabilities. Telling a child who says, "I don't like Susie because she can't walk" that "Yes, you do; we are all friends here" may lead to avoidance of Susie because unresolved fears interfere with getting to know her. Simply stopping children from expressing fears does not eliminate them. It just pushes fears underground, where they can freely fester, and will lay the foundation for prejudice and discrimination.

- Use accurate terminology when talking with children about disabilities. It is important that children begin to use correct terms, even if they are long and unfamiliar.

- If you do not know the answer to a specific question, be honest about it. Tell children you have to learn more in order to answer. Involve children in going to the library or other sources of information (e.g., Regional Centers for the Disabled), and then reading material together.

Never permit exclusion of a child because of her or his disability. Help children learn to include all children in all aspects of the classroom day.

"We don't want to play with Peter," 5-year-old Arthur says to his teacher, acting as spokesperson for four other boys and girls. "He can't catch the ball." (Peter uses a wheelchair.) Teacher: "Peter can throw the ball very well, and he can catch the ball if you throw it right to him. Peter has a right to play ball as much as everyone else in our class. You need to decide how to make it work so that he can play with you. Ask Peter what he needs and then all of you figure out together what to do. I know you can all figure out how to play together. I'll come over in a while and see what good ideas you had."

Children need skills and support for challenging accessibility and barriers

The world is still not designed to minimize barriers so all adults and children can participate to the fullest extent in it.

A class of preschoolers are walking to a pet store two blocks away. On the way there is one curb-cut and two curbs that are barriers to wheelchairs. Nikki can propel her own wheelchair down curb-cuts and needs only a little help to go up. As they come to the curb that is inaccessible to Nikki's wheelchair, she stops and looks at her teacher. The teacher says: "There is no curb-cut on this corner, is there? How do you feel about that?" Nikki: "Yucky old curb. I can't get down by myself." Teacher: "We'll always help you when you need help, but it isn't fair that this corner doesn't have a curb-cut so that you can get down by yourself."

Several children offer to help Nikki down. Teacher: "I'm glad you are being good friends to Nikki. Another way to be good friends to Nikki and other people who use wheelchairs is to get more curb-cuts." Children and Nikki: "How?" Teacher: "We can write and ask the office that makes curb-cuts to come and look at these corners. They will see that we need the curb-cuts. We can tell them why we think they should make more curb-cuts. We can get many friends to sign the letter." Angela, Nikki's best friend, firmly states: "Let's tell them to do it so Nikki can do things herself."

Activities

To implement what we believe in, we have to *do* something about it. Believing that children who are differently abled should have equal opportunities will not help them unless we create classroom and home environments in which they *do* have equal opportunities.

1. **Create an "inclusive" classroom.** Make sure that spatial organization, materials, and activities enable all children to participate actively.

- Attach ramps to the side of the sandbox to enable children who cannot sit or stand to lie on the ramps and play with the sand.
- Attach a paint brush to the protective helmet he wears to enable a child who cannot paint with his hands to participate.
- Use pillows and bolsters to position children who cannot sit on the floor.
- Put trays across the arms of wheelchairs so children can use manipulatives.
- Make sure materials available for children can be reached from a wheelchair.

2. **Actively introduce ways for disabled and nondisabled children to interact with and learn from each other.**

- *Model specific ways to interact:* For example, the preschoolers are getting ready to dance the "Hokey-Pokey." The teacher brings Melinda into the circle next to him and moves her wheelchair through the steps. (Melinda is not yet able to move her wheelchair herself.)

- *Pair children:* The next time the children dance the "Hokey-Pokey," the teacher asks a child to dance with Melinda. Eventually the children initiate involving her on their own.

  In another example, the teacher teams Melinda, who knows many color and shape names, with Susie, who is just beginning to learn them. They play a classification game together and Melinda teaches Susie color and shape names. Whenever possible, arrange partners or small groups so that a child with a disability who has an *advantage* in some other area (like knowing the colors) is put in the position of teaching another child who does not yet know whatever the skill or information is.

- *Consciously set up small groups that integrate children:* It is the first month of preschool. Ten children want to play in the block area this morning and there is only room for five at a time. The children and teacher agree to set up a schedule, so that one group plays for the first 45 minutes and the next group plays the following 45 minutes. The teacher creates the two groups herself this time to ensure that the four children with disabilities are integrated with the other children. She keeps an eye on their play and will intervene if necessary to help them figure out how to interact with each other.

3. Introduce a variety of disabilities through pictures, books, and dolls.

- There are many children's books that honestly depict children and adults with various disabilities (see Resources, pp. 119–132). Choose books and pictures that show people as full human beings and address both their disabilities and their abilities.

- Talk with children about their feelings and ideas. For example, using the story *Howie Helps Himself* (Fassler, 1975), ask, "What does Howie like to do what you like to do? How did Howie feel when he _____? Have you ever felt the same way? What helps Howie do what he wants to do? What does Howie do that is different from what you do? What questions would you like to ask Howie? Do you know anyone who uses a wheelchair as Howie does?" Make sure to directly address comments that show misconceptions, discomforts, or fears.

- Commercial and homemade dolls enable children to develop familiarity and ease with disabilities, open up dialogue among children and between teachers and children, and free children to play out their ideas and concerns. (The "New Friends" dolls created by the Chapel Hill Training Outreach Project can be made from an easy-to-follow pattern that comes with suggestions for adapting the doll to represent people with different disabilities.) Dolls also foster children's appreciation of how a person with a disability may be different in one respect, but the same in other ways. All dolls need to be fed, clothed, put to bed, hugged, carried, and so on.

4. Provide supervised times for children to explore adaptive equipment and devices used by people with disabilities.

- Handling and trying out wheelchairs, crutches, braces, walkers, hearing aids, glasses, magnifying reading glasses, Braille, canes, and prostheses satisfy children's curiosity, help take the mystery out of specific disabilities, and provide the information and experience that foster understanding and comfortable interaction with people. Equipment can be borrowed, rented, or bought. Contact physical therapy departments in your local hospital and organizations that have equipment pools for disabled people.

- Teach children how to use equipment. Hearing aids may be turned up too high and hurt their ears; using crutches inappropriately can result in falling.

- Pay attention to any fears children express about using specific equipment.

5. Invite differently abled people with varying disabilities to talk about their work, talents, and home life. This activity is more effective if your children have first had some experience learning about disabilities through other activities—books, dolls, trying out equipment.

- Prepare your visitors. Make sure that they are comfortable with answering the very direct questions of young children and can do so in a developmentally appropriate way. Also inform visitors about the activities you have already been doing and your goals for their visit.

With 4s and 5s, add the following activities.

6. Provide experiences that enable children to learn about specific disabilities. With concrete activities, 4s and 5s can begin to grasp what different forms of hearing, visual, and mobility impairments are like.

- *To gain awareness of what a person who is blind can know and not know about an object through touch,* children (in a group of about 10) sit in a circle. One child puts her hand through a hole in a box in which there are three objects. The teacher asks: "What can you know about what is in the box from touching?" As the child starts to explore, help with questions such as, "What is it? How do you know? What shape is it? Is it hard? Is it rough or smooth? What color is it?" When the child is finished exploring, open up the box and compare what the child knew from touching and from seeing. Then the second child covers his eyes, and the teacher gives him a box with three new objects. After everyone has had a turn, talk about what you can know about objects without seeing them and what things were easy and hard to know.

- *To learn about how hearing-impaired people can communicate and how hearing children can communicate with them, provide experiences with sign language.* Using finger spelling, teach children how to sign their names—first beginning letter and then their whole name. Then, sometimes sign each child's name when you want to call on them. Sign songs: All songs that use finger movements and simple, repeated refrains can be used for this activity.

- *To learn about accessibility problems faced by people who use wheelchairs,* try the following activity.

Teacher: (Shows children a child-size wheelchair at group time) Wheelchairs come in different sizes; this one is made especially for children.

Max: Are we going to be able to play with it?

Teacher: First we need to talk about the wheelchair. A wheelchair is not a toy. It is a special tool that people use. We borrowed this one so you could learn what it is like to use a wheelchair. We need to be very careful how we use it. Let me show you how we open it up. You pull it apart like this. This is where your body sits. This is a brake. You put it on when you want to stop. You push it forward like this and it locks. It is like the brakes of a car.

Maria: I want to try to go outside.

Teacher: Let's watch Maria and see what happens.

Kenji: (Now by the front door) How does the wheelchair get off the bump? (Looking at the raised door jamb on the floor)

Teacher: Good question. Maria, what are you going to do now?

(Maria gets out of the wheelchair and lifts up the chair.)

Teacher: Wait a second; if you were a person who needs to use a wheelchair, you wouldn't be able to get out of it like that. So how are you going to get over that bump?

Maria: I don't know.

Tiffany: Take a crane.

Peter: Push.

Teacher: But if you push what is going to happen to the wheelchair right here?

Peter: It's going to fall.

Teacher: What is going to happen to Maria's body?

Tiffany: She is going to fall out.

(The children work together and get the wheelchair over the bump and onto the porch.)

Teacher: How are we going to get the wheelchair down the step?

Kenji: Carry her.

Teacher: That would be one way. Every time Maria wants to get in and out of the room are we going to have to carry her?

Children: No.

Teacher: What could we do so Maria could do it on her own?

Holly: We could take one of those (pointing to a board), then she could trail down it.

Teacher: Let's try it.

(The children put the board down and try to push the wheelchair down, but find the board is not wide enough; so they have to find another board. When the boards are finally in position, they try to push Maria down but now find that the boards start to slip away. They solve that by having one child hold the bottom of the boards while one child pushes. Finally, they make it down to level ground and Maria can then move the wheelchair herself. At circle time, the teacher and children discuss how the ramp could be built so the boards wouldn't move.)

- Other activities come from the excellent book *Including All of Us: An Early Childhood Curriculum About Disability* (Froschl et al., 1984). Three units, with six activities each, provide experiences about different aspects of hearing, visual, and mobility impairment. For example, through an activity with teacher-made lenses, children experience what it feels like to have partial or no vision. In a parallel activity, they also learn about being able to hear only loud sounds. Other activities introduce children to American sign language and the equipment used to extend people's independence. We recommend buying this book to supplement the activities described here.

7. **Problem solve situations with persona doll stories.** Here are some examples from Kay Taus.

- With combinations of persona dolls, Kay involves the children in creating appropriate ways for the dolls to help each other.

- Make sure that the disabled persona dolls are also in stories about the common trials and tribulations of all young children (a new sibling, a grandparent dying, a trip to the doctor) and the same joys (a special birthday gift, a new pet, a special outing with a family member) and in stories about common classroom situations.

Problem solving situations involving hearing impairment:

- Using the doll who is deaf and whom the children have already "met," Kay asks the children, "How could you let Jennifer know you want to play with her if you don't know sign language?" One child suggests,"We could talk loud in her ear." Kay explains that Jennifer cannot hear voices, no matter how loud they are. The children think of other ways: "We can touch her," "We can show her what we want," "We can wave to her if she is too far to touch." Kay ends by telling children, "Jennifer and I will be teaching you how to sign your names and other words so you can begin talking with her."

- On another day, after the class had a fire drill, Kay tells the children that Jennifer hadn't heard the bell for the fire drill and when everyone jumped up suddenly she got scared. "What should we do the next time there is a fire drill?" she asks. From the children's various ideas, the group draws up a plan for next time.

- Another day, Kay raises the question, "How can Jennifer learn new songs? She told her mom last night that she feels left out at music time." Again the children propose solutions, and Kay helps them figure out which might work and which would not.

Problem solving situations involving visual impairment:

- Kay asks the children to close their eyes, and pretend they cannot see, just like Jerry (another persona doll). "Think about the activities you like to do and decide what you think you could do and couldn't do if you didn't see." At first, most children believe that they would be able to do very little. Then Kay asks, "What else could you use besides your eyes if you wanted to (do the various activities in the class)?" Kay writes down the children's ideas. Then she tells a story about how Jerry wanted to play baseball, and the children in his school figured out how to make it happen.

Problem solving situations involving physical impairment:

- With David, the doll who uses a wheelchair, Kay challenges the children to figure out what modifications to make in the room so that David could easily move about. With children using rented wheelchairs, they experiment in each area of the room and make a list of what needs changing or building.

8. Counter misconceptions and stereotyping.

- Make a list of the children's ideas about what people with different physical abilities can and can't do. (Can a person in a wheelchair be a mother or a father? Can she or he be a teacher? What other work can a grown-up with a disability do or not do?) Then, look at pictures, read books that show all the things people with disabilities can do, and visit work places that employ people with disabilities. Organizations that work for disability rights are good places to visit on field trips because children can see people working together to improve the quality of their own and others' lives. Finally, opposite the original list of children's ideas, make a new list that says whether their idea was correct or not.

- Make a book about the "unfair ideas" people have about people with disabilities. (Some people think a person who uses a wheelchair can't drive. We know he can because . . . .)

9. Research environmental adaptations to promote accessibility in your community.

- *Take the children on field trips to see adaptations for various disabilities:* Braille numbers on elevator buttons, sounds attached to street lights, adapted telephones, caption TV for the hearing impaired, handicapped parking zones close to exits, and accessible curbs, entrances into stores, restaurants, movies. (This activity may require some preliminary research on your part.)

- *Take a research walk around your school and find out for whom it is or isn't accessible:* Are there workable ramps and doorways sufficiently wide for wheelchairs? Are bathrooms, water fountains, telephones accessible? Are there curb-cuts on the streets near your school? Is there a handicap parking space? Are there sounds on the street light nearest your school? If accessibility is insufficient, this can lead to an action project, where the children and teachers choose an issue to work on together in order to make some changes. (See Chapter 9, "Activism With Young Children.")

References

Fassler, J. (1975). *Howie helps himself.* Niles, IL: Whitman.

Froschl, M., Colon, L., Rubin, E., & Sprung, B. (1984). *Including all of us: An early childhood curriculum about disability.* New York: Educational Equity Concepts, Inc.

LEARNING ABOUT GENDER IDENTITY 6

Gender identity consists of two components: a person's sexual identity, which is biological, and a person's role identity, which is cultural. If one's anatomy changes, so does one's gender identity; if one's roles change, gender identity remains the same. Young children do not yet know this. They need adult help to understand that their gender identity is based on their anatomy; it is not dependent on what they like to do, how they dress, what they feel, and how they express their feelings. They also need adult encouragement to go beyond stereotypic gender role constraints and try out new behaviors.

GOALS

1. To free children from constraining, stereotypic definitions of gender role so that no aspects of development will be closed off simply because of a child's sex
2. To foster children's healthy gender identity by enabling them to gain clarity about the relationship between biological identity and gender roles
3. To promote equality of development for both sexes by facilitating each child's participation in activities necessary for physical, cognitive, emotional, and social growth
4. To develop children's skills for challenging sexist stereotypes and behaviors

---

Developmental Tasks and Guidelines

Preschoolers know whether they are a boy or a girl and have some definite ideas about gender behavior. Further questions remain, however.

They are not yet sure what makes them a boy or a girl

Three 3-year-olds are changing out of their wet clothes and one matter-of-factly says to the other, "My mom doesn't have a penis; she has hair." The teacher, overhearing the remarks, comments also matter-of-factly, "Yes, and she has a vagina too. Women have vaginas, men have penises. That's what makes them a woman or a man. Do you have a penis or a vagina?" One child says penis, the other says vagina. "That's right," responds the teacher, "that's how we know that you are a boy and you are a girl." The third child looks bewildered. The teacher says, "You have a vagina too; you are a girl." Not all children are given this kind of information at home.

A considerable part of learning about sexual identity occurs in this informal way, if the teacher is willing to respond to the children casually and briefly. Here is "Lesson Number 2," initiated by the same children, also brief and to the point.

On a walk to the park a few days later, the same children see a dog. One child points out, "That dog is a boy because it has a penis." "Yes, that is a male dog. You remembered our talk about what makes a girl and a boy," responds the teacher.

"How do you know if you are a girl or a boy?" a teacher asks his group of preschoolers. Everyone has an idea: Boys wear pants, girl have long hair, boys play with trucks, girls play with dolls, boys like to run around, girls like to sit, boys don't cry, girls do. They respond with cultural criteria. When their teacher then asks, "What's the difference in our bodies?" the children giggle. Their teacher responds, "Boys have a penis and girls have a vagina. That's what makes you a boy or a girl. A penis or a vagina is part of your body, just like any other part—like arms and legs."

Children's comfortable acceptance of their gender anatomy is the cornerstone of constructing a healthy sexual identity and frees children to go beyond stereotypic gender role constraints.

Preschoolers are not yet sure if they will remain the same gender as they grow

"Teacher, will I always be a boy?" Johnny asked. His teacher, although startled, assured him that he would stay a boy forever. Thinking about Johnny's confusion, she realized that over the years she had heard other children express similar confusions: "Will my sister grow a penis when she grows up?" "When will my teeth fall out? What else will fall off?"

"Sara says I'm not a girl because I like to play rough," Heather complains to her teacher teary-eyed. "Do you think you are still a girl?" her teacher asks. Heather shrugs her shoulders. "Well, you *are* still a girl. You will be a girl no matter what you like to do. Your body makes you a girl, not how you play. I know you like to play rough and that's fine. Let's explain this to Sara and tell her she hurt your feelings by saying you aren't a girl."

Constructing gender constancy is an important part of developing a clear sexual identity. Otherwise, preschoolers can think that play preferences will change their gender.

By 4 years old, preschoolers are strongly influenced by societal norms for gender behavior and accept that girls and boys are supposed to do different things

Children may have narrow definitions of how women and men are supposed to look:

Cindy's teacher is wearing a pageboy wig in contrast to her usual hair style, an Afro. Cindy (3 years old) says, "You look like a real woman." Her teacher takes off the wig. Cindy: "Now, you are Regina." Regina: "And I'm a woman, and I have curly hair. The wig hair is straight. Women have many different kinds of hair."

In this interaction, Cindy seems to have formed a narrow, potentially stereotypic, image of women; her teacher's response directly deals with this.

Social norms may override children's own firsthand experience:

Judy and Marie ask John to play doctor with them. John wants to be the nurse, but Judy doesn't agree. "You can't be the nurse. You *have* to be the doctor," she firmly states. Their teacher intervenes: "Both boys and girls can be doctors and nurses. In fact, Judy, your dad told me that you used to go to a woman doctor." "She was a nurse," insists Judy. "Well," her teacher continues, feeling a little stymied, "you may not think that women can be doctors and men can be nurses, but I do and John does—so I want you to let John be the nurse." Judy agrees, albeit reluctantly.

A small group is playing with a teacher-made classification game. Cards depict girls, boys, men, women, and various toys and materials, and the children are deciding which objects go with which people. Peter declares that the play dough has to go with the girls because "only girls play with it," in spite of the fact that playing with dough is one of his favorite activities. His teacher questions Peter, "Don't you like to play with play dough?" Peter nods his head yes. "You were making wonderful things with your dough this morning. Lots of other boys also like to play with play dough. What other boys were at the play dough table with you?" Peter names one boy; his teacher helps him recall two others. Other children, who have been listening, chime in. "I like to play with play dough too," José says. "My dad plays with it at home," says Kimi. "So, is it true that only girls play with play dough?" the teacher asks. Peter and the other children say, "No."

Help children discover the contradictions between their ideas and their own experiences. Sometimes children will accept firsthand experience as the truth; somtimes they will cling to social norms or their own ideas about gender behavior. Don't get discouraged when stereotypic gender play and remarks continue despite a rich antisexist curriculum. Learning doesn't happen overnight; the socially prevailing beliefs about gender behavior are powerful. The key is to provide many opportunities for new ways of thinking and acting. Over time, many children will integrate nonsexist attitudes into their beliefs and behavior.

Children may also experience emotional conflict about acting differently than the social norms, especially when their families agree and act according to the norms.

Rose, an active 4-year-old, asks her teacher, "How do you think I look today?" Teacher: "I think you look fine. Why?" Rose: "Sometimes I think I look ugly." Teacher: "Why?" Rose: "I don't know, I just do. I look like a boy." Teacher: "Do you think you look ugly because you look like a boy?" Rose: "Yes." Teacher: "Why do you think you look like a boy?" Rose: "Boys wear jeans and shirts" (Rose's favorite clothes). Teacher: "Do you think you have to wear a dress to look pretty?" Rose: "Yes." Teacher: "You know you also look pretty in jeans and a T-shirt, and sometimes it's easier to play in jeans and a T-shirt because they don't tear as easily. You don't look like a boy; you look like Rose no matter what you wear."

For a period of time Rose struggled about whether she wanted to be a girl, because of what she liked to do. Encouraging a child to talk about her or his feelings when going beyond stereotypic rules of gender behavior is another important method for fostering nonsexist gender development.

Finally, acknowledging children's nonsexist behavior provides further support for their choices.

Rebecca is playing firefighter wearing a hat and jacket. Charles wants them for himself. "Girls can't be firemen," he tells Rebecca, trying to take off her hat. "Yes, they can," Rebecca insists, pushing his hand away and continuing to play. Their teacher steps in: "Charles, Rebecca is right. She *can* be a firefighter. You can play with the hat and jacket when Rebecca is finished. Rebecca, I'm glad you spoke up for yourself when Charles said girls can't be firemen."

Expanding Children's Play Options

One of the skills excellent teachers of young children have is the creativity to appropriately expand children's chances to learn.

Reorganize play areas

Observe children's play during choice time over a week. Note in what ways their choices divide along gender lines. Do girls tend to play in the housekeeping area (with dolls, dishes, dress-up clothes) and use small-motor, "quiet" materials (puzzles, books, drawing supplies) while boys tend to play with the blocks, trucks, woodworking, sand, and outdoor large-motor equipment?

Based on your data, the next step is to physically reorganize areas of the environment to encourage more cross-gender play choices:

- Expand the dramatic play center. Include props from other rooms in the house: Put the woodworking table and tools into the "house" for making home repairs as well as wood constructions; put a typewriter, adding machine, and other materials in a "study." Create dramatic play areas from the work world outside the home (include occupations of children's parents). Put the block area next to the dramatic play area for building work places (a market, a hospital, a gas station with mechanics). Expand the collection of work dress-up props (tool chest, lunch box, hard hat, doctor's bag).

- When the climate allows, move housekeeping/ dramatic play props (stove, sink, pots and pans, table, chairs) outside next to the sand area with the shovels and other sand toys.

- Add new materials to the centers. For example, here is how one teacher got more girls to use the woodworking center:

The staff set out the following activities in the woodworking center over a two-week period and waited to see what would happen.

10/23—Wood pieces with round plastic lids, pieces of woven wood, glue, nails, hammers, and saws. Six boys and three girls constructed walkie-talkies, a first for the girls.

10/25—Flat wood pieces with round lids, eye droppers with food coloring, hammers, nails, and saws. More girls than boys and more young children. Some children hammered nails into drops of water.

10/29—Wood, lids, woven wood, wood beads, tiny pieces of wood, glue, saws, and all the woodworking tools used. Five boys and five girls. Two girls stayed all morning making airplanes.

10/30—Same materials. Same two girls came back and made airplanes again.

10/31—Big pieces of styrofoam with saws, nails, glue, and hammers. Lot of children—boys and girls.

11/2— Lincoln logs, no tools. Five girls and six boys came.

At first, children new to the area, especially the girls, wanted teachers to help them. By encouraging the children to do things for themselves, with occasional help, teachers helped children become increasingly independent.

Directly involve children in new activities

Changing the environment encourages many children to try new activities. Some children, however, will need teacher intervention to try new activities. How much teachers should intervene in children's play choices is a thorny question. Free choice is a vital part of good early childhood education and should be a large percentage of the curriculum. However, thinking about free choice from an anti-bias perspective raises the question of how free "free play" is when preschoolers' behaviors are already influenced by gender socialization. Complete reliance on children's self-directed activities may limit rather than expand development. So, occasional teacher-initiated activities to correct "cognitive deficiencies" caused by nonparticipation in key activities are necessary (Serbin, 1980).

For example, here are some ways to involve girls in block play:

- Have an "everybody plays with blocks day" once a week for a month, or until many girls are comfortable choosing block play at free choice time. This method requires extra blocks: Team with another teacher, using her blocks on your "block day," and lending her yours on her "block day." Play alongside the children, working with individual girls who need support.

- Have a "girls only" block time once a week: Explain to the children that this is necessary; you've noticed that very few girls are playing with the blocks, while most of the boys do. It is important for girls to play with blocks too because it helps children's minds get smart. Work with the girls in the block area, explaining that "we are going to learn lots of ways to use blocks." When they have developed block-playing skills, have them work on their own in twos or threes.

- Next, have an all-block day and assign boy-girl teams to play together. Once girls begin choosing block play on their own, teacher intervention is no longer necessary, except to support those children who are still uncomfortable.

Boys may also need special times with certain activities. Occasionally limit boys' use of large motor activity during choice time. This requires them to choose other activities. Have a "boys only" art time, or sewing activity.

Work with individual children whose repertoire of play choices is still too limited by gender stereotyping by occasionally playing a special game with them involving new activities or materials. Be careful not to overdo. The goal is to facilitate each child's trying various activities, not mechanically insisting that every child do exactly the same kinds of activities for exactly the same length of time.

Expanding Children's Understanding of Gender Anatomy and Gender Identity

Remember that the purpose of these activities is to enable preschoolers to develop a clear, healthy sex identity through understanding that their being a girl or boy depends on their anatomy, not on what they like to do.

- Read *What Is a Girl? What Is A Boy?* (Waxman, 1976), and *Bodies* (Brenner, 1973). Both books have excellent photographs of children's bodies. Use correct anatomical terms with children.

- Make copies of an outline of a body as drawn by a preschooler, and in small groups ask children to fill in all the body parts, and to show if the person is a girl or a boy.

- Make a class book with the children based on the format of *What Is A Girl? What Is A Boy?*: "Some people say a girl is someone who likes to play with paints, but Robin also likes to play with paints, and he is a boy."

- Have anatomically correct dolls available for the children in the dramatic play area and to be used for specific activities with the teachers. For example, tell a persona doll story where a few of the dolls ask questions about what makes them a boy or a girl.

ADAPTATION

Some teachers and parents may strongly disagree with teachers' talking about genitals, using correct anatomical terms, showing books with photos of the naked body, or even using anatomically correct dolls in the classroom. Chapter 11, "Working With Parents," discusses strategies for talking and problem solving with parents if this issue comes up. Even if you ultimately decide not to use the direct approach of the activities suggested in this guide, it is important to find other ways to help your children understand that their body, not their behavior, makes them a girl or boy.

Expanding Awareness of Gender Roles

Many of the activities in this section are similar to those described in Chapter 7, "Learning About Cultural Differences and Similarities," and can be combined with them. In particular, see the activities for learning about different kinds of work.

- Read books about boys and girls that contradict gender stereotypes: *William's Doll* (Zolotow, 1972); *Stephanie and the Coyote* (Crowder, 1969); *Everybody Knows That* (Pearson, 1978).

- Have the children find and cut out magazine pictures of boys and girls, men and women, showing the diversity of looks, dress, activities, and emotions. Make books with the pictures: "About Girls and Women," "About Boys and Men."

- Create a display of photos and pictures of women and men doing the same kinds of tasks "in the home" and "in the world of work." Make sure there are racial and ethnic diversity and images of differently abled people. Use this to talk about the different tasks the children's family members do, and talk about what kinds of tasks the children do and would like to do when they grow up.

- As the teacher, role model learning new skills and sharing tasks in the classroom in nonsexist ways.

- Read books about different ways families are organized: two parents; single parents; children living with family members other than parents; two-parent families and a live-in grandparent; adopted two-parent, single-parent, same-race, different-race families; "blended" families; gay or lesbian families (two daddies or two mommies—you may decide not to use the words *gay* and *lesbian*, but the child deserves calm recognition of the reality of the composition of his family); only child; many children; cousins living as a family; families without children; single adults who do not live with their families (nieces, nephews, parents, etc.). These last two family types are very hard for children to understand. And don't forget foster families. We usually do. Talk about the different kinds of families of the children and staff. (See Resources, pp. 119–132.)

- Make a picture display of different kinds of families called "Beautiful Families Come in Many Different Ways." Help children understand that all families serve the same functions—to provide a home, to take care of children and adults in the family, and so on.

- Invite members of the children's families (including extended family) who do nontraditional

jobs to visit and talk with your class (male flight attendant, nurse, secretary; female construction worker; and so on.)

- Support children's dramatic play in nontraditional roles and about different kinds of families.

- Insist that all children take equal responsibility in carrying out the necessary jobs for maintaining the classroom or child care center. Rotate tasks so that girls and boys carry out all tasks.

- Tell stories about the persona dolls that support nontraditional behaviors and describe the conflicts they sometimes feel when acting in ways that challenge stereotypic gender roles.

ADAPTATION

Two issues affect how learning about gender identity is implemented in different settings:

1. Expectations about gender roles are not only affected by the general sexism in our society; ethnic and cultural background also influences people's beliefs about gender behavior. This is one area where the creative tension between respecting diversity and countering sexism can be very apparent. Teachers must be careful not to act in racist ways while trying to be antisexist. This requires: (a) doing activities about gender roles within the context that there are many choices, rather than making some choices superior to others; and (b) finding alternative ways to promote each child's full development. For example, if a family really doesn't want girls in pants, see if you can agree to special times in the school day when pants are worn for specific large motor physical activities, or for constructing and painting a new piece of equipment. Provide smocks so that good clothes do not get dirty. If a family really doesn't want a boy encouraged to cry, find other ways for that child to express his feelings (dictating/writing a story).

2. Some adults fear that encouraging nontraditional gender behavior leads to homosexuality (boys who play with dolls, or who cry; girls who prefer large-motor activities or don't like to wear dresses). This is a reflection of the deep homophobia in our society. There is no research evidence that nontraditional gender behavior creates homosexuality. Nevertheless, teachers may need to spend time in educational discussions with parents who are frightened by their children participating in certain activities, and may have to make choices about what activities they will stand up for and which they will modify or let go.

Discuss these issues with staff before implementing activities with children and when problems arise. See Chapter 11, "Working With Parents," for strategies for resolving disagreements between teachers and parents.

Developmental Tasks for Kindergarten Children

1. Five-year-olds have established sex identity and constancy (they know they are and will remain a girl or a boy), but they do not necessarily have accurate information about their gender anatomy. They have also learned the societal embarrassment about gender anatomy, which shows up as giggling, teasing, and sometimes surreptitiously trying to see or play with each others' genitals.

2. Five-year-olds are curious and want information about how babies are born.

3. Five-year-olds are defining their individual gender identity and may struggle with prevailing gender stereotypes and norms. They need information and role models about expanding gender roles, and support for their appearance and personal preferences in dress and play.

Supplementary Activities for Kindergarten Children

1. Make sure your children do have accurate terms about gender anatomy.

2. Do not permit giggling or teasing of any individual. If children giggle as a group, say, "I expect you not to act so silly after you know more about bodies. Then you can act more sensible and grown up." Forbidding giggling may prevent a child from communicating his uneasiness about this subject. Then you would not be able to help him develop a healthier attitude. Persona doll stories can help children explore their embarrassment and inappropriate teasing of each other.

3. Encourage children to respect and care for their bodies.

4. Do a series of activities that provide accurate, simple information about how babies are born:
   - Find out children's own ideas about conception and birth. Five-year-olds have some interesting and unique theories. Your subsequent activities should provide feedback about misconceptions. Keep in mind that many children do not have a known father.
   - Read books about how babies are born. Be careful to choose books that handle the topic respectfully and accurately and that are developmentally appropriate.*
   - In addition, read books about adoption as another way that women and men become mothers and fathers. If you have adopted children in your class, be sure to find out how their parents are explaining adoption to the child.

5. Continue activities that explore different family styles and women and men doing various kinds of work at home and out of the home. *Also* do any activities that enable children to gain critical thinking skills about gender stereotyping. Introduce the word *stereotype*—explaining that it is an unfair belief that a girl/woman or boy/man can only act in one way, instead of having choices. Make a chart or a book about gender stereotypes.

6. Tell persona doll stories about girl and boy dolls challenging a stereotype about gender behavior.

7. Read books about children countering gender stereotyping (See Resources, pp. 119–132). Discuss how the children handle disapproval from peers or some adults and alternative strategies for handling these problems.

8. Celebrate "International Women's Day" (March 8) by honoring the important women in the children's and staff's lives and women who have made important contributions to our lives. Celebrate "Mother's Day" in an antisexist way by honoring all the different kinds of ways to be a mother, and all the different kinds of tasks mothers do in and out of the home (this idea courtesy of Jane Stone).

*You may not approve, or choose to discuss this with children, but you should know that more and more mature, never-married women are electing to become mothers through insemination. If a child in your group announces that this is her situation, remember, this child, like all others, deserves staff respect. Say, "Yes, that is another way some women who very much want a child get one. Other mothers adopt children."

References

Brenner, B. (1973). *Bodies.* New York: Dutton.

Crowder, J. (1969). *Stephanie and the coyote.* Upper Strata, Box 278, Bernalillow, NM 87004.

Pearson, S. (1978). *Everybody knows that.* New York: Dial.

Serbin, L. (1980). Eliminating sex bias in early childhood education. *Equal Play, 1*(4), 5.

Waxman, S. (1976). *What is a girl? What is a boy?* Los Angeles: Peace Press.

Zolotow, C. (1972). *William's doll.* New York: Harper & Row.

LEARNING ABOUT CULTURAL DIFFERENCES AND SIMILARITIES

7

Cultural diversity is about the myriad ways people solve the daily challenges of being human. First through experiences in their families, and then in ever-widening circles of influence—neighborhood, school, church or temple, media—children construct their cultural or ethnic identity and way of being in the world.

GOALS

1. To affirm and foster children's knowledge and pride in their cultural identity
2. To foster children's curiosity, enjoyment, and empathetic awareness of cultural differences and similarities
3. To teach children to overcome any inappropriate responses triggered by cultural differences

---

Developmental Tasks and Guidelines

Activities for teaching cultural diversity are the basis of most multicultural curricula. However, too often, the suggested activities fall into the trap of a tourist approach, which trivializes and frequently stereotypes the cultures being studied. (See Chapter 1.)

Use the following guidelines to avoid the "tourism" error

Connect cultural activities to individual children and their families. Three-, 4-, and 5-year-olds construct their cultural identity in relation to their families—their individuality and their group connection. Awareness of other cultural ways of being builds on children's understanding of their family context.

Remember that while cultural patterns are real and affect all members of an ethnic group, families live their culture in their own individual ways. Young children are often confused about the criteria for ethnic group membership and need help understanding why they belong to their ethnic group. (Even if you don't speak Spanish, you can still be Mexican-American. Even if you celebrate Christmas, not Chanukah, you can still be Jewish, because people can be culturally *and* religiously Jewish, or just culturally Jewish.) Do not stereotype a family's lifestyle by making them a representative of a whole group. Always say, "This is how Rosa's family lives. Her family is Mexican-American," not "This is how Mexican-American families live."

At the beginning of the school year, find out: the term each family uses to name their own ethnic group; what/how each family teaches their children about their culture; and how the family celebrates which special days.

Connect cultural activities to concrete, daily life. Culture is not an abstraction to young children. It is lived and learned every day through the way family members interact; through language, family stories, family values, and spiritual life; through household customs and the work family members do.

Holidays are only one aspect of a culture, although the easiest part for an outsider to "see."

Explore cultural diversity within the principle that everyone has a culture. White children come from ethnic groups with specific customs or mixtures of customs, just like the more "visible" ethnic groups, even if some White families do not consciously carry out their ethnic culture. However, their daily lives do reflect a set of beliefs that are derived from identifiable ethnic world views and traditions.

Have cultural diversity permeate the daily life of the classroom, through frequent, concrete, hands-on experiences related to young children's interests. When learning about different ways of living is part of the regular classroom environment, then children's questions and responses arise naturally, and each child can experience diversity in her or his own way and time.

Avoid the editorial we ***when talking with children.*** "*We* do such and such" makes assumptions about homogeneity that may not be true. Say "This is what I do," or "This is what we do in our classroom; you do it differently at home—both ways are OK."

Explore the similarities among people through their differences. Everyone laughs, cries, eats, works, and plays because we are all human beings, *and* people do all these activities in different ways. No one way is superior to another: All ways meet the same human needs.

Begin with the cultural diversity among the children and staff in your classroom. Then extend children's awareness by introducing diversity "outside" the classroom.

In all-White classrooms

The main task is to intervene in children's developing the belief that the dominant White culture is superior to other ways of life. Children learn this bias through lack of contact and information as well as through direct exposure to prevailing racist beliefs.

- Establish the concept of the desirability of diversity in your classroom environment. (See Chapter 2.) This in itself will open up some questions. For example, if you offer black and brown paint and play dough frequently, and some children say "yuck," you can raise the issue with all the children—discover their feelings, their information; then begin to do activities that foster children's learning about physical and then cultural differences.

- Establish the concept of families having their own ways of living through the differences and similarities among families of the children and staff in your class. Remember that Whites come/came from different places, have different ethnic heritages, and have/had different languages.

- Introduce a new cultural/ethnic group through specific individuals and families. Begin with a group that lives in your city or state, or a group the children are aware of through the media. Use the persona dolls, books, visitors, and field trips, with the same guidelines as for learning about the children's own culture.

In all-Black, Mexican-American, Asian-American, Native American, or Latino classrooms

The first task with children of color is to build their sense of personal and group identity. Children of color also learn the prevailing social prejudices against members of other groups of color, so a second task is to foster their awareness and empathy for the life of other ethnic groups of color.

Children of color have the third task of learning how to live in the dominant culture. Early childhood programs already address this task: Teaching the rules of behavior for being in school and teaching English are two examples. An anti-bias perspective emphasizes the first two tasks without eliminating the third. The goal is bicultural development: for children to function well both in their "mother" culture and in the dominant culture (Hale-Benson, 1986).

- Differences are first explored through children learning about each other and their group identity. (Black children have different skin tones, but all are part of the same group. Mexican-American children do not all speak Spanish and also have a range of skin and hair color.) Children learning about their own group continues throughout the year.

• After children have had a number of experiences learning about themselves, introduce learning about a new group. Choose a group that lives in your city, or larger community, or one of the major groups of color in the United States. Use the persona dolls, books, visitors, and field trips, with the same developmental guidelines as for learning about the children's own culture. In addition, help children understand that other children and families of color experience racial bias and that it is important for all people to stand together against racism. Personalize the concept through stories about the persona dolls of color and stories from visitors.

ADAPTATION

When a child or a few children come from a different background than the rest of the children:

• Remember that these children are in a vulnerable position. They may not want to be different in school; however, it is important that they get support to be who they are and to feel comfortable even though they are in the numerical minority.

• Never single out the "minority" child. Include learning about his or her family in the study of every child's family; then extend diversity by learning more about the group to which the child belongs. Help the class see that there are many other people like their classmate.

• Before beginning these activities, talk with the child's family and the child about what you plan to do. Tell the child, "I want the other children to know more about people who are Vietnamese like you—so I'm going to read some books, tell a story about our doll Trang, and invite some friends of mine to school."

• Don't do these activities all at once—include them regularly throughout the year.

• A tougher problem is making the child who feels different for reasons such as the suicide of her mother or the disappearance of his father feel included. It is hard to see how we can help the class see that these are many other people like their classmate. But we must develop sensitivity to children like this, who *also* come from a different background than the rest of the children.

Activities

These activities cross-reference with activities for learning about gender diversity and physical abilities.

Who's in your family

1. Borrow and take photographs of all the people who live with each child and staff member. Make a bulletin board of "The People in Our Families." Label each photo with the names and family relationships of each person. Talk with children about the similarities and differences in who lives together as a family.

2. Make a class book about "Our Families" with a page for each child and staff member, telling who lives with each child, and what work family members do in and outside the home. "This is Jamal's family. He lives with his _____. His mom, dad, grandma, grandpa, aunt, uncle takes care of him, works at. . ." Be aware that some children's primary family members are temporarily or chronically unemployed. Focus on what they *do*, not on where they work. Let children take these stories home to read to their families.

3. If your children/staff speak different languages, make a poster and a book about "The Ways We Speak," illustrating with four or five words children commonly use: names of family members and pets, thank you, water, milk, and so forth. Use the book at circle time and with individual children.

4. Read children's books about families reflective of the ethnic groups in your class. Always read more than one book about each group. Talk about the differences and similarities between the children's lives in the book and the children from that ethnic group in your class. Discuss the books— "Is this how you do it in your family?" Expand on this with books about families from ethnic groups not present in the classroom. Include books about interracial and intercultural families. (See Resources, pp. 119–132.)

5. Tell stories with persona dolls. (See Chapter 2 for a description of the persona doll method.) Dolls' stories can both reinforce a specific family's way of living and add new variations on a group's cultural patterns. They are also wonderful for expanding diversity.

Use three or four persona dolls who are part of the racial/ethnic group you chose to introduce. Each doll's family background should reflect differences within the group. For example, in learning about Mexican-Americans, one doll would come from a bilingual family, one from a Spanish-only family, and one English only. One family would have been here several generations, another be newly arrived; a third doll would have been born in the United States. Vary the family structure—in one case grandparents, an uncle, or an aunt; in another, a two-parent nuclear family; in a third, a single-parent family. Vary the work and socioeconomic status—one a professional, another a blue-collar worker, a third a farm worker.

Gradually introduce the dolls: "Here are some dolls whose lives you do not know about because they do not go to our school, or live in your neighborhood. It is important for you to know about other people who live in your city (or state). I am going to tell you about them on different days so they will seem like friends."

Tell stories that personalize each doll's experiences—with their family, in their school, in their neighborhood. Include stories about daily life and about special holidays—for example, Dia de los Muertos (see Chapter 10). Introduce language, objects, food, and music through the dolls. Include stories that talk about some of their problems with cultural differences and with racism. For example, talk about a Spanish-speaking doll's experience when beginning school. Read a book in Spanish to the children and talk about how they feel when they don't understand the words and how they think the doll felt. Tell a story where one of the dolls was teased for being Mexican; talk about how the doll felt and what the doll did to stand up for him- or herself.

Help children see the similarities between themselves and the new group by telling stories about common 3- and 4-year-old themes and problems—a new sibling, a visit to the doctor, a birthday party. Also help children see the differences within the culture. Each of the dolls is Mexican-American, but they do not do everything the same way.

Get the information for telling stories from your own reading about the group you are introducing, from discussions with people who are part of the group, from photos you take of people in their neighborhoods.

Read many different children's books about the group you are studying. Read each book a number of times so it becomes a part of the children's repertoire. These books should be regularly available to children to read on their own.

Who's in your community

Take neighborhood photographs, no matter how poor the area may be. Locate attractive buildings, shops, and gardens—places where children's families go. Find people doing work and recreational activities. Tell them about your program's "Build Community Pride" activities and ask permission to photograph them for a bulletin board display and for a picture book. Enlarge and duplicate the best photographs; mount one set with labels (bilingual if appropriate) of names of specific places and people.

Make a picture book, "Our Neighborhood Matters to Us," with the second set of photographs, with a few sentences under each. Let children take them home to share with their families.

Take trips to new neighborhoods. Carefully plan field trips as part of many different kinds of activities. Visit places that relate to a family's daily life—just as you did in the children's neighborhood project. Make a number of trips to a new neighborhood: Going only once is a tourist approach. Make purchases of materials or other services for the classroom as part of your trips.

Visiting a neighborhood of an unfamiliar racial/ethnic group can create discomfort or reinforce children's stereotypes. Prepare the children beforehand about how to behave when visiting a new place, and ask about their reactions after the trip.

Family artifacts

Connect objects to their use in individuals' lives. Have a range of objects from each culture, including White families'. Most objects should be part of daily life, some a part of ceremonial life—and teach children the difference. Have limits about appropriate use; intervene when children make fun of a culture, or engage in stereotypic play.

- Place objects from various cultures in the dramatic play area, where children can use them by choice. For instance, you might include a wok, a rice steamer, and rice bowls; a bongo drum and a guitar; a hard hat, work shoes, work shirt and pants, and work gloves. Start with objects that come from the families of children and staff in your classroom. If a child makes fun of an unfamiliar object, intervene, explain it isn't fair to make fun of an object used by another child's family, and demonstrate how the object is used. Then allow the child to use the object.

- Do small- or large-group activities where children take turns sharing objects meaningful to them and their families. Begin with a few daily life objects from the teacher's home; explain their names and uses. Ask children, "Do you have something at your house you want to bring in to show to us?" Make a list of different days for each child. Send a note home to each parent the night before their child's turn, explaining the activity. Accept all objects the child chooses and help them explain their use to the group.

- Repeat this activity, this time sharing objects from each family's ceremonial life—for instance Rosie's Shabbat dress and Shabbat candles; Maria's Sunday dress and shoes for going to church.

- After exploring the objects from the children's and staff's families, use a similar procedure to introduce objects from new cultural groups. Say that the objects come from the family of a friend, or introduce them as the objects one of the persona dolls uses, or ask a friend to come to the class. Then place these objects in the environment—for dramatic play, for cooking, for room decoration.

Be sure that new objects are part of a number of other activities about the same cultural group.

What families eat: Cooking

Cooking is a frequently used activity for learning about cultural diversity. However, children often do not like the new food they are supposed to be learning to appreciate. Unless cooking activities are done thoughtfully, they can backfire.

Cook what children regularly eat at home. Include foods eaten by *every* child's family.

Don't stereotype: For example, if you cook black-eyed peas, emphasize that "this is one of the things that Selena eats at home with her family—one of the foods *some* Black people eat." Do *not* say, "This is what Black people eat." If other children from the same group eat differently from each other, point that out. Explain the difference between daily foods and holiday foods.

Don't mix cultures up. Families from El Salvador do not eat the same foods as families from Mexico. Families recently from Mexico may not eat the same foods as third-generation Chicanos.

Integrate culturally diverse cooking regularly at snack and lunch. Include meats, vegetables, and fruits, as well as sweets. Remember that foods that the dominant culture considers "regular" are usually foods originating in White ethnic groups.

Teach children ways to decline food without disparaging it. Invite, but don't force them to try. Help them understand that sometimes we like new things and sometimes we don't. If children make fun of the food or call a food "yucky," intervene immediately, explaining that it is not OK to respond in those ways and offering other ways: "I've never tasted that before; what does it taste like?" or "It tastes different to me"; or, if a child really doesn't want to try, say "No, thank you; I don't want any today."

How families speak: Language

Language is a basic element of culture, and one that interests preschool and kindergarten children. Fill the environment with written and oral languages other than English. Begin with the languages currently or previously spoken by the families in your classroom, then extend to other languages. You do not have to know a language yourself; there are plenty of resources—children, parents, friends, dictionaries, records.

Written language. Display different writing systems (e.g., Chinese, Hebrew, Braille), and label materials in more than one language. Use newspapers in different languages to cover tables for artwork. Many children will become aware of these materials and ask questions.

Teach children how to make a few letters from different alphabets—initial letters and then their whole name.

Spoken language. Teach children other languages' names for common things in the environment—numbers, days of week, colors, food, objects, family members, pets—and frequently used phrases. Use these words informally and frequently: at snack time to refer to foods in a second language, at greeting and good-bye times, when singing "Happy Birthday."

Read children's books in different languages. Read the same ones on different days. If you don't know how, have someone teach you. You can tell the children you are learning too. Ask parents to help. It works best either to read a story simultaneously in both languages, or to read a book that children already know well. Talk with the children about what it is like to listen to stories in a language they don't understand. If you read the same book a number of times, children will begin to recognize words.

Have someone you know who is fluent in a language make tapes of favorite books for children to listen to individually.

How family members work

Help children understand that work is what family members do when they take care of children and the house, and what family members and other adults do when they leave their homes to go somewhere else to work. Include all kinds of work: blue- and pink-collar, white-collar and professional. Introduce the concept that people get money in return for their work outside the home so that they can buy the things necessary for their families to live, that low-paid work is as important as high-paid work (e.g., artists, musicians, child care and preschool teachers). Include the issue of unemployment—when people cannot get work, they worry or get upset. Counter stereotypic images about work: that professional work is more valuable than blue-collar work; that people with disabilities cannot work; that work must be decided by gender. Finally, develop the concept that children also work when they help in the care of their home and family members and when they do jobs like cleanup, preparing snacks, and helping to fix objects in their classroom or center (Wilson, 1985).

Activities about work integrate learning about diversity in culture, gender roles, and physical abilities. Any of the following activities may include learning about all three issues.

- Make a picture display showing parents at their work with photos or magazine pictures to illustrate each job. If you take the photos, bring small groups of children with you to visit parents' work sites if possible. Over several days, talk about how each job helps people's lives, and that each person's work is equally important to their families.

  Supplement this with photos and pictures of other adults doing work important to children's lives. Be sure to show people of color, differently abled people, and women of all races doing nontraditional jobs. Include musicians, writers, artists, and actors in your learning about work.

- Visit a variety of work sites showing a range of work. Search out sites that also counter gender, racial, and handicappism stereotypes about who can do what kind of work. Include places where people of color are in supervisory roles.

- Read and discuss books about work that both reflect and extend the work of the children's families. (See Resources, pp. 119–132.)

- Make a list with the children of all the kinds of work family members, including themselves, do at home to take care of the house and people. Make a book about "Work That Takes Care of Us at Home," with photos of family members, supplemented by magazine pictures, to illustrate each job.

- Make a list with the children of all the jobs they do at school: cleaning up, food preparation, fixing things, shopping. Think about other areas of work where children can participate: clearing and sorting shelves, sorting lost and found and extra clothes, outside cleanup, constructing new equipment (e.g., a cage for an animal) (Wenning & Wortis, 1985). Talk about how each job helps everyone in the class, which is why it is important always to do a careful job.

- Make a list of the jobs the staff does at school. This may be hard for preschoolers to see: Begin by asking them, "What grown-ups work at our center? What do they do?" Then on different days have staff members add to the list by explaining what they do. Include cooking, maintenance, and office staff. Take photos of each person doing her or his work and write a few sentences under each picture—use them to make a wall display or a book.

- Organize the space and objects in the dramatic play and block areas so children can act out the various jobs they are seeing and talking about.

- Read the few available children's books about unemployment: *My Mother Lost Her Job Today* (Delton, 1980) and *Tight Times* (Hazen, 1983). Use the persona dolls to supplement or substitute for the books. Help children understand that it is not the person's fault when he or she is laid off, that the unemployed person isn't "bad," and that unemployment is hard for the person and his or her family.

- If members of any of the children's or staff's families are on strike, or if there is a strike in their community or in the media, talk about what a strike is for. Use persona doll stories to explain why people go on strike, and how families help each other during this time.

Families' holidays

Using holidays to teach about cultural diversity should only be a small part of the curriculum. (See Chapter 10.)

Families' music

Teach songs that are really sung by an ethnic group, not songs made up by an outsider. Choose songs that reflect concrete aspects of life in a culture that interests preschoolers: work, lullabies, adventures, funny stories. Use these songs regularly. Use music from various cultures for move-

---

CAUTION

WARNING: TOURIST CURRICULUM IS HAZARDOUS TO THE DEVELOPMENT OF YOUR CHILDREN.

Watch out for the signs of tourist curriculum:

Trivializing: Organizing activities only around holidays or only around food. Only involving parents for holiday and cooking activities.

Tokenism: One Black doll amidst many White dolls; a bulletin board of "ethnic" images—the only diversity in the room; only one book about any cultural group.

Disconnecting cultural diversity from daily classroom life: Reading books about children of color only on special occasions. Teaching a unit on a different culture and then never seeing that culture again.

Stereotyping: Images of Native Americans all from the past; people of color always shown as poor; people from cultures outside the U.S. only shown in "traditional" dress and in rural settings.

Misrepresenting American ethnic groups: Pictures and books about Mexico to teach about Mexican-Americans; of Japan to teach about Japanese-Americans; of Africa to teach about Black Americans.

ment and dance activities, for relaxing children at rest and nap times, and as background music at eating times.

Famous people

Stories about famous people, past and present, who have made important contributions to everyone's lives can extend diversity and provide role models for 4- and 5-year-olds. They are not appropriate for younger children, who are still completely focused on people in their own immediate experience.

Be very concrete and relate famous people's contributions to children's interests and to their everyday life. Examples: When someone is in the hospital and needs extra blood—do you know who figured out how to do this? (Charles Drew, a Black man.) Stevie Wonder, who is blind, is a composer and singer who has made important contributions in popular music. He wrote a special birthday song for Martin Luther King, Jr., which is sung by many Black families on the birthdays of their own children. Delores Huerta helps farmworkers and their children have better homes, food, toys, and education.

Developmental Tasks for Kindergarten Children

In kindergarten, activities about cultural identity continue to center on the children's families but also expand to set the child and family in the broader context of their community. Of course, kindergarten children must first learn about their immediate family, and then move outward.

1. Five-year-olds can begin to make connections between their individual and family cultural identity and their larger ethnic group.
2. Five-year-olds can begin to understand peoples' struggles for justice and a better quality of life.

Activities for Kindergarten Children

When children have not had activities designed for younger children, start with those. Then . . .

Learning about children's family history

This series of activities (developed by Susan Freeman) adapts the methodology of oral history to the capabilities of 5-year-olds. The activities are teacher initiated, but the content emerges from the children's families and the children's ideas. Other areas of the kindergarten curriculum—language arts, math, and spatial relationship concepts—can be an integral part of family history activities.

Most activities are done in small groups of up to eight children, which stay the same for the series. Some activities are for the whole group.

Step 1: Making individual "family maps"—who is my family? Each child brings in pictures and names of everyone she considers part of her family. Some bring in best friends and pets as well as family members. Each child has a chance to share pictures with other children at small-group times.

Step 2: Making a group family map. Set aside a whole wall for this project. An outline of a giant tree has each child's name next to one branch, with space near it for photos, drawings, and sentences about the child's family members. In small groups, each child glues material about his family in its place on the tree and dictates what he wishes to say. (This activity takes about a week.)

Step 3: Sending home a Family History Questionnaire (see p. 67). Each child takes home a questionnaire for the family to fill out, with a note explaining the purpose of the questions as a part of the family oral history project. (Translate the questions into the languages spoken by families as necessary, and ask families whom a question may embarrass ahead of time how they want the question handled on the form. Individualize the form if appropriate.) Encourage children to find someone at home or in the neighborhood who can write the information parents and grandparents give if the parents "don't have time to." Be sensitive. Many parents can't write well.

Step 4: Charting the Family History Questionnaire. Explain this step to the children as doing research—to find out how their family histories are the same and different. In the small groups, first focus on information about parents. Collate the information from Questions 1 through 3 on a large piece of paper by asking each child to say the names of his or her parents and where they came from while writing down the information under each child's name. The next day have children dictate sentences to add to the group family tree (e.g., Marti's father was born in New York).

Step 5. Repeat Step 4 with the information about grandparents (Questions 4–6).

Step 6. By now, the children will probably ask questions about the location of the different places family members came from. With wall-mounted, large maps of the United States; North, Central, and South America; Europe; Asia—depending on the geographic origin of your children's parents—pushpins; and different colored yarn for each child, help the children make a route between each parent's place of origin and where the family now lives.

This activity can elicit much conversation ("Look at how far my mom had to go," "My mom didn't have to go anywhere," "My dad was born farther away than my mom"), which leads to simple measurement activities on subsequent days.

This activity has been used to bring in additional math concepts: Children cut pieces of yarn to match the distance of their parents on the map. Then they use blocks to count and compare the different distances. They make a graph chart of all their parents' places of origin.

Step 7. Using the Step 6 methods, the children chart where their grandparents were born.

Step 8. The teacher reads the responses to questions 7 and 8 about each family's cultural or ethnic heritage and special customs and traditions. Introduce the word and concept of an *ethnic group* —people who once came from the same place and who share languages and customs. The children get excited about how special each family is.

Step 9. At large-group circle time, children share favorite stories about their grandparents and special objects their grandparents have given to their families.

Step 10. At large-group time the teacher reads books and folktales representing the cultural background of each child.

Step 11. Ask parents and/or grandparents to write down why their parents came to the United States and what experiences they had when they first arrived.

Step 12. Read the stories at a few large-group times, telling the children they are going to be researchers about immigration. Explain that adults use the word *immigration* when people leave the country where they were born to move to a new country. Then ask the children questions such as: "What do you notice about why people immigrate? What happens to them when they come to their new country? Is it easy or hard? Do they know the language? How do they find a place to live? How do they find a job?"

Help children understand that in many cases people immigrated to the United States because of lack of work or freedom or because of war and that the first experiences in this country were sometimes very hard. If none of your children have experienced immigration themselves, tell persona doll stories about contemporary experiences (a Vietnamese or Salvadorian family).

Step 13. Individually during choice time, or in small groups, make a family book with each child, pulling together all the data and photos about her or his family. Encourage children to show or read their books to each other.

Step 14. As a follow-up activity, children, pretending to be TV reporters, interview each other about their families during small-group times. Tape the interviews and use them to make simple books for the children to read.

Learning about people's work

The activities already listed under "How family members work" can be expanded into units with kindergarten children—for example, learning about farmworkers. In one classroom, the teacher introduced the unit by serving grape jelly at snack and asking the children, "Where do you think grape jelly comes from?"

Subsequent activities included:

- Looking at photographs and magazine pictures of grape farms in the San Joaquin Valley in California and of farmworkers caring for and harvesting the grapes, and talking about all the tasks necessary

- Inviting a parent of one of the children whose own parents had worked as farmworkers to tell about their experiences, including how hard the work was

- Looking at photos of different working conditions of farmworkers and talking about what were fair and unfair situations

- Reading a story about Delores Huerta and Cesar Chávez, and helping children explore the concept of a union and a strike, and why the farmworkers felt they needed both

- Telling a persona doll story about the doll's mother and father participating in a farmworkers' strike. The doll "taught" the children to sing "De Colores," one of the songs farmworkers sang on the picket lines

- Planting their own garden during this unit, so that they could experience growing, caring for, and harvesting food

Talking about religious beliefs of different ethnic groups

As children learn about each other's families, differences in religious practices may come up. Families will worship in various ways: churches, synagogue, Buddhist temple, mosque; some may not worship. Families may be Buddhist, Catholic, Jewish, Muslim, Protestant, or atheist. Differences in what holidays are honored will also arise. Accept children's talking about their religious ideas as part of their family's way of life and explain to children that each family has its own ideas about God, and that all ideas are treated with respect in the classroom.

Teasing may also occur. In one classroom, Andrew, a 5-year-old, casually announced at circle time, "All you kids are going to hell." His teacher asked, "Why do you say that?" Andrew: "Because they didn't go to my church yesterday like I told them." Teacher: "Everyone does not go to the same church and that is fine. You cannot tell children which church to go to, and you cannot tell them they will go to hell. If you believe in God, only God can say that."

Exclusion or name calling about another child's religion should never be permitted and should be handled as any other discriminatory behavior based on a child's identity. (See Chapter 8, "Learning to Resist Stereotyping and Discriminatory Behavior.")

In an anti-bias curriclum *all* religious beliefs are treated with acceptance: Each family has the absolute right to believe as they do, but no one has the right to tell other children that one way is better than the other. In a religiously based school, where a particular viewpoint is a part of the curriculum, anti-bias activities should include teaching respect for people who are not part of one's religious orientation.

Summary

Learning the cultural attributes of one's own ethnic identity takes time. Even more so does learning about someone else's culture. Young children are just beginning their journey. Centering curriculum in children's families and then expanding diversity through learning about other children's families provides sufficient material and issues to last a whole school year. Since early childhood teachers have been exposed to or are using multicultural curriculum approaches, it is particularly important to keep in mind the traps of a tourist approach when planning anti-bias activities about cultural differences and similarities.

References

Delton, J. (1980). *My mother lost her job today*. Niles, IL: Whitman.

Hale-Benson, J. (1986). *Black children: Their roots, culture and learning styles*. Baltimore: Johns Hopkins University Press.

Hazen, B.S. (1983). *Tight times*. New York: Penguin.

Wenning, J., & Wortis, S. (1985). *Made by human hands: A curriculum for teaching young children about work and working people*. Cambridge, MA: The Multicultural Project for Communication and Education.

Wilson, G.L. (1985). Teaching pre-schoolers about work: A complex task. *Interracial Books for Children Bulletin, 16*(4), 9–13.

FAMILY HISTORY QUESTIONNAIRE

This questionnaire is part of our Kindergarten Family History/Multicultural Project. Please work with your child to fill in the answers and return to school by _____. Thanks! (Answers reflect the *child's* history.)

1. I was born in _____.
                                            city/state

2. My mother's name is _____. She was born in

   _____ on _____ , _____ .
           state (or country)   date   year

3. My father's name is _____. He was born in

   _____ on _____ , _____ .
           state (or country)   date   year

4. My mother's parents live or lived in _____.
                                                    state (or country)

   They were born in _____ and _____ .
                          state (or country)   state (or country)

5. My father's parents live or lived in _____.
                                                    state (or country)

   They were born in _____ and _____ .
                          state (or country)   state (or country)

6. Did my grandparents or great-grandparents come from another country?

   Which person? _____

   Which country? _____

7. What is my family's cultural/ethnic heritage? _____

8. Does our family have special customs or traditions? What are they? _____

   _____

9. Tell a story about a special relative who's important to our family. _____

   _____

   _____

   _____

LEARNING TO RESIST STEREOTYPING AND DISCRIMINATORY BEHAVIOR

8

Learning non-oppressive ways of interacting with differences requires more than introducing diversity into the classroom. It also requires gentle but active and firm guidance by adults. Unfortunately, many teachers and parents are uncertain about what to do when a preschooler exhibits biased behavior. All too often, uncertainty results in nonaction: "I was struck speechless," "I was afraid of saying or doing the wrong thing," "It made me so upset (angry), I couldn't do anything" are typical comments.

Discriminatory acts are one form of aggressive behavior, as hurtful as physical aggression, and should be immediately and directly addressed. Teachers must become aware of any attitudes or feelings that prevent them from intervening in discriminatory interactions between children and practice appropriate responses through techniques like role playing. (See Chapter 12, "Getting Started.")

GOALS

1. To help children change discomfort and inappropriate responses to differences into respectful, comfortable interaction
2. To expand preschoolers' developing concept of fairness and feelings of empathy for each other
3. To foster children's critical thinking about stereotyping
4. To enable children to gain the tools and self-confidence to stand up for themselves and others against biased ideas and discriminatory behavior

---

Handling Discomfort With Differences

Children sometimes react to cultural differences with discomfort and hurtful behaviors. Whether these are "natural" responses to newness or learned responses to differences, it is necessary to intervene so that pre-prejudice is not allowed to ripen into prejudice.

A 4-year-old White child asks a visitor to her day care center, "What is your name?" The visitor answers, "Rayko." "Yuck, yuck, yucky," responds the child. Her teacher admonishes, "Be nice to our visitor." Rayko joins in and asks the child, "Does my name sound funny to you?" (She nods yes.) "Have you ever heard it be-

fore?" (The child shakes no.) "It is a new and different name to you," continues Rayko. "I like my name; it is a Japanese name." "Oh," says the child and goes off to play.

Although the teacher intervened, her response was too vague. Teaching politeness is not sufficient. Children need help understanding why they are uncomfortable.

As their teacher begins reading a story in Spanish to an English-speaking group, a few children begin to giggle. The teacher stops reading and tells the children, "I am stopping because some children are giggling while I am

69

reading. That is not OK—it is rude. I know Spanish is a new language to some of you. Sometimes we are not comfortable with something we do not know and we laugh to make ourselves feel better, but laughing at how people talk is hurtful and unfair. Laughing is not OK, but it is OK to raise your hand and ask me questions about what I am reading."

In preparation for their Thanksgiving feast, the child care staff decide to each cook a dish from their cultural background with the children. A Chinese teacher announces she is going to make a Chinese dessert. Alexis says, "Yuck, I hate Chinese food." The teacher replies, "I eat Chinese food every day." "I only like Whitesican food," Alexis retorts, laughing. "What is Whitesican food?" the teacher asks, and gets Alexis to talk about what she eats every day. Then the teacher continues, "You like the food you eat every day, and I like the food I eat every day. I don't like it when you say you hate Chinese food; that hurts my feelings. When I cook my dessert, you can say instead, 'No, thank you; I don't want any. I don't know how it tastes.' Or you might just taste a very little bit because even though it is new, maybe you will like it."

Tanya, a Black child, says to Soon Yung, who is speaking in English, "You sure do talk funny." Their teacher responds, "Tanya, Soon Yung does *not* talk funny; she is learning to speak English. At Soon Yung's home she and her family speak Korean. Soon Yung can speak Korean very well; now she is learning to speak English. Soon she will be able to speak two languages. In our class we can help each other speak different languages."

In sum:

1. Immediately address a child's negative response to a cultural difference.

2. Help the child figure out why he or she is uncomfortable.

3. Explain what responses are hurtful and offer alternative responses.

Dealing With Discriminatory Exclusion

Here are some examples of discriminatory exclusion. Do you agree with the teacher's handling of each situation?

Three girls, Marisol, Angie, and Janet, were playing with dolls on a spread-out blanket. When Dimitri attempted to enter their play, Angie asserted forcefully, "No boys can play." The other two agreed. Dimitri walked away. The teacher got Dimitri and they joined the girls. "Being a boy is not an OK reason for not letting Dimitri play, just like I wouldn't let anyone say they wouldn't play with you because you are a girl," the teacher stated. "Boys cannot change being boys and girls can't change being girls—that is who they are. It is unfair not to let someone play because of who they are." The girls chorused, "Yeah, we like playing with boys in the morning and in the afternoon, but not right now." Their teacher asked, "Why not right now?" "The dads are at work," Angie insisted. "Dimitri would like to join you now. Is there a way he could play with you that would be OK?" Dimitri interjected, "I'll be the daddy. I'm at work, but I'm coming home soon." The girls agreed; their teacher left them to play.

The children found a solution, albeit one that reflects traditional gender roles. However, the teacher felt this was not the time to further interrupt their play.

Brandy and Nina, both girls, are playing house. Tomas comes over and asks, "What are you playing?" Brandy: "House." Tomas: "Can I be the dad?" Nina: "We don't need a dad." Tomas: "Can I be a brother?" Brandy: "We don't need any more people." Their play goes on with Tomas watching.

The teacher did not intervene in this interaction.

Children do not always have to play with each other every time. Groups do not always have to be "mixed." In this incident, the teacher judged that the children did not use discriminatory reasons. And, not every family has a dad or a brother!

The teacher has noticed that a number of children have not been including Laurie, a child with mild cerebral palsy who uses a wheelchair, in their play. Children aren't using a discriminatory reason; they say, "We don't want anyone else playing." After a few weeks, the teacher decides to take action. The first day, she reads the book *About Handicaps* (Frank, 1974), which addresses the issue of hostility and fear about a differently abled child.

The next day the teacher tells a story about Julie, their persona doll who uses a wheelchair. She first speaks to Laurie, saying, "When Julie [the doll] first came, the children didn't want to play with her. I'd like to tell everyone her story. Do you think that is a good idea?" Laurie nods yes and smiles. After describing Julie's experiences and feelings, the teacher asks, "What could the children do to help her like coming to school?" Children's responses reveal misconceptions, which the teacher addresses—"Julie is a baby because she can't walk, so the kids don't want to play with her," "Maybe she doesn't know how to play." Then they are open to figuring out solutions: "Tell her next time she can play," "I'd be her friend," "They should say they are sorry."

The teacher observes, "I see the same problem in our class. Many children aren't letting Laurie play with them. This makes her feel sad just as it made Julie feel sad. From now on, I want you to make sure that she gets to play with whomever she wants to. After circle time, I want these children to join Laurie and me in a math game . . ." (the teacher names a few of the children who play with Laurie and a few who haven't).

Billy, a White child, refuses to sit next to George, a Cherokee child. Billy cries to his teacher, "I'm afraid that George is going to kill me." To learn about the source of this fear, the teacher asks, "Why do you feel that way?" Billy says, "Because Indians kill White people. I saw it on TV last night." Teacher: "Billy, most TV programs are just make-believe, so there is no reason to be afraid of Indian people. The cowboy and Indian movies you see on TV do not tell the truth about Indian people. Many White people did mean things to Indian people, like taking away their land and their homes. That is why the Indian people fought back, to protect their homes and families. George is a member of our class. He and his family live in our neighborhood, just like you and your family do. We will not insult him and his family by

saying things about Indian people that are not true. Whenever I hear anyone saying untrue things about Indian people, I tell them to stop. I'd like you to help me do that." (CIBC, 1983, p. 17)

After building a house in the block area, Barbara and Lisa, two Black girls, have a disagreement about where to put the furniture. Unable to reach a compromise, Lisa screams at Barbara, "Well, I don't like you anyway because you've got short nappy hair. *My* hair is *good*." Teacher: "Lisa, you are upset because Barbara wants to put the furniture one place and you want to put it some other place. However, you must *not* hurt Barbara's feelings by saying something that is mean and disrespectful. All hair grows differently. Many Black people's hair grows slowly. It is usually short and springy. How your hair grows depends on the kind of hair your family has. Lisa, in this classroom you may not call your hair better than anybody else's! Barbara, if some people say mean things about your hair, you just tell them that your hair is pretty just as it is. Now let's figure out a way to solve the problem of where to place the doll furniture. By learning to cooperate, you won't say mean things that hurt feelings." (CIBC, 1983, p. 18)

Guidelines for Dealing With Children's Discriminatory Exclusion Behaviors

Set limits. Make it a firm rule that no aspect of a child's or adult's identity, be it gender, race, ethnicity, disability, religion, socioeconomic class, or any other aspect is *ever* an acceptable reason for exclusion, or teasing: "In this class, it is never OK to say you won't play with someone because of the color of their skin or because she is a girl or because she uses a wheelchair."

Intervene immediately, reminding children of the limits.

Comfort/support the target of the discriminatory behavior: "It was unfair for Johnny to say you couldn't play because you are Black." Help the target child verbalize his feelings to the other child: "I don't want you to say that, I don't like it." Teach children not to accept being victims. Help the excluder understand that discrimination hurts another child just as much as a physical hurt.

Determine the real reasons for the conflict. If the excluder does not ordinarily use biased reasons for exclusion and you find out that the real reason for this particular incident of exclusion is a specific action on the part of the child who was excluded

(she wanted to be the fire chief and someone else already was chief), help the children understand that their real reason for the exclusion was not related to the child's identity; and involve the children in problem solving (taking turns at being fire chief, starting a new fire house, or whatever seems suitable).

If you believe prejudice does underlie the exclusion—the excluder has previously engaged in similar behavior and/or verbalizes a biased reason—offer the excluded child further support: "I am angry that Johnny doesn't want to play with you. He is missing out on a great friend. I do not like what he is saying, and I am going to help him change his ideas about playing with you. Now, let's find someone else to play with."

Then take further action with the excluder: Tell the child, "In this classroom it's not OK to refuse to play with another child because he's Black (or speaks another language)." Try to learn more about the thinking underlying the child's bias.

Work on a long-term plan: Collect more data about Johnny to figure out the dynamics of his exclusionary behavior, including further observation and talking with other staff and with his family. Develop a plan for work at school *and* at home. Keep in frequent touch with his home. After an agreed-upon period, re-evaluate the child's progress and develop further plans if necessary.

Within these guidelines, children may need different kinds and amounts of intervention to overcome pre-prejudice and discriminatory behaviors.

For many children, one firm intervention is sufficient:

This morning, Sandy refused to play with Tiffany, a new Black child. It was the first time Sandy's teacher saw this behavior. When asked why, Sandy replied, "Elaine (another child in the class) said we shouldn't play with Tiffany because she is Black." Her teacher replied, "That is not a good reason. You don't even know Tiffany yet. I want you to get to know her." Sandy did reach out to Tiffany, and they became friends. There were no further discriminatory behaviors on Sandy's part.

For other children, a series of activities is necessary:

Jane's mother, Ann, told the teacher that Jane had said she doesn't like Mei (a Vietnamese student teacher) because Mei talks funny and is too dark. Ann explained to Jane that Mei is from another country where people have darker skin than she does and that Mei is learning English. She told Jane to like all her teachers. Jane insisted that she didn't like Mei. Ann was upset, saying she didn't know what else to do.

The teacher felt that Jane was having discomfort because Mei was very different from anyone else she knew. She talked with Ann about how to help Jane learn more about Mei, both at home and at school. That night, Ann talked to Jane about Mei's country of origin and showed Jane some picture books. Ann reported that Jane expressed interest.

In school, Mei talked to Jane's small group a number of times about her life, using photos and daily life objects. Ann followed up by inviting Mei to their home for a meal. This plan worked. Neither her mother nor teacher saw any repetition of Jane's discomfort.

For a fewer number of children, discriminatory behavior is a part of a more general emotional problem and more difficult to change:

Elaine, a White child with serious emotional problems, used racial exclusion to express her general anger and hostility. Her teacher's first strategy was to support the children Elaine excluded, but not directly address Elaine's racial bias because she wanted to work on Elaine's more general emotional problems first. In hindsight, this was a grievous error. Not only did Elaine's discriminatory behavior continue for far too long, but also other children began to imitate her. Led by Elaine,

they made one Black child a particular target.

Finally, the teacher realized she had a serious problem. At circle time, she talked with the children about their exclusionary behavior and emphasized that this was very serious and upsetting. She made clear that, from now on, the teachers would make sure no one ever again said they wouldn't play with another child because of her skin color. She asked the children to help each other remember this.

During the next few weeks, the teacher did some further small-group activities about different skin colors, read stories about Black children, and told stories about the Black persona dolls. Some children needed reminders of the limits; a few needed further teacher intervention. When children played well, the teacher supported them: "Today you played really well with Linda." Except for Elaine, the rest of the children's negative behavior stopped. The staff set Elaine much stricter boundaries and immediately enforced limits on her discriminatory behavior while continuing to work with her and her parents on Elaine's other problems. Her teacher was not able to completely eliminate her hostility toward the Black children, but she did stop her involving the other children.

After this whole experience, the teacher concluded that she would never again hold back on directly dealing with discriminatory behavior at once, no matter what the reasons for such behavior.

Margaret, a 4-year-old, refuses to play with Anna. "Go away, you no good Mexican," she yells. Anna backs off, looking first surprised and then near tears. Their teacher immediately intervenes. She puts her arm around Anna and hugs her, then firmly says to Margaret, "That is a very hurtful and unfair thing to say to Anna." Before the teacher gets any further, Margaret insists, "My dad told me not to play with her. He says Mexicans are dirty." The teacher responds, "Margaret, in our classroom everyone plays with each other. I have a different rule than your father. I also do not think the same as he does. I do not think it is true that Mexicans are dirty. I am going to talk with your father about our different ideas and rules." To Anna, the teacher says, "Let's go find something special to play with together." Anna chooses to read books. In the book corner, the teacher first takes Anna on her lap and says, "I am sorry that Margaret said such unfair, untrue things to you. I will talk to her again and remind her that in our classroom we take care of each other and do not leave anyone out. Now, what book would you like me to read to you?"

In this situation, the teacher's immediate intervention and firm limit setting was essential. She also knew from previous conservations with Margaret's parents that they had strong anti-Mexican attitudes. After school she phoned them, related what had happened and how she handled the incident, and explained that it was not acceptable for parents to tell their children that they could not play with a specific child. She set up a time for a conference with them to discuss what to do about the different messages they were teaching Mar-

garet. (See Chapter 11, "Working With Parents," for ideas about how to handle such a conference.) The teacher also spoke with Anna's family, explaining what had happened and what she did, and asked them to let her know if Anna showed or expressed further distress about the incident.

CAUTION

When handling discriminatory behaviors,

Don't ignore. "It will go away on its own if I don't respond." This position does not support the target of discriminatory behavior and implies permission to act in discriminatory ways, thereby making the environment unsafe.

"If I respond, it will make things worse." It is true that some children will test these limits as they do others. However, we would not ignore throwing blocks or sand in children's faces because we are worried that intervention will make the behaviors worse. We act, thereby reaffirming our limits.

Don't excuse. Saying, "Johnny didn't really mean it or know what he meant when he said Susan couldn't play because she is a tomboy," or "Johnny has socializing problems; let's not focus on this remark," excuses discriminatory behavior. Conversely, saying, "Susan wasn't upset by Johnny's remarks. She just walked away," trivializes the excluded child's feelings. Excusing responses teach one child it is OK to be hurtful and the other that she will not be protected against oppressive behavior.

Don't be immobilized by fear. Making a mistake is far less serious than not acting at all. You can always go back to a child and say or do something else if, on reflection, you feel you didn't respond correctly. However, if you were unable to respond immediately at all, think about what to do afterward, and go back to the children involved in the incident.

Learning To Recognize and Criticize Stereotyping

The objects young children use often reflect and teach stereotyping: lunch boxes, books, food packaging, toys, TV cartoons, commercials, sitcoms, home decorations. Another form of social stereotyping that affects young children are "sayings" like "No way, José" and "Indian giver." Hearing adults and older children use such terms, preschoolers will imitate, unless they learn that it is hurtful.

Most adults are so accustomed to stereotypes that they often don't even recognize them as such. If teachers train themselves to notice, they can help 4- and 5-year-olds begin to do the critical

thinking essential for resisting the damaging effects of stereotyping.

Here are examples of what 4½- and 5-year-olds learned after staff-directed activities to counter prevailing stereotypes about Native Americans:

Jill arrived this morning with a stereotypic "Indian Warrior" figure. Sue and Kenji immediately told her, "Don't show that to Suzanne (a Cherokee-Cree staff member); it will hurt her feelings. It isn't the way Indians look."

Malcolm brought Suzanne a copy of *National Geographic*, and, showing her pictures about Native Americans in the colonial period, asked, "Are these true?"

Activities

Provide experiences that challenge children's stereotypic ideas. Invite people who challenge stereotypes by the work they do—a male nurse, a Black female doctor, a female firefighter, a female truck driver, a male dancer, a hearing-impaired teacher, a Latino lawyer, a White factory worker—to visit your classroom.

Read books that challenge stereotypes: *My Daddy Is a Nurse* (Wandro, 1981); *My Special Best Words* (Steptoe, 1974), about a single father; *Don't Feel Sorry for Paul* (Wolf, 1974); *Grandma's Wheelchair* (Henriod, 1982); and *All Kinds of Families* (Simon, 1975).

Display side by side photographs and pictures that challenge stereotypes: images of men and women, of various racial and ethnic backgrounds and different physical abilities, doing similar work.

Confront children's ideas and do follow-up activities: For example, a preschool teacher overhears this conversation in the dramatic play area: Three White children, two boys and one girl are playing; Mark, a Black boy, joins them. One White child who often plays with Mark says, "You can't play now. Blacks can't marry Whites." The teacher steps in and says, "That is not true. Many Black men are married to White women, and many Black women are married to White men. It is not OK for you to say Mark cannot play with you." The teacher then leaves them to play. In the next few days, she follows-up by reading *Black Is Brown Is Tan* (Adoff, 1973), about an interracial Black-White marriage, and by bringing pictures from her picture file of various examples of interracial and interethnic marriages for display and discussion at small group times.

Compare authentic and stereotypic images in books and other materials

Comparing images is effective for looking at book illustrations, comic strips, TV cartoons, posters, greeting cards, lunch boxes, holiday decorations, even educational materials. Explain the concept of critiquing pictures to decide if they are fair or unfair. "Unfair pictures aren't true (Chinese skin is not yellow) and make fun of a person (exaggerating features)." Introduce the word *stereotyping* for unfair pictures if you wish.

Show the children a stereotypic picture and say, "I wonder if this picture is fair. Let's find out." Compare with an accurate picture, talking about what is different. Help the children verbalize how the picture is unfair, and why stereotypes hurt people's feelings. Then figure out together what to do about the stereotypic material: cover it with an accurate picture, stop using the material.

Make a book about fair and unfair pictures with the children

On facing pages paste a "fair" and an "unfair" picture about gender role, a racial or ethnic group, a person with a visible disability. Use pictures from magazines or photocopies of illustrations in books. Under each picture write a few sentences that the children dictate about why they think a picture is fair or unfair. Add new pictures to the book as you or the children find them. As children learn, they may change their minds about a particular picture —if the group agrees, then change its category with them. Read the book at circle time periodically and leave in the book shelf for children to look at by themselves.

Critique books

Here is the place to use books that have been removed from daily circulation in the classroom. For example: A child care center teacher reads the book *Popcorn* (Asch, 1979) to her 4-year-olds. The central figure, a bear, dresses up as an "Indian" for a Halloween party. After reading the story, the teacher asks, "What do you like and not like about the book?" and writes the children's responses on a large sheet of paper. The children like that the "popcorn popped all over the place and creeped upstairs . . . because it (the house) filled so much up with popcorn you couldn't see anyone." They don't like that "his parents left the bear alone in the house—he would be scared," and that the bear "dressed like an Indian—it hurts Native Americans' feelings; they will think that they are making fun of them." "How else could the bear dress up?" asks their teacher. Children suggest a horse, a ghost, a lion, and a dinosaur.

Acknowledge and support children's awareness of stereotyping

Benjamin was playing with his Lego™ toys, one of his favorites. Suddenly, he looked at his teacher and announced, "You know, all of the characters in this set are White people!" His teacher responded, "Hey, you're right. There should be Black and Asian and Hispanic figures too. I think in the country where Legos are made, almost everybody is White. I'm proud of you for noticing because it is important to notice when things are unfair like that."

Learning To Problem Solve Discriminatory Behavior

1. Teach children ways to stand up for themselves. The following activity (developed by Molly Scudder and Susan Parker) is an example of one way to help children learn effective, appropriate skills for expressing their anger when hurt by another and for stopping physical or verbal aggression from another child. This activity helps children dare to defend their personal space. It can be used when dealing with hitting or verbal abuse of any kind.

   Material: A hoop 36″ in diameter, and 3 preschooler-size cloth dolls (male/female and different racial/ethnic backgrounds).

   Method: At group time:

   • Tell children, "We are going to play a game that will help you take care of yourself."

   • Teacher and assistant demonstrate first: The assistant puts the hoop over her and drops it to the ground. The teacher explains, "You are in a special space that belongs to you. You have the right to control that space. If anybody comes into your space when you don't want them to, or hurts you by their actions or words, you have the right and responsibility to stop that person."

   • Role play a doll "invading" the personal space of the assistant in the hoop. The teacher outside the hoop holds the doll in front of her and hits the assistant with the doll's arm. The assistant whispers, "Don't do

that." The doll hits her again. The assistant hits back. The doll hits her back. This time the assistant takes the doll's wrist firmly in her hands, makes eye contact, and says in a strong, loud voice, "I am angry with you. I don't like it when you hit me. Stop it." The doll stops.

   • Then some of the children take turns—one in the hoop, a second manipulating the doll. After each team acts out the situation, the rest of the group critiques how the child in the hoop responded. Ask: "Does she sound like someone who is angry? Would she stop the doll from hitting her? What does she need to do to stop the doll from hitting her? Does she need to change her voice, her words?" Try out and discuss the merits of the children's suggestions.

   The teacher can also make suggestions, "Let me hear you sound angry. Say it like you really mean it."

   • Repeat the hoop activity a number of times, so that all the children get a turn to be inside the hoop. The same procedures can also be used to practice stopping verbal aggression, such as name calling and teasing. The hoop activity establishes an acceptable way to stand up for oneself in the face of unfair behavior in the classroom.

2. Read children's books that address prejudice such as *The Swimming Hole* (Beim & Beim, 1947) and *The Sneetches* (Seuss, 1961). These

two books open up discussion about judging people because of their physical characteristics. A third book, *A Look at Prejudice and Understanding* (Anders, 1976), addresses cultural prejudices.

3. Use persona doll stories about incidents of discrimination between dolls to foster children's problem-solving skills. Set the scene and then ask children what they think the doll who has been the target of discrimination might do. Encourage children to think of various strategies and stress the importance of doing something.

   Tell other persona doll stories where the problem to be discussed is what a third child might do when seeing two other children involved in a discriminatory incident.

4. Help children learn how to help each other when a discriminatory incident occurs in their classroom.

5. Help children learn to take action against bias. The next chapter, "Activism With Young Children," extends the activities for learning to resist stereotyping and discriminatory behavior into the larger area of taking action against bias beyond the classroom.

References

Adoff, A. (1973). *Black is brown is tan.* New York: Harper & Row.

Anders, R. (1976). *A look at prejudice and understanding.* Minneapolis: Lerner.

Asch, F. (1979). *Popcorn.* New York: Parents Magazine.

Beim, L., & Beim, J. (1947). *The swimming hole.* New York: Morrow.

Council on Interracial Books for Children. (1983). *Childcare shapes the future: Anti-racist strategies.* New York: Author.

Frank, D. (1974). *About handicaps.* New York: Walker.

Henriod, L. (1982). *Grandma's wheelchair.* Niles, IL: Whitman.

Seuss, Dr. (1961). *The Sneetches.* New York: Random House.

Simon, N. (1975). *All kinds of families.* Niles, IL: Whitman.

Steptoe, J. (1974). *My special best words.* New York: Viking.

Wandro, M. (1981). *My daddy is a nurse.* Reading, MA: Addison-Wesley.

Wolf, B. (1974). *Don't feel sorry for Paul.* New York: Harper & Row.

ACTIVISM WITH YOUNG CHILDREN

Children learning to take action against unfair behaviors that occur in their own lives is at the heart of anti-bias education. Without this component, the curriculum loses its vitality and power. For children to feel good and confident about themselves, they need to be able to say, "That's not fair," or "I don't like that," if they are the target of prejudice or discrimination. For children to develop empathy and respect for diversity, they need to be able to say, "I don't like what you are doing" to a child who is abusing another child. If we teach children to recognize injustice, then we must also teach them that people can create positive change by working together.

Young children have an impressive capacity for learning how to be activists if adults provide activities that are relevant and developmentally appropriate. Through activism activities children build the confidence and skills for becoming adults who assert, in the face of injustice, "I have the responsibility to deal with it, I know how to deal with it, I will deal with it."

Many teachers and parents may be unaccustomed to doing activism with young children, so it is essential to carefully think through how to introduce this aspect of the curriculum. This chapter discusses the issues, goals, and kinds of activism activities meaningful to young children, through an edited transcript of an Anti-Bias Curriculum Task Force meeting.

Laying the Groundwork: Learning Assertion and Empathy With Each Other

Anti-bias activism begins in young children's daily interactions with each other. Learning to express their feelings to another child who has hurt them and to care when another child has been hurt creates the foundation upon which activism activities build. Anti-bias curriculum alerts us to helping children be assertive in situations that reflect bias or in situations of physical aggression.

MARIA (teacher of 2s): The first thing that we do is give children permission and support to speak their feelings about having an injustice done toward them. If they can't do it, we help them find words, even say the words for them. We want our children to get used to saying to each other, "I don't like it when you hit me," or "I don't like it when you call me a baby," or "Girls can *so* climb." They get daily practice in speaking up for their own rights.

REGENA (teacher of 2s): We have one 2½-year-old girl who is passive and fearful when another child takes something from her or picks a toy she wants. We're in the process of building up her courage. An adult stands right next to her and says to the other child, "You really need to listen to her words. There's something she wants to say," and then says to the first child, "You can say this in a strong voice. Tell them that you don't want . . . ."

MAE (preschool teacher): I have a similar situation with a 3½-year-old girl. She is able to stand up for herself with other girls but passively withdraws if a boy tells her she can't play. I am now intervening as soon as that happens. I bring her back and say, "I saw you wanted to play with the blocks, or sand, or whatever. Frank can't stop you. You tell him that you *are* going to play." The first few times she did it in a whisper, holding on to me. Recently she comes to get me and then says loudly, "I am going to play; you can't boss me." I hope soon she will be able to stand up on her own.

CORY (preschool teacher): Sometimes a child's been insulted, and I encourage the two children to talk about it, but the child who's been insulted doesn't want to talk. I might say, "Well, I really don't like what's happened myself, and I'd like to say something about it." And then I use what-

ever words are appropriate, like "When you said Rosa couldn't play with you because she looks funny, you were not fair to her. You hurt her and now she feels sad. What you did makes me feel sad too, and angry at you. In this classroom we are fair to each other," so that I model expressing feelings and don't let a situation like this go by without doing something about it.

MOLLY (kindergarten teacher): In kindergarten we do some very direct teaching about respecting each other's physical and emotional space, and about ways to assertively tell someone "no." We practice holding the offending child's wrists and saying what you feel as if you really mean it, whether you've been the recipient of abusive language or physical violence. I find that many of my kids begin by using a "wishy-washy" voice that wouldn't convince a cucumber. I want them to say it like they really mean it strong and firm.

FRANCOIS (child care teacher): By doing this we are saying to children, "You are respect-worthy human beings who have a right to your feelings, to express your feelings, to be listened to, to be taken seriously."

CORY: I think another important precursor of activism is children's developing the ability to care when another child is hurt or feels scared or sad. Usually children show empathy toward a child who is physically hurt, or feeling sad because of separating from a parent, or feeling sick. We need to help them also develop empathy for a child who is emotionally hurt by teasing, name calling, or rejection because of his or her gender, or race, or physical ability.

MAE: Learning to appreciate different needs or special needs of each other is another part of extending empathy. This is hard for preschoolers, but they are capable of learning if they see adults accepting a child's uniqueness, and not insisting that everyone act the same and do the same things. I also give children a lot of encouragement when I see them helping each other: "You're really showing your friend how much you care about her or him." I think we can build on this work, start with areas where preschoolers do show empathy, and then connect anti-bias issues to what they already do.

KAY (after-school care director/teacher): I teach my children to call on friends when they are faced with an unfair situation. For example, last week two boys were playing on the rope swing, and two girls were waiting for a long time. The girls kept asking for a turn, and the boys ignored them. I watched and waited to see what would happen. Finally, the girls came to me and complained. I asked them, "What should we do? *I could go and stop them, but that won't help you in the future.*" One girl then said, "Maybe we could get some of our friends to help us." I responded, "Yes, that is a good idea." The two girls collected about four children, girls and boys, and with their friends around them told the boys to give them a turn. The boys got off the swings and complained to me that they had been chased off. I talked with the two boys about what they had done to create the need for the girls to get their friends to help them.

MOLLY: I absolutely agree about children learning to help each other. I have another example. Last year we had a White child who frequently used racial slurs against the Black children. I had been working with him for months, making it very clear that such language was not allowed. His behavior stopped finally. However, at a birthday party outside of school, he insulted Carol, one of the Black children, who came to school the next day very angry and hurt. I decided new action was necessary. I called the six Black children to a meeting, explaining to the other children that we had a special problem that was affecting the Black children and that if others wanted to they could also come. A few did. At the meeting I explained what had happened to Carol and asked what they thought we should do. All of the Black children told about times the White child had insulted them and how mad it made them. They had a lot of ideas about what to do—some more acceptable than others. One child told Carol that she should kick the White child in the balls if he called her names. I responded, "I cannot allow that action, even though I understand that you are angry enough to do it." Finally we agreed that the six Black children would meet with the White child, his mother, and myself as soon as he arrived and tell him that we never wanted to hear him say the N word again. By this time Carol was tooting on a cylinder-shaped block as if it was a trumpet, clearly feeling restored. I praised the children for their good work together. We did meet with the White child, and it did change his behavior for a while.

Friends learning to help each other deal with unfair situations prepare children for group activism activities.

Group Activism in the Classroom: Working Together To Create Change

While developing assertiveness and empathy are the activism goals for 2s and 3s, 4- and 5-year-olds are capable of working together to change biased situations beyond individual interactions with their peers. Group activism activities about concrete issues that are real to young children are empowering experiences. Through them children learn to interact with the world with initiative, responsibility, and strength. It is interesting to think about whether group activism activities also serve as a challenge to "superheroes." Instead of one superhuman figure (usually a White male) righting wrongs all by himself, activism activities teach children that real people, adults and children, can make life better by working together.

CORY: In the preschool we did an action around the multicultural dolls we bought from Lakeshore. One day, as I was using dolls to tell a story, one child commented, "They don't have any penises or vaginas." The other children checked out the dolls and agreed. We discussed whether it would be better if the dolls had either one or the other. The children felt that they would prefer to really know if the dolls were boys or girls. So, I suggested that we write to Lakeshore and tell them about our concern. The group dictated a letter, we sent it, and a few weeks later Lakeshore offered to replace our dolls with a new set that did have genitals. I felt that this was a very successful activity.

BILL (special education teacher): In my classroom (3- to 5-year-olds) we have an ongoing project dealing with the parking space for people with special needs at our school. It began a few years ago when a parent who was in a wheelchair had enormous difficulty getting to my classroom for a conference because there was no "handicapped" parking space at the school. I was furious; the irony of this happening in a school for physically disabled children added to my anger. I decided that the children in my class and I would remedy the situation.

I initiated the activity by taking the children to look at parking spaces for people with disabilities and asking them if they knew what the symbol stood for. We talked about why it is important to have a special parking spot for differently abled people, why it needed to be near the entrance of the school, and what would happen if a differently abled person who couldn't walk had to park far away. Then we looked at the parking lot at school, and the children couldn't find a special "handicapped" parking space. So, we agreed to make one from the spaces already on the lot. I got blue paint, made an H stencil to paint on the ground, and brought a "handicapped parking" sign for the other end. Everyone participated.

The next step was to deal with the people who inappropriately park in the spot. My classroom overlooks the parking lot so we could see when this happened. Many of the children suggested tickets—something they already knew about. Each child dictated a few tickets, and we either put the ticket on the car or gave it directly to the person. We haven't stopped all the able-bodied people from parking in the handicap space, but it has cut down on the number who do.

LISSA (child care center teacher): My favorite activism activity is the one I did on "flesh-colored" Curads™. One day, while getting an adhesive bandage for one of my 3-year-olds, the label "flesh-colored" suddenly hit me. So I said, "Look at this—it says on the box that these bandages are flesh-colored. That means they are the same color as our skin. Let's see if it is really true." We then put bandages on each child's arm and discovered that they were only like the color of some of the children, but not like the color of those with brown skin.

The next day I suggested that we do an experiment. We would invite other children from the Children's School to put on an adhesive bandage and see if it matched their skin. So, other children came to our yard and we took photos of each child's arm with a bandage on it. We made a chart and realized that the bandage didn't match a lot of children's skin.

On the third day I suggested that we write a letter to the company and tell them what we learned. The children dictated what they wanted to say, and I added an explanation of our experiment. We took a trip to the post office the next day to mail our letter. We also involved the parents, sending letters home about what we were doing, and talking about it when parents came to pick up their children.

We got a letter back from Colgate-Palmolive Co., which politely said, "We read your letter, but we don't think it's a problem. Enclosed find some transparent strips which are more flesh-colored." I felt it was important that we did the letter writing, even if the company didn't agree with us. We told them how we felt; they told us how they felt. I think the children felt it was a success because we could get transparent bandages. I let it go after that. Some children remember; I've heard them say, "This doesn't match me." Now I'm wondering if I should have taken another step such as saying to the children that if we still don't think it's fair, we can decide not to buy this brand anymore, or ask the parents to write letters too. We are just beginning. If we get the parents involved, then we are laying a longer lasting foundation.

MOLLY: One activity we did was to paint over a wall in a park that had racial slurs written on it. The day we saw it, I stopped the group and said, "Do you know what is written on this wall? It makes me very angry." I read the words, we talked about what they meant, how they are very hurtful to people. Then we talked about what we could do and decided to paint over the words, which we did the next day. We probably could have written to the Parks Department, telling them about the wall and what we did. It would have been interesting to see what kind of response we got.

LOUISE: A friend of mine, B. J. Richards, who teaches in New York City, told me about the following activity. One day, on a walk around their neighborhood, they came upon a sign, "Man Wanted," in a store window. They read the sign and talked about it, deciding it was unfair to women. They wrote a letter to the store owner and then visited him a few days later. He told them he thought they were right and would change the sign to "Person Wanted."

MOLLY: What else is common in children's lives? We could write to authors of children's books, either about what we like because we think it's fair, or about books that we think have stereo-types. We could write to toy manufacturers about the kinds of toys we want, or don't like, cereal manufacturers, TV shows. We could visit toy stores, bookstores, greeting card stores.

BILL: Sounds like good language arts activities as well as good activism activities.

MAE: How would you feel as a child if you wrote a letter or talked to a store manager and then it didn't do a bit of good? I deal with powerlessness a lot as an adult. I have a lot of trouble with some activism because I feel it's so hopeless.

SHARON: Is success a part of what needs to result in order to promote activism for young children?

A few voices at the same time: Right. Right.

MARIA: I'm hearing that you must have a positive outcome or else do nothing. Life isn't like that. There are ways of coping with not always winning, like with the adhesive bandage activity. The company didn't say they would make bandages that matched, or take the label "skin colored" off the box. Well, we can say, "Then I'm not buying your nasty bandages." That's success that's built into a situation that could be a failure.

REGENA: And that's what teaching children acti-vism is all about. It doesn't necessarily have the outcome you want, but you have to keep on. Again, those are building blocks. You just have to keep putting one block on top of another until you get there.

Beyond the Classroom:
Participating in Community Events

Is it appropriate for young children to participate in community-wide campaigns for social justice? The Anti-Bias Curriculum Task Force did not agree at the meeting. Some thought that if the issue was one the children could comprehend, and parents agreed, then joining a community-wide action would be a meaningful educational experience. Seeing many people coming together because they share a common conviction and are willing to stand up for what they believe can make quite a strong impression on a child. It provides role mod-eling and enhances children's sense of connection. On the other hand, some task force members questioned involving children in what are primar-ily adult issues. They pressed the group to think carefully through what might be appropriate or inappropriate community events in which to in-volve young children.

BILL: When Louise and I were teaching at a child care center, we took our 4- and 5-year-olds to some community demonstrations. For example, when a child care center in Echo Park was going to be closed by the city, the teachers went with the children and parents to a protest at the Los Angeles City Hall. We explained to our children that a friend of Louise's and mine, who was a

teacher at a center just like ours, was upset because the city government was going to close her center. Her children and parents wanted to tell the city government people not to close their center, and they wanted us to help them. Our children wanted to go, and their parents agreed. It was very successful. The Echo Park Center was given another building and our children learned about standing up for their rights. We found this out when, a week later, our children—with a little help from school-aged siblings—made signs and picketed the teachers demanding to eat candy, which we did not allow. (We compro-mised with a candy time one afternoon a week!)

REGENA: In my experience too, children can un-derstand a community action. When McDon-ald's was being boycotted by the NAACP, some of the families in my preschool class partici-pated. Every morning I had one child say, "I still can't go to McDonald's," and we would talk about it.

MOLLY: Well, I think demonstrating about the closing of a child care center or boycotting McDonald's because of discrimination is a little different than, say, picketing the South African Embassy.

SHARON: Is that because you don't see apartheid in South Africa as a concern children can understand and care about?

KAY: I did a series of activities about the Nelson Mandela Tent City the college students set up at UCLA. We often take walks around the campus, and in the course of one of these walks we came upon the Tent City. The children (5- and 6-year-olds) were fascinated and wanted to know why it was there. I explained, simply and briefly, about apartheid in South Africa and why the students had set up Tent City. The children were able to relate what I said to our previous discussions about fairness and about civil rights struggles in this country.

As part of the environment, the college students had created a cemetery with gravestones of dead activists, including Steven Biko. I had previously taught them a song about Biko, so the children immediately recognized that name (some thought he was really buried there and I had to explain about that).

The group wanted to go back for several days and hang out with the college students. The Black children were particularly involved and excited. I then wrote a letter to the parents explaining about our first visit to Tent City and why we wanted to take the children a few more times. I asked for their responses, and it was unanimously supportive. It was an appropriate activity for my class because it was happening right on our campus and was a current issue children were hearing about from TV and their parents.

LOUISE: There are a few children's books about people working together for social change that support what our children do. One is called *Swimmy* (Lionni, 1973). It is about how a school of small fish stop a big fish from eating them. Another is about Mother Jones, a famous union organizer, who worked with children for better working conditions in the cotton mills during the time when child labor existed.

BILL: Another, *King of the Mountain* (Cassidy, 1980), is about children saving a big heap of dirt from a construction project they play on. The city wants to knock it down, but the children take action to save their "mountain."

LOUISE: Activism activities can include stories about historic heroes and heroines who have worked to stop injustice. But, I think it's important that we explain that it wasn't that hero or heroine alone who made change happen. No one is a leader without other people participating with them.

MAE: This discussion makes me feel a bit more comfortable about involving kindergarten-aged children in community action events.

MARIA: But you still aren't comfortable?

MAE: No. But I will try some activities and see.

Teacher as activist

SHARON: If we ask children to be activists, don't we also have to be activists?

LOUISE: I think so. We need to look at our own attitudes and experiences in taking action against injustice by individuals and by institutions and what has kept us from acting. If a teacher thinks activism is wrong, it will be harder to implement this part of the anti-bias curriculum.

BILL: We don't want a "tourist" approach to activism—visit the problem, but don't get involved yourself.

MOLLY: I talk with children about "Here is something that bothers me very much—this is what I'm doing about it." It's sort of storytelling.

MARIA: I think activism means risk taking. I know that is so for myself. Through my parent education meeting, this year the parents know more about me than I think I've ever shared with any group of friends.

MAE: We can't teach more than what we are.

Inventing activism activities in your classroom

In every classroom and community, issues arise that can spark activism activities. Since these activities must be concrete and meaningful in the life of each group of children, there are no exact recipes. Each teacher has to create his or her own activities using the principles discussed in this chapter.

Young children's anti-bias interactions with each other are the first activism activities. Foster their developing empathy, their ability to express their needs, and their skills in standing up for themselves and other children.

Group activism activities should address issues that children understand and care about. Involve children in deciding what strategies to use.

Involve parents through informing them of, discussing, and encouraging participation in activism activities.

Teachers' own experiences as activists can strengthen their skills for doing activism activities with children.

You may find the examples in this chapter relevant to your class. Here are some further examples of possibilities:

Example 1

Your school is an all-White school in a middle-income community. You have done a number of activities about physical differences and similarities. The children became particularly interested in the dolls with disabilities. You tell them that you noticed that the local bookstore (or toy store) doesn't have books about people with special physical situations (the toy store doesn't have dolls with disabilities). You ask the children what they think about that, helping them see that other children will miss out on the chance to learn what they have been learning. You and the children may decide to ask the store manager in a letter to visit your school and see your books and dolls; or you may decide to write and ask the manager if you can visit and show her or him your materials. What you will do next depends on how the store manager responds and your follow-up discussions with the children. If she or he is not interested, you may

decide to involve parents and other preschool teachers in sending letters. If the manager cooperates, you may want to send letters telling preschool teachers and parents that new materials about differently abled people will be available at that store.

Example 2

You are in a Head Start program with a diverse group of children: Black, Mexican-American, White. You realize that you have mainly White dolls, and want to diversify them, but do not have a budget for purchasing new dolls. You raise the problem with the children, comparing the diversity among them with the token diversity among the dolls—do they think we need more dolls to be fair? You then suggest that they, the staff, and their parents can help make cloth dolls at a workshop and at home. Children can dictate a letter to parents explaining the problem and inviting them to a workshop of parents and staff. Children can go on a trip with teachers to buy materials. Get dark, medium, and light brown, sand color, and beige cotton; a variety of colors and materials for hair, including wool; check pattern books for dolls or find someone who already makes dolls to help. Figure out tasks the children can do. After the workshop, some parents may be able to continue to help at home. Make little gifts with the children to send to all the parents who have participated in the project.

Example 3

You are in a child care center where a number of the children are Vietnamese and Korean immi-

---

ADAPTATION

To invent activism activities:

- Be alert for unfair practices in your school or neighborhood that directly affect your children's lives. You may be the first to identify the problem, or the children may bring a problem to your attention.
- Consider the interests and dynamics of your group of children. Do they care about the problem? What kind of actions would work with them?
- Consider your comfort. Is the issue one you feel comfortable addressing? What strategies do you prefer?
- Consider the parents' comfort. Do you want their agreement beforehand? Do you just plan to inform them of your plans? Do you want to include them in the activity?
- Try out the activity. If it works, great! If it doesn't, try again with a different activity!

grants. You do not have books or tapes or materials in the children's languages. You need the help of people who are bilingual to make tapes reading children's books, to make signs for materials, to make alphabet and number posters, and to teach you key words. Discuss the problem with the children—involve them in writing letters to leaders in the Vietnamese and Korean communities who would know of people who can help. Then write letters to these people asking if they can help with specific jobs.

Example 4

The neighborhood in which your children live does not have a decent playground. You have heard that some community people are organizing to get funds to develop a new playground. Discuss the problem with the children, go on a field trip to playgrounds in other neighborhoods, and then talk about the lack in their own neighborhood. Contact the community organizing group and figure out how the children can help. This may include letter writing, speaking to city officials, helping to plan equipment, suggesting ideas for accessibility. This same series of activities could also tackle the need for a traffic light, or for curb ramps.

References

Cassidy, G. (1980). *King of the mountain*. New York: Leisure Books.

Lionni, L. (1973). *Swimmy*. New York: Knopf.

HOLIDAY ACTIVITIES IN AN ANTI-BIAS CURRICULUM

10

Celebrate: to honor (as a holiday) by solemn ceremonies or by refraining from ordinary business; to demonstrate satisfaction in by festivities or other deviation from routine.
Holiday: a day on which one is exempt from work.

(from *Webster's Ninth New Collegiate Dictionary*, 1987, Springfield, MA: Simon & Schuster).

In many early childhood programs, holidays are a mainstay of the curriculum: Columbus Day, Halloween, Thanksgiving, Christmas, Valentine's Day, and so on become the focal point for themes and activities. Curriculum guides and educational supply companies make teaching holidays convenient by packaging sets of activities and materials. Curriculum courses frequently suggest using holiday units to teachers-in-training. Why this has happened seems to be an educational mystery, for there are no meaningful developmental reasons for such an abundant emphasis on holiday activities. In fact, the overuse of holiday units interferes with a developmental approach to curriculum as too many prepared, "canned" activities take the place of activities tailored to the needs of specific groups of children.

The problem becomes even more serious in regards to the overuse of holidays to teach about cultural diversity. Because holidays, as the above definitions indicate, are special times, when the usual business of life is temporarily suspended, they do not teach children about the daily life of people. When early childhood curriculum uses holidays as the primary source of activities about cultural diversity, children do not learn about the common tasks that all people do in culturally different ways. Focusing on holidays is tourist curriculum: Children visit a culture by participating in a few activities and then go home to their regular classroom life. This leads to stereotyping and trivializing a culture—"All people do is dance, wear special clothes, and eat."

Early childhood teachers must rethink *why* they use holiday activities. What do children learn? What purposes do such activities serve? As one preschool teacher said with relief, "When I stopped doing holidays every month I found I had so much more time to do other things!"

If used sparingly, holiday activities can contribute to anti-bias curriculum. One, they are fun to do and children get involved. Two, participating in celebrations and rituals helps build a sense of group collectivity. Especially in child care centers, recreating the home experiences of preparing for holidays can enhance children's feeling of being part of a close-knit group. Three, holidays are a part of our society's cultural life. Learning about holidays in school can broaden children's awareness of their own and other's cultural experiences if they are *thoughtfully used as part of a more inclusive curriculum about cultural diversity.*

Guidelines

1. Use holiday activities as part of many other kinds of activities about a cultural group. Ask yourself: What is the purpose of teaching about this holiday? Is it developmentally suitable to my group of children? Is it related to their lives? If not, why am I introducing it?

2. Set holiday activities in the context of people's daily life and beliefs by connecting them to specific children and families. With kindergarten children, include holidays that honor struggles for justice and relate these holidays to children's own experiences with unfairness.

3. Establish the distinction between learning about another person's holiday rituals and celebrating one's own holiday. Invite children to participate as "guests" in a holiday activity not part of their culture. Encourage the children whose holiday it is to share feelings as well as information.

4. Honor every group that is represented in your classroom (children and staff). Do not treat some holidays as "exotic" and others as regular. Everyone is "ethnic": Everyone's traditions come from specific ethnic or national groups (including national holidays such as Thanksgiving and Christmas).

5. Do not assume everyone from the same ethnic group celebrates holidays the same way. Make sure that any differences in how each family celebrates are evident and respected.

6. Demonstrate respect for everyone's traditions throughout the curriculum.

The kindergarten had spent a few days getting ready for and then celebrating Passover. During the Seder ceremony, the meaning of matzo was explained and Esther, one of the Jewish children, explained that she could not eat bread during the whole week of Passover. The next day, cake was served at a birthday celebration for another child. A student teacher gave Esther a piece of cake in violation of the Passover week requirement. She explained later that she felt sorry for Esther because Esther was being deprived of the cake and would feel left out. Luckily, the teacher noticed the pained, conflicted expression on Esther's face and intervened: "Esther, do you know that cake is made with leavened flour and that you can't eat it?" (Esther nodded her head yes.) "Let's freeze your piece and you can eat it after Passover." Esther relaxed, gave her cake to the teacher, and went off to play.

7. Plan strategies for working with the children whose families' beliefs do not permit participation in holiday celebrations. Include the child's parents in creating satisfactory alternatives for the child within the classroom.

8. Be sensitive to the possibility that families with very low incomes may find certain holidays stressful because of the enormous amount of commercialization and media pressure to buy, buy, buy. Stores' advertising of Halloween costumes, media and store emphasis on eating special foods at Thanksgiving, and the commercial equation of love with expensive and numerous gifts at Christmas time are prominent examples.

In the classroom, challenge these pressures by focusing on meaningful ways to celebrate holidays without spending money. Emphasize that homemade costumes and gifts are very special because they are unique and made with each person's wonderful ideas and with love. Make Halloween costumes and Christmas gifts at school—using these times to encourage and support children's creativeness. Talk about the underlying meaning of holidays as times when your family and other people you care about come together to enjoy each other. Critique the way TV and stores make it look like the important thing is to buy, buy, buy!

Don't solve the commercialization problem through charity. Many poor families deeply resent the once-a-year Thanksgiving or Christmas "box." Open up discussion with parents about ways they have found to celebrate holidays, and the pressures they experience. Explain how you challenge the commercialization of holidays in your curriculum, and explore with parents how to find and make inexpensive toys and holiday decorations and how to have inexpensive celebrations.

Celebrating National Holidays

National holidays are events institutionally celebrated from work, or at least schools, stores, and media give them major attention. Underlying these acts is the false assumption that *all* Americans celebrate holidays such as Halloween, Thanksgiving, Christmas, or Easter. In an anti-bias curriculum, activities about national holidays should challenge this inaccurate assumption. Furthermore, because some holiday customs incorporate stereotypes about other cultures, activities must also help children identify and think critically about such stereotypes.

Thanksgiving

The history and customs of Thanksgiving highlight the complexities of disengaging harmful bias from "national" holiday celebrations. Michael Dorris, of the Native Studies Department of Dartmouth College, states the situation succinctly:

> Native Americans have more than one thing *not* to be thankful for on Thanksgiving. Pilgrim Day, and its antecedent feast, Halloween, represent the

annual twin peaks of Indian stereotyping. From early October through the end of November, "cute little Indians" abound on greeting cards, advertising posters, in costumes and school projects . . . . Virtually none of the standard fare surrounding either Halloween or Thanksgiving contains an ounce of authenticity, historical accuracy or cross-cultural perception. (Dorris, 1978, p. 6)

Dorris cites as one example the misinformation in a "ditto" about Thanksgiving brought home by his young son. Under a picture of the "first Thanksgiving" was the sentence, "They served pumpkins and turkeys and squash; the Indians had never seen such a feast!" Dorris refutes the statement:

> On the contrary! The Pilgrims had literally never seen "such a feast," since all foods mentioned are exclusively indigenous to the Americas and had been provided, or so legend has it, by the local tribe. If there was a Plymouth Thanksgiving dinner . . . then the event was rare indeed. Pilgrims generally considered Indians to be devils in disguise, and treated them as such. And if the hypothetical Indians who participated in that hypothetical feast thought that all was well and were

thankful in the expectation of a peaceful future, they were sadly mistaken. (Dorris, 1978, p. 9)

Dorris concludes:

It must somehow be communicated to educators that *no* information about Native peoples is truly preferable to a reiteration of the same old stereotypes, particularly in the early years. (p. 9)

As an alternative, Dorris suggests that Thanksgiving be a time for appreciating Native American peoples as they were and as they are, not as either the Pilgrims or their descendents might wish them to be.

Suggestions for activities: 4- and 5-year-olds

1. The starting point: Ask your children what they think and feel about Native Americans. Ask them: Who knows about Indians? Where do they live? What do they do? How do they look? Does anyone know an Indian person? Make a note of their misconceptions and stereotypes (*All* Native Americans wore buckskin and feather headdresses, lived in tepees, made war all the time, and consequently were bad and scary).

2. Teach about the *daily contemporary* life of specific Native American groups. Always use a group's specific name (Navajo, Hopi, Cherokee). Use photos, accurate pictures, paintings, drawings about contemporary life to make wall displays and books.

   Read the few children's books that do accurately portray contemporary life. Since there are so few, use books whose pictures are authentic, even though the text is too difficult for young children, and adapt the story. *Kevin Cloud: Chippewa Boy in the City* (Bales, 1972) is about a child living in Chicago. *The Goat in the Rug* (Blood & Link, 1980) is a true story about a weaver and her goat who lived in the Navajo Nation at Window Rock, Arizona. *Indian and Eskimo Children* (Bureau of Indian Affairs, undated) contains pictures of how different children live today. *Sharing Our Worlds* (United Indians of All Tribes Foundation, 1980) contains text at junior high level, but the pictures are excellent for any age.

   Tell stories with persona dolls. Lakeshore Educational Materials has a boy and girl Native American doll. Although not perfect, they are an effective way to build concrete curriculum about contemporary life of a particular Native American group for preschool children. Based on your reading about the group you select, create a family, daily family life, and stories about each doll. Use these dolls many times to introduce gradually different aspects of their daily life to the children.

   Invite visitors who can come a number of times and ask them to talk about contemporary life. Sources for guests may be a Native American Center, bookstore, or crafts store, or a Native Studies Program in a nearby university.

3. With kindergarten children you can include the following activities.

   Make a collage depicting diversity in the contemporary lives of Native Americans (e.g., in the country and in the city; in the Southwest and Northeast), where children can look for and talk about similarities and differences.

   Help children identify the differences between daily life and ceremonial activities: Have them bring in photos of themselves dressed up for a particular ceremony in their family—and a photo of how they dress when they go to school, or to play. Bring in pictures of Native American children and adults in their daily life and ceremonial dress. Discuss the differences in everyone's life. Read the book *Pow Wow* (Behrens, 1983).

   Compare past life with present life: Have children bring in photos of great-grandparents in the dress of the 19th Century and compare with how their family dresses now. If children's families don't have these photos, bring in pictures from the era of their great-grandparents. Then contrast pictures of past and present life of a Native American group.

   There are many wonderful folktales from different Native American peoples, tales that played and play an important role in the education of children. Used in conjunction with the activities listed above they are a delightful part of the curriculum. For example, tales about the Navajo Spider Woman—a powerful, important figure in the Navajo traditional belief system—introduces a strong woman figure and information about important activities and values in Navajo life.

   Introduce the term *Native American.* Explain that "many Native American people like to be called by this instead of 'Indian.' It means they lived in this country first. Let's try to help each other remember to use the word *Native American.*

ADAPTATION

Unless you are teaching Native American young children, it is not effective to introduce activities about past Native American life. After all, children do not study the lifestyle of colonial Euro-Americans in preschool, or in kindergarten (except for the very simplistic stereotypes of the "Pilgrim").

If you teach Native American children, activities about traditional and past ways of living *are* an appropriate part of a comprehensive curriculum for developing children's individual and group identity.

4. Critique stereotypes about Native Americans.

Show children stereotypic Thanksgiving cards purchased in local stores, including some depicting animals "dressed" as Native Americans, and compare them with real, accurate pictures, saying, "These cards really bother me. Why do you think they do?" Accept all their ideas and help them understand that unfair pictures and showing people as animals are insulting and teach wrong ideas.

Do not allow children to play "cowboys and Indians" and do "war dances."

Critique Thanksgiving TV specials. Make a video to show and discuss with children. Ask parents to watch a program with their children and talk with them about which images are unfair and not true. Prepare parents by having a discussion about Native American stereotyping and/or send home a letter with a list of common stereotypes (see Appendix, pp. 141–142).

Critique books. Compare books that depict Native Americans accurately with books that depict stereotypes. Talk about what is fair and unfair, what helps us learn about Native Americans, what hurts their feelings.

5. Tell the story of Thanksgiving from the perspectives of Native Americans as well as of the European immigrants. Children must learn both sides if they are to become critical thinkers and not repeat or continue the injustice of the past and present. Here are examples of two stories that relate the story of Thanksgiving from the point of view of Native Americans.

Christopher Columbus's Mistake

A long time ago there lived a very rich queen named Isabella, and she lived in a country far across the sea, called Spain. A man named Christopher Columbus came to her castle to see her one day. He had a dream of looking for a land called the Indies. He believed there was a beautiful place far away across the ocean that he wanted to find and get for Queen Isabella. Christopher Columbus told the queen about the gold and spices he expected to bring her back from the Indies and so she finally agreed to give him the money for his ships, men, and food.

With Queen Isabella's money, Christopher Columbus built three ships. He called them the Nina, the Pinta, and the Santa Maria. He got sailors to sail them, and stocked them with all the food he thought the sailors would need. He then set sail for the Indies.

After many weeks filled with storms and hardships, Christopher Columbus landed at a place near the countries we now call Cuba and Puerto Rico. Columbus thought he found the Indies, so he called the people already living there "Indians." Soon, European people who came to America called all the people already living here "Indians."

We all know that everybody can make mistakes. Teachers, children, and even moms and dads make mistakes. Columbus made a mistake, too, because his ships didn't land in the Indies. They landed here in America. So the people he found already living here were not the native people of the Indies. They were really Native Americans.

My House and the Strange People

More and more people came from Spain, England, and France to live in the beautiful country of the Native Americans. The people coming to live here were called colonists. As more and more colonists came, they needed more and more land for their houses and farms.

The sad part of this story is that the Native Americans were already living on the land the colonists wanted, and so the colonists took the land away from the Native Americans. Here's a story to help you understand the way the Native Americans felt about having their home taken away.

Suppose you lived in a house that you and your family loved very much. Every day, your parents tell you that the trees, streams, mountains, and animals around your home are your brothers. Every night, before you sleep, you think about how wonderful it is to have such a beautiful home. Your parents teach you never to harm any living thing, except to use for food, or shelter, or clothing.

One day, some people came to your home from far away in big ships. They look very different from you, and at first you are very afraid. Then, you remember your parents' teaching that all living things are brothers.

Your mom and dad invite these people into your beautiful home. These strangers have a long stick that kills your brothers, the animals. They call it a gun, and its loud noise frightens you because you've never seen one before.

Mom and Dad teach these people how to grow things and how to live in your house. One day, the Strange People tell your family that they like your house so much that they have decided to take your house away from you and keep it for themselves. The Strange People make your family leave your home. How does that make you feel?

Every year after your family has left, the Strange People have a big party in your old house to celebrate taking it away from you. They eat the animal brothers that your family taught them were good to eat. They have the vegetables and breads your family taught them to grow and make. They even enjoy the berries you used to love to pick and eat. How does this party make you feel?

The Strange People called their celebration Thanksgiving.

After the story, the teacher should emphasize that this happened a long time ago and that in our class we're learning how to be fair to Native Americans. As a follow-up to this story, have the persona dolls celebrate their own Thanksgiving together. Bring out all the dolls and sit them at a table. With the children, prepare different kinds of ethnic foods—based on each doll's favorite—and then have the dolls share their Thanksgiving feast with the class. At the end of the dinner, Mary, the Navajo doll, says: "I'm thankful that all of us friends, who all have different colors of skin, speak different languages, and have different kinds of families can be together!"

Halloween

The Halloween image of the "witch," old, ugly, wicked, and dressed in black, reflects stereotypes of gender, race, and age: Powerful women are evil; old women are ugly and scary; the color black is evil (a connection which permeates our language). Moreover, the mean, ugly, evil witch myth reflects a history of witch hunting and witch burning in Europe and North America—from the Middle Ages through the Salem witch hunts of the 17th Century directed against midwives and other independent women.

Adults are so used to seeing this witch image as part of a "fun" holiday that it may seem "picky" to some of you to make this critique. However, some teachers are challenging it because it is so offensive, especially to many women. At an after-school care program (children 4 to 6 years old), the teacher did these activities during the two weeks before October 31st.

Witches and Healers

DAY 1: Kay asks "What are your ideas about witches?" "Bad, ugly, old" is the children's unanimous response. Kay: "Many people do think that. What I know is that the real women we call witches weren't bad. They really helped people. These women lived a long time ago. Maybe you know about some good witches too?" (The only one the class can think of is Glinda in "The Wizard of Oz.") Kay: "Yes, Glinda was pretty and helped people, but she didn't do what most of the women called witches did. They healed people who were sick or hurt." (The children start talking about doctors.) Kay: "Yes, the healers were like doctors." Then Kay reads the children a story she has written and illustrated.

DAY 2: Kay brings in a number of different herbs: mint, clove, cinnamon, and ginger root. She introduces the herbs to the children, letting them smell them. They talk about what they think they could use them for and then Kay tells them briefly about how the herbs have really been used to help people.

DAYS 3, 4, 5, and 6: Kay sets up a number of activities children can choose to do over the next week: a "witch-healer" table, where the children can make their own potions; a tea-making table, where children can make and drink mint and cinnamon tea; planting herbs; and making collages with herbs.

FOLLOW UP: After a week of these activities, Kay has another brief discussion with the children about witches. "What do you know now about witch-healers?" she asks. The consensus is that witches fell into two categories. Some were bad, some good. So although the activities don't completely change the children's minds, they do stretch thinking by creating a category of "some good witches." (Later in the year, Kay raises the question of witches again to see what ideas the children have kept over time. They still hold to the "some good/some bad witches" categories.)

Witches, Evil, and the Color Black

To contrast the prevailing imagery of black and evil (witches, cats, darkness), Kay teaches the children an already existing Halloween chant:

"Stirring, stirring, stirring the pot;
Bubbly, bubbly, bubbly hot;
Look to the moon, laugh like a loon,
Throw something into the pot."

(This chant is usually accompanied by hand movements. Kay, integrating another aspect of anti-bias curriculum, substitutes signing.) Then Kay puts a large black cloth in the middle of the children's circle and asks children to symbolically throw beautiful black things into the "pot." At first, children throw in typical Halloween objects (e.g., black cat, spider). With Kay's encouragement to think of other black things, they begin throwing in

objects such as licorice, pepper, chocolate ice cream, blackberries, magic markers. Kay then lists all the beautiful, useful, black things on a chart and briefly talks about how people sometimes think that black is bad because of how the color black is used. Later in the day, children who want to find and paste on pictures of the black objects listed on the chart.

Two further spin-offs come from the Halloween activities. (1) In response to the children's interest in healers, Kay brings in books and tells stories about healers in other cultures, including Native American, Mexican-American, and African. She talks about how people stereotype "witch doctors" as scary, just like the healers who were called witches. (2) Kay introduces the children to the Mexican and Mexican-American holiday, "Dia de los Muertos" (Day of the Dead). In contrast to the way death and ghosts are treated on Halloween, Dias de los Muertos is a time for remembering and celebrating the dead in one's family. Skeletons are an important part of the ritual, but they have a different meaning than the skeletons of Halloween. Kay sets up an altar, children dictate or write the name of a person or pet animal who is dead, and Kay tells the story of how Marisela's family celebrates Dias de Los Muertos.

Christmas

Although Christmas is celebrated as a national holiday, it really reflects a specific religious belief system. For children who are not Christian—be they Jewish, Buddhist, Muslim, atheist—Christmas can be a problem. How do teachers handle the dual reality of Christmas, as a Christian holiday and a national holiday, in a way that is supportive and fair to all? Here are some solutions other teachers have used.

Alternative 1: Integrate December holidays from several cultural groups. In one child care center, many of the children and staff celebrate Christmas, three families celebrate Chanukah, and a staff member, Suzanne, wants to share her Native American tradition of celebrating the Winter Solstice.

First, the staff identifies common themes and observances: All three holidays use firelight (candles and bonfire) and have special music. All involve nighttime (Solstice celebrates the longest night of the year as well as the shortest day; Christmas celebrates "Christmas Eve"; and Chanukah has the ceremony at sundown). All three holidays are celebrations of community, sharing, and caring for one another and for the planet.

A series of group times, lasting 10 to 20 minutes, is held in the late afternoon using these themes.

DAY 1: Children and staff sit inside on the rug in a "special" holiday circle. The lights are turned off. Teachers explain about using the candles to symbolize special things we appreciate. The children light the first candle in appreciation of all of us in the group and how lucky we are to know each other. Then the children think of and light seven more candles for things about nighttime that are special. Placing the candles in the middle of a circle, children and teachers dance around holding hands. After the candles are blown out, group time is over.

DAY 2: This time is like Day 1, except that the children light candles to things they like in the night sky.

DAY 3: Children talk about things that make light but are not electric, and how, long ago, when people first celebrated Christmas, Chanukah, and Winter Solstice, they didn't have light bulbs. They had to use candles, oil, and wood to make fire and light. Teachers and children light candles and an oil lamp.

DAY 4: Group time is an outside bonfire. Children talk to each other, look at the stars, look at the neighborhood Christmas lights across the street, and watch the fire. Children and staff talk about what is special about each person in the class.

DAY 5: Teachers point out that the night is beginning earlier, the day ending sooner. A small, live tree is set up in the circle. Everyone dances around our tree, we light candles for it, Suzanne talks about how her family decorates their trees for Solstice, and children talk about how their families decorate Christmas trees.

DAY 6 (Chanukah): Children light the Menorah and talk about Chanukah. A 4-year-old child shares how his family celebrates this holiday; the teacher reads a story and teaches two Chanukah songs.

DAY 7 (Christmas): The group dances around the tree, lights candles, and sits in a circle in the dark with candles and sings. Earlier, the children have made eggnog; as parents arrive, their children offer them a glass of eggnog as special holiday cheer.

DAY 8 (Winter Solstice): The celebration begins with a special lunch feast and listening to Native American music. In the late afternoon activity, children notice how early it gets dark. Everyone dances around the Solstice tree and says goodbye to each other, as it is Friday, and time to go home for the holidays.

The celebration of La Navidad could also be included in this series of activities.

Alternative 2: Do December holidays other than Christmas. In one kindergarten class, the children learn about the holidays of Kwanzaa (an Afro-American holiday) and Chanukah (a Jewish holiday). Their teacher emphasizes how these two celebrations reflect beliefs of each group and honor Afro-American and Jewish people's struggles for justice. Her goals are to expose Christian children to other important December traditions and to support the children who do not celebrate Christmas.

KWANZAA: Seven days of activity are organized around the seven principles of Kwanzaa: Unity, Self-Determination, Collective Work and Responsibility, Cooperative Economics, Purpose, Creativity, and Faith. Each day, activities, stories, and discussions explore the meaning of each principle as it relates to classroom life, Black families, and the Black liberation movement.

On the first day, the children collectively decorate the room—they make a wall-to-ceiling poster about Black life; string red, black, and green paper chains; weave paper place mats; and put up posters and photos of important Black individuals. Music of Black artists is regularly played all week. At group time, children talk about what unity means in their classroom —how they are learning to help each other, talk to each other, and solve problems. The candle-lighting ritual begins (candles are lit each day for the principle of the day).

The next day, group time begins with the candle ceremony and then a brief discussion about the meaning of self-determination. For the children it means being able to make choices; the teacher then relates this to Black Americans' struggle to build a freer, fairer life. They talk about the three colors: red for struggle; black for Afro-Americans ("Like me," one of the Black children says); green for children—the hope for the future ("Like me," a White child calls out. The teacher says, "Yes, like all of us.").

The teacher then reads a story about Fannie Lou Hammer, one of the leaders in the 1950s–60s struggle for Blacks to vote. The children are concerned about how she lived as a child—her family were poor sharecroppers. Their teacher explains that Fannie Lou Hammer wanted Black people to vote so that children wouldn't have to live the way she had to. Then the teacher asks, "Who in our class would have been able to vote before people like Fannie Lou Hammer worked to make sure Black people could vote?" As the children realize that many of them would not have been able to vote, they get very quiet for a moment. Then one of the Black children firmly says, "But now we can."

On day three, for collective work and responsibility, children have a fix-it day for objects and furniture in the classroom needing mending.

Days four, five, six, and seven proceed in a similar vein, ending with a big feast the children cook together.

CHANUKAH: Chanukah is a Jewish December holiday that honors an ancient Jewish struggle against invasion of their land by a neighboring people and the destruction of their Temple. Chanukah lasts eight days; it focuses on the lighting of candles in the Menorah each day and the telling of the story of the Maccabees, leaders of the guerrilla fight to stop the more powerful invader.

Chanukah activities can tell the story. There are some good picture books to read to children (Green, 1986; Hirsh, 1984; Schlein, 1983). Randy Fishfader, a teacher in a child care center in Oregon, shares this activity, which helps children understand the destruction of the Jewish people's Temple.

At circle time, she tells the children she is going to tell them a story about a Jewish holiday called Chanukah, which she celebrates because she is Jewish. She asks each child to get one block to bring to the circle. The children then construct a building together. Randy explains how long, long ago, the Jewish people had built a special building together called a Temple (like a church) where they came together to think about their God and to celebrate their holidays. Then Randy suddenly knocks the building over. (The children gasp.) Randy explains that this is what happened to the Temple when another group of people, who didn't like the Jewish people, came into their country and knocked down the Temple. Randy asks the children how they felt when she knocked over their building, and they relate their feelings to how Jewish people felt so long ago. Then Randy tells them the story of the miracle of the oil: When the Jewish people made the invaders leave, they found only enough oil to light the Temple lamp for one day. But it burned for eight days, which gave the people courage to rebuild their temple. That is why the Menorah is lit for eight days. The children light the first candle and then add one more each day for the next seven days.

Invite Jewish family members of children and staff, or a person you know, to tell/show the children the ritual of Chanukah: lighting the Menorah, playing with dreidels, making potato latkes (pancakes).

Tell a persona doll story about how the doll's family celebrates Chanukah (some families give a gift for each of the eight nights). Tell another story about how the doll felt when only Christmas was celebrated at his school and some children teased him.

Even if you have no Jewish families in your class, it's useful to introduce Chanukah so that children can learn that not all Americans celebrate Christmas—one important lesson for countering the ethnocentrism of the dominant culture. Be sure to get accurate information from books and/or Jewish people. Use the guidelines for "Expanding Diversity In Your Classroom" in Chapter 7.

Alternative 3: Don't do December holidays at all in the classroom. When children return from winter break, they can share what they did. Encourage children to identify the similarities and differences in the way they spent their time.

Holidays: Historic struggle for justice

All people have celebrations that commemorate struggles for freedom, for self-determination, for justice, and for peace. July 4th commemorates the adoption of the Declaration of Independence, in which the United States proclaimed its self-determination. Martin Luther King Jr.'s birthday honors a man and a civil rights movement involving millions of people. Passover celebrates an ancient struggle and victory of the Jewish people over slavery. International Women's Day, March 8th, is about working women's struggles to gain equality and decent working conditions. Mexican Independence Day and Cinco de Mayo commemorate historic fights for independence from Spain and France respectively.

With 4- and 5-year-olds, do activities about holidays that honor people's civil rights struggles. Relate these activities to children's desires to be treated fairly and to their own day-to-day problems with unfairness. Do not expect young children to completely understand all the facts and complexities of the historic events holidays commemorate. They will learn that many grown-ups do not just passively accept injustice, but have worked and continue to work hard to make the world a safe, fair, and good place. They will learn that their teachers honor and deeply care about people who participate in these struggles.

Tell persona doll stories, based on historically accurate facts, about individual dolls' grandparents or parents who participated in a particular civil rights struggle you are honoring. Read about the specific historic events you are honoring to get information. Talk about why the individual decided to participate, how life for children today is better because of what that movement did, how the family of the persona doll feels proud of the family member who participated in the civil rights activity, how it makes the doll feel good when people celebrate the particular event.

Invite individuals who have participated in a particular civil rights action to tell the children about their experiences. Talk to the visitor before she or he comes to help her or him determine what your group of children will be interested in.

Tell stories about your own civil rights experiences (e.g., "This was something that I thought was very unfair, and I decided to do something about it. This is what I did. This is how I felt. This day has special meaning for me because I was/I am a part of it.").

Make collages or books about a specific civil rights movement or event. For example, for International Women's Day, ask children to bring in photos of women special to them and bring in pictures of women special to you, including women who have been or are presently active in the movement for women's equal rights. Make a large collage, then ask the children to tell you about the women they chose (this activity courtesy of B. J. Richards).

Make the celebration of a civil rights event as special as other kinds of holidays. Decorate the room, have a special snack, invite family.

As part of your celebration, involve the children in an action project that addresses an unfair issue in the children's lives. For example, on Martin Luther King's birthday, visit your neighborhood toy store to see if it sells dolls of various racial and ethnic backgrounds, and, if not, write a letter asking the store manager to sell them.

Do role playing with kindergarten-age children. Choose a specific incident from the civil rights movement you are honoring, and have the children act it out. One example is the following role play about the Montgomery Bus Boycott:

- Prepare by telling the children about Rosa Parks and how she protested the rule that Blacks had to sit in the back of the bus. Explain that you are going to do a play about what happened. First, children who can roll their tongues get to sit in the front of the bus, and children who cannot roll their tongues get to sit in the back (emphasize that this is only for pretend, that it really doesn't matter whether you can roll your tongue or not). The second time, children who cannot roll their tongue will get to sit in the front of the bus.

- Appoint a bus driver, a policeman or policewoman (you may want to play the policewoman/ policeman the first time), and one child to be Rosa Parks. Review the plot with the group: The bus driver will tell some people to go to the back, others to the front. Rosa Parks will refuse to go to the back. The bus driver will call a police officer, who will insist that Rosa Parks get off the bus. Other non-tongue rollers will get off with her, and then link arms and refuse to move. Then they will all sing "We Shall Overcome."

- The play: The bus driver checks each child, asking them to roll their tongue, and assigning seats in the back or front. When Rosa Park's turn comes, she refuses to sit in the back and the action proceeds (the teacher may have to do some directing, reminding children about the plot). Pay attention to what children say as they act out their roles, so that you can bring up their comments later during discussion time. Then, everyone reverses roles and the play repeats.

• After the role plays are finished, talk with the children about how it felt. Children usually get emotionally involved. Say, "Listen to yourselves. You sound angry. How come you are so angry?" Kindergartners are able to understand the unfairness of the bus incident. As one White child said very indignantly to her Black friend, "You couldn't sit next to me. I wouldn't like that at all." "Yeah," responded the Black child, "It would be stupid." Some children may want to ask further questions or look at books about Rosa Parks after this discussion. Children may do this role play for several days by choice.

Sing protest songs, folk songs, about specific civil rights struggles. There are records you can use. Explain what each song is about and why people sang them. Teach children the wonderful poem "I Am Freedom's Child"*:

> I like me, no doubt about it,
> I like me, can't live without it,
> I like me, let's shout about it,
> I am Freedom's child.
> You like you, no doubt about it,
> You like you, can't live without it,
> You like you, let's shout about it,
> You are Freedom's child.
> We need all the different kinds of people we can find,
> To make Freedom's dream come true,
> So as I learn to like the differences in me, learn to like the differences in you.
> I like you, no doubt about it,
> You like me, can't live without it,
> We are free, let's shout about it.
> Hooray for Freedom's child!

---

*Copyright © 1970 by Bill Martin. Published by DLM Teaching Resources, Allen, TX. Used with permission.

Some of the stories about people's struggles for freedom and justice are upsetting and scary. People got hurt, people went to jail, people died. Can 4- and 5-year-olds handle this? Just as with other curriculum subject areas, teachers need to use their child development knowledge to create and try out new activities and evaluate what works and what doesn't. At the same time, adults must not confuse their own discomfort about "unpleasant" realities with children's developmental needs. Integrating holidays honoring struggles for justice into anti-bias curriculum asks adults to face their own positions on social issues.

References

Bales, C.A. (1972). *Kevin Cloud: Chippewa boy in the city.* Chicago: Reilly & Lee.

Behrens, J. (1983). *Pow wow: Festivals and holidays.* Chicago: Childrens Press.

Blood, C., & Link, M. (1980). *The goat in the rug.* New York: Macmillan.

Bureau of Indian Affairs. (undated). *Indian and Eskimo children.* Washington, DC: Author.

Dorris, M. (1978). Why I'm NOT thankful for Thanksgiving. *Interracial Books for Children Bulletin, 9*(7), 6–9.

Green, J. (1986). *Nathan's Hanukkah bargain.* Kar-Ben Copies, Inc., 6800 Tildenwood Lane, Rockville, MD 20852.

Hirsh, M. (1984). *I love Hanukkah.* New York: Holiday House.

Martin, B., Jr. (1970). *I am freedom's child.* DLM Teaching Resources, One DLM Park, Allen, TX 75002.

Schlein, M. (1983). *Hannukah.* Behrman House, 1261 Broadway, New York, NY 10001.

United Indians of All Tribes Foundation. (1980). *Sharing our worlds.* Seattle: Author.

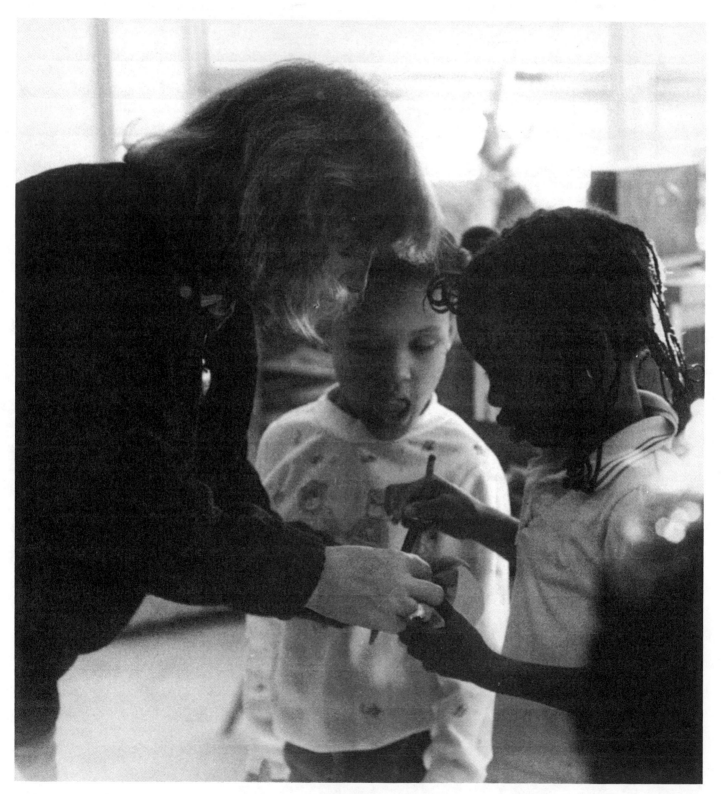

WORKING WITH PARENTS

11

Parent work is vital to an effective anti-bias curriculum. If teachers are to do educational work that may be new and controversial, they set themselves up for failure if parents are not included.

Teaching from an anti-bias perspective means seeking to respect and support each child's and parent's background and reality while introducing a working concept of diversity that challenges social stereotypes and discrimination. With parents who agree with the underlying values of anti-bias curriculum, these two goals work together. With parents who disagree, tension occurs. However, *respecting parents does not necessarily mean acquiescing to all their beliefs*. Teachers also demonstrate respect when they challenge parents to struggle with them when there are disagreements, keep communication open, and search for solutions agreeable to both. It is necessary to acknowledge that a coming together with *all* parents may not be possible.

Inform and Educate Parents

In his discussion of the U.N.'s Declaration of Human Rights articles on education, Jean Piaget (1973) asserts:

> . . . if every person has the right to education, it goes without saying that parents also have this right, and "prior right" as well. They have the right to be . . . informed and even instructed about the better education that their children should receive. (pp. 83–84)

Piaget was writing in the context of new educational methodology related to his theory of cognitive development; his statement is equally true for implementing anti-bias curriculum.

GOALS

1. To establish genuine parent/teacher dialogue that opens up discussion of each other's points of view and seeks to gain clarity, understanding, and solutions agreeable to both teacher and parent

2. To provide information that facilitates parent awareness of how young children develop racial/ethnic and gender identity and the ways in which sexism, racism, and handicappism negatively affect healthy socioemotional and cognitive growth

3. To create safe settings for parents to discuss with each other the issues raised by anti-bias work and to increase their ability to integrate anti-bias perspectives in their childrearing

4. To facilitate development of children through joint parent/teacher problem solving and mutual support

5. To involve parents in curriculum development, implementation, and evaluation

Many parents are unaware of how soon racial, gender, and disability awareness begins to develop. Some have had to deal with the negative impact of bias on their children's developing self-concept and attitudes toward others. Other parents deny the evidence, willing to believe that young children "do not notice" or think about such topics.

Not only do parents have the right to know what we are doing and why, but their knowing also works to the child's and the teacher's advantage. We teach a child for a few years at most; parents teach them over their entire childhood. We have often found that what first appeared to be parental disagreement with anti-bias curriculum turned into support when they had sufficient information about the underlying reasons and specific methods of anti-bias curriculum. Even if information does not resolve all parental concerns, it plays a crucial role in promoting meaningful dialogue and problem solving.

Written communication

Send letters and newsletters throughout the school year to inform parents and to keep them up-to-date on what happens in the classroom and in parent group meetings. A newsletter also gives parents the opportunity to share their ideas with other parents. An example is on pp. 99–100. Tailor letters to the style, vocabulary, and language(s) of your particular group of parents.

Children's work

Send home chidren's work, with an accompanying letter explaining the purpose of the activity. Children's paintings and drawings of themselves in accurate skin colors, the class book "Each of Us Looks Special," the class book "About Our Families," and a xeroxed copy of the class-made book of "Favorite Stories From Each Family" for reading at home are some examples of ways to make anti-bias curriculum concrete and personal to parents.

Parent group meetings

Hold group meetings that educate parents about anti-bias issues. Minimally, one session introduces parents to the concept and practice of anti-bias curriculum. A few follow-up sessions enable parents to explore how children develop identity and attitudes and how to facilitate anti-bias development at school and at home. These meetings help the teacher identify parents who support anti-bias work and are willing to help implement the curriculum, as well as identify parents who disagree. All the following sessions can be led by the classroom teacher, school or child care center director, or parent educator.

Session 1: Introducing Anti-Bias Curriculum

Goals:

- To inform parents about anti-bias curriculum
- To identify areas of agreement/disagreement

Preparation:

Review Chapter 1. Think about questions parents might have; plan how you would respond.

Materials:

- "Anti-Bias Curriculum" video (Derman-Sparks & Atkinson, 1988)
- Large paper or chalkboard for writing down parents' questions, concerns, and areas of agreement

Activities:

1. Show the "Anti-Bias Curriculum" video. (30 minutes)
2. Have parents meet in fours and discuss their responses to the video. Ask them to share what they liked and didn't like in the video and what questions they have. (15 minutes)
3. Meet as a whole group; write down likes, dislikes, and questions. (5 minutes)
4. Tell parents why you are introducing anti-bias curriculum into your program. Respond to parents' questions. (30 minutes)
5. Plan follow-up sessions for further exploring questions and disagreements. Recruit parents who might like to work with you in implementing the curriculum. (10 minutes)

Variations of these activities:

Variation 1:

(*a*) Instead of the video, begin by telling parents about questions and interactions you have seen in the classroom that illustrate how their children are grappling with anti-bias issues. Describe the goals, rationale, and examples of anti-bias curriculum.

Founded by Friends   *213/795-9161*

Dear Parents,

As a part of our anti-bias curriculum, we are taking a careful look at how we talk about and celebrate Thanksgiving with the children. As some of you may already realize, most of the images of Native Americans found on Thanksgiving cards, decorations, school ditto sheets, etc. are very stereo-typic. They are typically inaccurate distortions and rarely show people within any context of daily or real life. Often they are based on a "composite" inaccurate White vision of Native Americans rather than on any reality based in the diversity of Native American lifestyles and traditions. Therefore, most of the visual impact of Thanksgiving serves to teach or reinforce children's misinformation and stereotypic thinking about Native Americans and lays a foundation for the later development of prejudice and racism.

Moreover, the "story" of Thanksgiving is almost always told from only one side, that of the Europeans who came to America (i.e., Pilgrims). Rarely is it told from the perspective of the people who were already here. Consequently, the vital contribution of the Northeast Native American peoples who contributed to the initial survival of the Pilgrims is typically downplayed or ignored. To many Native American peoples today, Thanksgiving is a day of mourning because it is a reminder that in return for their help, knowledge, and tolerance of original European settlers, they were "repaid" with theft of their land and the genocide of their people.

Therefore, with these considerations in mind, Thanksgiving becomes a more complicated holiday than we previously thought. What then do we propose to do? We are NOT suggesting that we stop celebrating Thanksgiving. Rather we will spend time helping children understand that, first, Thanks-giving means different things and is celebrated in different ways in different families; second, some families do not celebrate it at all and why (in appropriate language for young children); and, third, that greeting cards and decorations may be unfair and not true images of Native American peoples and those unfair pictures hurt the feelings of people who are Native Americans.

What we do do about Thanksgiving is also part of a larger curriculum effort to help children learn accurate information about Native Americans of the past and present. Given the pervasive and terrible distortions of Native American life presented in the media and in many children's books, young children's typical conceptions of Native Americans are not only false but are also a foundation for later full-blown racism. One common way their thinking about Native Americans becomes evident is in their make-believe play (i.e., Indians are the "bad" guys having fun killing the "good" cowboys). We do not allow children to play Cowboy/Indian at Pacific Oaks because we believe permitting this kind of play based on stereotypes reinforces racism. Moreover, being "Indian" is not a role, it is a part of a person's identity.

(b) Form groups of four: Ask parents to share what questions or experiences they have had with their children about gender, race, ethnicity, or physical-abledness (disabilities), and what questions they have about anti-bias curriculum.

(c) Follow Steps 3, 4, and 5 above.

Variation 2:

(a) Begin with parents sharing in small groups how they remember learning about their own gender, racial/ethnic, and physical-abledness identity and their first encounters with people different from themselves.

(b) Talk about what research tells us about children's development and the goals and method of anti-bias curriculum.

(c) Ask for questions and plan follow-up sessions to explore parents' questions.

Follow-Up Sessions

The topics and sequence of further sessions depends on what issues arose in the introductory meeting about anti-bias curriculum and what topics you plan to work on with the children. Here are some possibilities:

Session 2: Gender Identity and Sexism

Goals:

- To increase parents' awareness of what they want to teach children about gender identity
- To increase parents' awareness of the stereotyping about gender to which children are exposed

Preparation:

Review research summary in Chapter 1, developmental tasks in Chapter 6, and relevant activities in Chapter 12.

Materials:

Large sheets of paper, markers, chalkboard and chalk

Methods:

1. In small groups of four to five, parents talk about what they want to teach their daughters and sons about being a girl or a boy. Set the

ground rule that people are to listen to each other, not tell others what to do. (20 minutes)

2. Back in the large group again, each small group reports the goals it talked about for boys and girls. The group leader writes them down on large paper or chalkboard. (10 minutes)

3. The leader summarizes gender identity research and developmental tasks, and the constraints that gender behavior norms impose on young children's growth. The difference between sexual and gender role identity as two aspects of gender identity are made clear. The activities used in the classroom to foster children's gender development are briefly summarized. (20 minutes)

4. The group leader seeks to elicit concerns parents have about their children not being raised to fit traditional role definitions. (20 minutes)

Pay attention to cultural differences in how gender roles are defined and the concerns parents have about opening up options. Help parents see the variation of views among them, and help each parent understand her or his own concerns, including conflicts parents may feel between traditional and nonsexist ideas about gender socialization. Do not impose one "right" way for teaching their children about gender. Listen for homophobic fears—that opening up gender options will promote homosexuality—and let parents know that there is no evidence that nonsexist gender development causes homosexuality.

Session 3: Creating Nonsexist Environments for Young Children at Home

Goals:

- To increase parents' awareness of materials, activities, and interactions that promote nonsexist development

- To help parents evaluate whether they are teaching their children what they really want to teach about gender identity

Preparation:

Review Chapter 1 and Chapter 6.

Materials:

Develop a handout consisting of a shortened list from Chapter 2 of what to look for at home in relation to influencing gender identity. Include questions about what clothes parents buy, what activities they encourage, and what role modeling they do.

Methods:

1. Set goals of the session and give parents the handout. (5 minutes)

2. Ask each parent to evaluate the home environment in relation to the handout points and what parents might want to change. (10 minutes)

3. In twos (pairing people from different families), have parents share their self-evaluations. (10 minutes)

4. In the large group, ask parents what issues or questions came up. As parents respond, list their ideas on large easel paper. Then summarize how you set up an antisexist environment in the classroom, and briefly discuss the issues raised by parents. (35 minutes)

Session 4: How Children Develop Racial Identity and Awareness

Goals:

- To increase parents' awareness of how early children begin to develop racial identity and awareness

- To explore what parents want to teach their children about race

Preparation:

Read developmental tasks in Chapter 4, research review in Chapter 1, and relevant sections of Chapter 12.

Materials:

Prepare a handout of developmental tasks taken from Chapter 4.

Methods:

1. Summarize key research points and developmental tasks. Using examples, emphasize that *all* children need to learn about who they are and to develop pride but not superiority. If you have an interracial group, talk about the different tasks for children of color and for White children. (15 minutes)

2. In small groups, ask parents to tell what they want their children to know about their racial and ethnic background, and how they themselves learned about who they are. (If there are

only a few people from one racial/ethnic group, put them in the same group so they do not feel isolated.) Set the ground rule that people are to listen to each other, not tell each other what they should do. (20 minutes)

3. In the large group, ask parents what questions and concerns came up. Highlight the following issues: color-blindness versus noting and appreciating differences; protection of children of color from the pain of racism versus teaching skills for coping and confronting; confusion of parents in interracial or intercultural relationships and of parents who have adopted racially or ethnically different children about what identity to teach their child. (15 minutes)

Session 5: Creating Antiracist Home and School Environments

Goals:

- To raise parents' awareness of how they are fostering positive self-images and anti-bias awareness of differences in their homes
- To inform parents of methods used at school

Preparation:
Review activities in Chapters 4, 7, and 8.

Materials:

- Index cards of children's common questions
- Home inventories with questions about what toys, pictures, books, and activities parents have that promote their children's racial/ethnic self-concept and positive awareness of differences in others, and places in the community they know of that sell multicultural toys, books, cards, art, and so on.

Methods:

1. As parents arrive, ask them to fill out the home inventory (10 minutes). Collect and collate these while the parents are in small groups.

2. In small groups, pass out index cards with children's questions (two questions per group), and ask parents to discuss how they would answer each question. (15 minutes)

3. Ask the small groups to report how they would answer the questions. Watch for inappropriate responses: ignoring, indirect answers, insufficient information. (10 minutes)

4. Without mentioning names, share the responses to the home inventory: List various materials and activities parents use and community resources; and mention what percentage of parents are doing many, moderate, little, or no activities about racial/ethnic identity. (10 minutes)

5. Briefly summarize the kinds of materials and activities you do in the classroom for promoting self-identity and skills for resisting discriminatory behavior. (15 minutes)

Session 6: Sexism and Racism in Children's Books

Goals:

- To raise parents' awareness of how children's books teach stereotyping
- To provide guidelines for selecting nonsexist and nonracist books

Preparation:
Read relevant chapters in "Guidelines for Selecting Bias-Free Textbooks and Storybooks" (CIBC, 1980), including "Ten Quick Ways" (see Appendix, p. 143).

Materials:

- Filmstrips "Sexism in Children's Books" (CIBC, undated) and "Racism in Children's Books" (CIBC, undated).
- Handout: "Ten Quick Ways" (photocopy)

Methods:

1. Show filmstrips. (20 minutes)

2. In the small groups, ask parents to discuss what they learned, their questions, and their disagreements. (10 minutes)

3. In the large group, ask for a summary of each group's responses. Pay attention to indications of distress if favorite books were critiqued and point out the pull between wanting to make change and also wanting to share books, or other experiences, that were meaningful to us as children. (20 minutes)

4. Talk about criteria for selecting books to use in class, show a selection of positive books, and list ways to use books with stereotypic images with 4- and 5-year-olds to foster critical thinking. (20 minutes)

Session 7: Talking With Children About Disabilities

Goals:

If all participants are parents of able-bodied children:

- To inform parents about young children's questions and fears about differently abled people

- To raise parents' awareness about bias against differently abled people

- To discuss how to respond to children's questions and comments to foster nonbiased attitudes and behavior with differently abled people

Preparation:

Review research summary in Chapter 1, activities for learning about different physical abilities in Chapter 5, and relevant activities in Chapter 12.

Materials:

- Chalkboard or large sheets of paper and markers

- Card sets with questions children ask about disabilities (see "Developmental Tasks," Chapter 5)

- Handout: "Caution" box for answering children's questions, Chapter 5

Methods:

1. Summarize the developmental issues for young children, what you want children to learn, and the kind of activities you do in the classroom. (20 minutes)

2. Parents meet in groups of four or five. Give them each a set of cards with examples of children's questions or negative comments about people with disabilities. Ask parents to discuss how they would respond. (30 minutes)

3. Have each group report the answers they came up with and discussions about disabilities they have been having with children. (15 minutes)

4. Lead a discussion on the feelings and attitudes that interfere with adults answering children's questions on this topic. Refer to the handout. (30 minutes)

Variation:

If parents include parents of differently abled children, add:

Goals:

- To enable parents to foster their children's knowledgeable and confident self-concept

- To increase parents' skills for answering their children's questions about themselves

Methods:

In step **1**, include discussion of the developmental tasks for children with physical challenges.

In step **2**, include questions that differently abled children ask about themselves.

Session 8: Children's Books About Differently Abled People

Goals:

- To raise parents' awareness of stereotyping about people with disabilities in children's books

- To provide examples of anti-bias children's books about differently abled people

Preparation:

Read the chapter about handicappism in "Guidelines for Selecting Bias-Free Textbooks and Storybooks" (CIBC, 1980) and the bibliography of children's books in Resources, pp. 119–132.

Materials:

- A collection of anti-bias children's books about differently abled people

- Handouts: a list of common stereotypes about people with different abilities ("Guidelines for Selecting Bias-Free Textbooks and Storybooks" [CIBC, 1980]); and a list of good children's books

Methods:

1. Read parents two excellent children's books. (8 minutes)

2. Parents meet in groups of five or six. Give each group two books and ask them to take turns reading to each other. Using the list of common stereotypes, have them list what they like or don't like about each book. (20 minutes)

3. With the whole group, make a list of the likes and dislikes for each book. Explore the reasons behind parents' dislikes. Pay attention to indications of discomfort, misconceptions, or stereotyping. (20 minutes)

4. Use the likes list to discuss criteria for good books. Hand out the list of children's books and go over each book. (15 minutes)

LOS ANGELES UNIFIED SCHOOL DISTRICT
PROCEDURAL SAFEGUARDS AND APPEAL PROCEDURES
FOR INDIVIDUALS WITH EXCEPTIONAL NEEDS

I. GENERAL RIGHTS

A. The parent or guardian of an individual with exceptional needs has certain rights which arise when the educational agency:

1. Proposes to initiate or change the identification, evaluation or educational placement of the child or the provision of a free, appropriate public education to the child.
2. Refuses to initiate or change the identification, evaluation or educational placement of the child or the provision of a free, appropriate public education to the child.

B. The parent or guardian has the right to:

1. Receive a full explanation of procedural safeguard rights and appeal procedures.
2. Privacy and confidentiality of all educational records.
3. Inspect and review all educational records and, if necessary, challenge them in accordance with the Family Educational Rights and Privacy Act of 1974.
4. Receive, inspect and review copies of all educational records prior to meetings.
5. Revoke consent to assessment and/or services at any time.

C. Individuals with exceptional needs have the right to:

1. A free and appropriate public education.
2. Placement in the least restrictive learning environment that promotes maximum interaction between handicapped and nonhandicapped pupils appropriate to the needs of both.
3. Enjoy the same variety of programs as are available to the nonhandicapped; remain in school through age 21 to complete the prescribed course of study and/or meet regular or differential proficiency standards; any pupil who becomes 22 while participating in a program may continue participation for the remainder of the then current school year.

II. RIGHTS RELATED TO ASSESSMENT

A. Parents or guardians have the right to:

1. Initiate a request for an educational assessment.
2. Give or withhold consent within 15 days after a request for assessment by the educational agency.
3. Receive a description of the procedures and tests to be used and to be fully informed of the assessment results.
4. Receive a copy of assessment findings upon request.

B. Individuals with exceptional needs have the right to:

1. An assessment by a multidisciplinary team in all areas related to the suspected disability.
2. An assessment that is nondiscriminatory.
3. An assessment that is validated in the pupil's native language.

III. RIGHT TO AN INDEPENDENT ASSESSMENT

A. Parents or guardians have a right to an independent educational assessment if they disagree with the assessment conducted by the educational agency.

B. The educational agency must provide information about independent assessment upon request.

C. The independent assessment must be at public expense unless the public agency shows at an administrative hearing that its assessment is appropriate.

D. If the assessment of the educational agency is determined to be appropriate, the parent is still entitled to an independent assessment but not at public expense.

E. An independent assessment must be considered by the public education agency regarding the provision of an appropriate education for the child and may be presented as evidence at any hearing regarding the child.

IV. RIGHTS RELATED TO THE INDIVIDUALIZED EDUCATION PROGRAM

A. Parents and guardians have the right to:

1. Be notified prior to and choose to participate or be represented at all meetings.
2. Have the meeting conducted in their primary language or form of communication.
3. Participate in the development of the Individualized Education Program at a meeting held within 50 days of receipt of signed consent to assess.
4. Implementation of the Individualized Education Program immediately or within a few days unless necessary timeline extensions are agreed upon.
5. Participate in a review of the Individualized Education Program at least once a year.
6. Appeal decisions of the Individualized Education Program team regarding assessment, eligibility, placement and/or designated instruction and services.

B. Individuals with exceptional needs have the right to participate in the meeting(s) as appropriate.

C. If the Individualized Education Program team determines that no appropriate public school placement is available, the pupil may be served in a nonpublic, nonsectarian school at no cost to the parent.

Session 9: Advocating for the Rights of the Differently Abled

Goals:

- To inform parents about the activism component of anti-bias curriculum
- To inform parents of the rights of differently abled children and their families
- To encourage parents to participate in advocacy for their own and others' rights

Materials:

Prepare handout on your state's "Procedural Safeguards and Appeal Procedures For Individuals With Exceptional Needs" (see p. 104).

Methods:

1. Explain how activism activities help children build their self-concept and teach able-bodied children to stand up for the rights of others.

2. Parents meet in groups of four or five to share ideas for their families participating in advocating for the rights of the differently abled.

3. Groups share their ideas and questions. Give them the handout on the rights of differently abled children and parents in school and explain. If you have parents of physically challenged children and parents in your class, plan a further session to teach them how to actively participate in an Individualized Educational Program meeting.

For group leaders

It is preferable that parent meetings use a dialogue model where everyone learns from each other, rather than an "expert" model where the teacher only tells parents what to do. Sensitive leadership is needed to create a safe environment for sharing experiences, beliefs, questions, and disagreements. It is usually more effective if the leader is someone parents know. Outside "experts" tend to provide information rather than facilitate dialogue, unless the person is engaged to do a series of anti-bias educational sessions.

Two kinds of preparation are necessary for leading dialogue-based anti-bias parent sessions. The first is knowledge of the specific subject. The second is self-awareness of beliefs and attitudes relating to the specific subject of each session.

Group leaders do not have to be experts in each subject. The self-education activities described in Chapter 12 provide a beginning, experience will lead to further skills. As important as knowledge is willingness to explore and engage in dialogue about anti-bias subjects.

——— Involve Parents in Individual Problem Solving ———

Involve parents whenever you observe a *pattern* of biased exclusion, teasing, or name calling on the part of a child. Include the parents both of the child who was the target and of the offender.

Guidelines for talking with the parents of the offender

1. Inform parents immediately by phone. Tell them what happened and what actions you took. Set up a conference to discuss what they think may be causing the child's behavior and what strategies can be used at home and at school to help the child.

2. At your parent conference:

   (*a*) Share your observations and concerns about the child (be specific with anecdotal data). If you have not previously done so, share the reasons for your concern.

   (*b*) Ask the parents to share observations about the child's behavior and experiences. How have the parents responded? What might be influencing the child's behavior? Consider the home and community environment of the child. Does the child have interaction with people different from him- or herself—friends, doctors, and other community "helpers"? What are the attitudes of close family, siblings, friends, and neighbors? What does the child watch on TV? What books and toys does he have? What stressful situations has she recently encountered?

   (*c*) Discuss the methods you are already using or plan to use at school to work with their child; find out if any of your ideas seem inappropriate or unacceptable. If so, find strategies agreeable to everyone.

   (*d*) Develop strategies for successful intervention at home and at school. You may suggest to the parents to decide what they will say if their child makes biased remarks at home. Encourage friendships with children of different backgrounds. Encourage ways to expand the child's contacts with diversity—going to public events; acquiring books that depict people of color, disabled people, or men and women in nontraditional roles. Suggest that parents carefully select and watch TV shows and commercials with the child, reinforcing "fair" or "true" images and pointing out "unfair" and "untrue" images.

Sometimes parents resist, insisting that the child's behavior at school comes from other children rather than from home. (Sometimes teachers also fall into a similar trap—locating the source of the problem only in the child's home and resisting looking at what is or isn't happening at school.) It is important to remember, and to help parents recognize, that it may not be possible to pinpoint exactly why the problem exists. In any case, efforts must be made both at home and school for children to develop anti-bias identity and attitudes.

Guidelines for talking with the parents of a child who is the target of discriminatory behavior

It is as important to inform the parents of the child on the receiving end of biased behavior as it is to tell the parents of the child who was responsi-

ble. Don't assume that the child isn't affected if she or he is not obviously upset. Tell the parents what you have done to support their child's self-esteem and how you handled the incident. Find out how the family teaches their child to deal with prejudice. Try to help plan how the parents will handle the incident at home.

Guidelines for talking with the parents of a child exhibiting poor self-concept

Before speaking to parents, hold a staff meeting to discuss the child. The anecdotal data from this meeting will be useful in presenting the problem to the child's parents.

Phone the parents to say, for example: "Mary's behavior makes me concerned about how she feels about her identity. I would like to set up a conference to discuss this further."

At the conference, ask if the parents have seen similar behavior at home. (This is very important because it may be dynamics at school that are creating the problem.) Find out what and how they are teaching their child about the aspect of identity under discussion. Together, depending on what you and the parents have observed, try to figure out what underlies the problem. Plan what you can do at school and at home to build the child's self-awareness and esteem.

Involve Parents in Curriculum Development, Implementation, and Evaluation

Involve parents in planning, implementing, and evaluating anti-bias activities. Their perspective is important.

Find out early in the year what parents want to teach their children about racial and ethnic identity, disabilities, and gender. Find out the terms and methods they use. Find out the experiences their children have with people different from themselves and how they respond to their children's biased remarks.

Ask parents to collect data about their children: comments they overhear and conversations indicating bias. These anecdotes extend teachers' awareness about how young children think and provide feedback about curriculum.

Ask parents for materials: photos of the family, written stories about family members, household

artifacts, books, picture books, and records or tapes of songs in languages other than English. Ask parents to invite children to visit their places of work.

Ask parents to participate in the classroom by reading to children in languages other than English, teaching words and phrases, helping the children make a poster and signs in their language, making a snack or lunch of the family's favorite foods with the children, or telling stories about special family members and about family experiences related to their culture and/or movements for social justice.

Ask parents to evaluate the environment, taking you to places that have relevant ethnic materials. Involve them in finding places to purchase culturally relevant materials.

Ask a parent committee to collect data by observing in the classroom the impact of the anti-bias curriculum on the children and by interviewing other parents about what they hear and see at home. This committee can be very helpful to the teacher in evaluating the effectiveness of activities and in identifying areas where new activities are needed.

When Teachers and Parents Disagree

Teachers may also find themselves faced with parents who make overtly bigoted statements or demands, or disagree with specific topics and activities. How would you handle the following real situations reported by teachers in various schools?

1. A child says, "My dad said Indians are bad."
2. A parent tells you she doesn't want her child sitting next to any Mexican kids.
3. A White parent tells you he doesn't want his 4-year-old daughter playing with a Black doll because that will lead to interracial dating and marriage.

The easiest response is to assert simply: "In this classroom, we do not think Indians are bad; all children sit with everyone; and children can play with any doll they want." Period! Parents then can decide if they want to keep their child in your class or find another place (that is, if they have a choice).

However, the easiest approach ultimately is the least effective because it undercuts our anti-bias work with the children. It cuts off the possibilities of expanded information, understanding, and change in the parents and limits our own understanding of the specific life history and dynamics of our children's families. Moreover, it violates the spirit of anti-bias work. To say to ourselves, "These parents are so racist, sexist, or whatever, it's good we have their children for a while so that we can teach them better values" hardly reflects respect for people. An anti-bias commitment calls on us to respect adults enough to challenge prejudiced behavior in ways that optimize the likelihood of effecting positive change.

Invest time and energy with individual parents by engaging them in a series of conversations. Find out what underlies the parent's racist (or sexist, or handicappist) stance. Remember that none of us is free from bias. Each of us needs other people to help us sort through our experiences and identify contradictory attitudes and areas we want to change. Sometimes bias is based on lack of, or incorrect, information; sometimes a negative experience is overgeneralized into bias against a whole group; sometimes a lack of validation in one's own life may be a contributing factor to a strongly held prejudice. Remember, also, that our society gives people permission to use racism, sexism, or handicappism as outlets for frustration, anger, greed, and fear. These facts do not make the bias OK, but they help us to look at the whole person and not just at the biased behavior.

Engage the parents in exploring their fears about what may happen to their child as a consequence of anti-bias education and in exploring your ideas about the benefits. Remember that this is a dialogue, not a monologue; make sure that parents have ample opportunity to express their views and that you are open to learning from their views as well as hoping they will learn from yours.

Anti-bias dialogue requires risk taking for both teacher and parent. This requires trust that has previously been built through interactions about other less threatening aspects of the child's development. Dialoguing with a parent may not always succeed; some parents will not want to talk, and some, even after a number of conversations, will retain their original stance. In these situations, the "bottom line" approach will be necessary. Now it is appropriate to say, "We will not allow prejudice and discrimination in our classroom."

If disagreement occurs about various aspects of the anti-bias curriculum try the following steps:

1. Talk with the parents who disagree to explore their concerns further. These discussions may be sufficient to resolve the disagreement. If they are not, then carry out the next steps.
2. Inform all parents in writing (a letter, a notice on the parent bulletin board) about the disagreement and call a parent meeting to discuss the issue.
3. Structure the meeting so each point is clearly stated and the difference in viewpoint fully expressed. Then involve all participants at the

meeting in deciding what to do. If no resolution occurs, there are four further options:

a) Ask parents who still disagree if they are willing to have you carry out disputed activities, and then evaluate the results together for further discussion;

(*b*) state that further discussions will be held, and that meanwhile the activities under disagreement will be held;

(*c*) if only one or two people continue to disagree and the rest are satisfied with the solution, state that the activities will take place and expect the few disagreeing parents to go along with the majority; or

(*d*) drop or modify the few activities that are causing the most controversy with a large number of parents, but don't back off anti-bias curriculum in general.

4. Inform parents of the solutions reached at the meeting, or of the lack of resolution for the time being. If necessary, schedule further discussions about the issue.

5. Do the agreed-upon activities with children. Inform parents about what happens, and ask them for feedback.

The following situation is one example of handling a curriculum disagreement, in this instance over Thanksgiving holiday anti-bias activities in preschool.

A letter was sent to all parents about the staff introducing new activities about Thanksgiving. Feedback from a few parents was supportive; no parents objected. However, after a teacher told the story of Thanksgiving from a Native American perspective, a few children came home sad and upset. Some of their parents voiced angry objections; the staff became upset.

A meeting was held for all parents and staff. Some parents complained about one or more of the following: the staff was (1) revising history; (2) teaching the children that life isn't always fair, and they weren't sure they wanted their children to learn that yet; (3) doing non-child-centered activities; (4) turning children against other family members who didn't share the same ideas of Thanksgiving.

Point 1 was challenged by some of the parents as well as the staff. The director, acting as group leader, asked the parent who raised the issue to further talk about his feelings. What emerged was his discomfort and sadness at the tarnishing of his image of Thanksgiving. After discussion, he still wasn't sure he wanted Thanksgiving to be a bittersweet holiday for his child, but at least he recognized the source of his anger was not the "rewriting of history."

Point 2, the anxiety and sadness children might experience upon learning about painful events, was hard for many parents. Staff talked about how the issue of fairness is meaningful for children in their daily interactions and that feeling bad about unfairness toward others reflects their developing empathy. Staff and parents discussed advantages and disadvantages of providing children with information and experiences that challenge misconceptions and stereotyping.

Point 3 was most easily resolved: Teachers explained specific examples of activities, enabling parents to realize that methods were appropriate to the children's developmental level. Teachers also made clear that they didn't have all the answers, were trying out different activities, and wanted parental feedback.

Discussion about the last issue, creating tension with other family members, revolved around the more general question of anti-bias education. Children who learn to question injustice and to stand up for themselves will irritate those adults who believe children should be seen and not heard. Some parents felt fine about their children speaking their minds; some were ambivalent, wanting their children to speak up against unfair comments but also wanting them to be polite with family; and some felt they would tell their children *not* to criticize adult family members.

After the meeting, parents and staff had greater clarity about each other's issues. The staff realized they had to think about whether they were trying to do too much too quickly. Many parents expressed support for the anti-bias work as a result of gaining greater understanding of its objectives and methods. Some remained concerned about its appropriateness. However, the channels of communication had been opened.

The staff also learned to hold a parent meeting *before* initiating Thanksgiving activities with the children, in addition to an informational letter. As a result, the following year the negative after-the-fact responses did not recur. Even after planning together, not every parent completely agreed, but everyone was clear about what would happen in the class and knew that the majority of the parents agreed with the activities.

The next example involves a disagreement over the use of anatomically correct dolls and genital names. Joel Gordon, the director of a child care center in a small, rural, Northern California city, wrote (personal communication, January 1987):

In explaining your anti-bias curriculum workshop at a meeting attended by teachers, practicum students and parents, I ended up touching off a furor that caught me by surprise. The problem arose when I described teaching children about their identity by telling them that boys have penises and girls have vaginas, and by using anatomically correct dolls. Three of the parents became outraged that I would use genital names in the classroom. Their argument against using explicit words were (1) children don't need to know those words; (2) if they learn those words in school, they might say them in a check-out line at the supermarket; (3) terms like "private parts" should be used; and (4) putting anatomically correct dolls in the dramatic play area would allow unsupervised play and children might have the dolls "engage" in sexual acts.

Using all my powers of persuasion, I explained why using accurate terms for genitals was necessary and empowered children when faced with a discriminatory situation. I explained that this was not sex education in the sense of teaching them about reproduction, but naming body parts, like a hand or an elbow. They just wouldn't buy it.

I called a second meeting with all the parents to continue the discussion. Some parents liked the idea of using the dolls and explaining to children about what anatomically makes you a girl or boy. Other parents continued to strongly argue that any use of genital terms constituted bringing sexuality into the classroom and was wrong.

Joel finally decided that the loss of trust and confidence in the program by a number of parents was more serious than losing one piece of the anti-bias curriculum. However, his program does include other activities that encourage nonsexist play and development.

A similar disagreement about using anatomically correct dolls, this time in a public school class of 4- and 5-year-olds, was resolved in another way. In this case, it was agreed that the teacher use the dolls for specific teacher-directed activities, but not put them out in the dramatic play area.

Working thoughtfully with parent disagreements may slow down implementation of anti-bias curriculum and may lead to some adaptations and modifications. In the long run, taking time to try to resolve parent disagreements pays off, in support in the classroom and reinforcement of anti-bias activities at home. Remember that anti-bias curriculum is recreated in each setting through the interactions of children's interests, teachers' professional knowledge, parents' values, and societal events. What matters is to keep the basic principles operating.

Strategies

The specific way you implement and balance the three components of parent work—educating, dialoguing, and involving—depends on your particular parent group. Consider the following questions as you develop strategies:

1. *What resources do you have for parent work?*

If you have an active parent program and high parent/teacher communication, then addressing anti-bias issues will be easier. You will have mutual trust and a repertoire of methods which work.

If you have a minimal parent program, think through what you can do to build more parent/teacher interaction on less sensitive issues, as well as around anti-bias topics.

2. *Which anti-bias issues might be more relevant, which might create controversy or resistance, and which support?*

It is not necessary to begin activities in all areas of anti-bias curriculum at once. It may be more effective to begin with a topic that is of interest to the

parent group. Implementing activities on that topic will facilitate the later introduction of other topics.

3. *What is the most effective initial method with your group of parents?*

Consider whether it would work best: (a) to do some initial anti-bias curriculum with the children first, to get your feet wet, gather data about the kids' ideas, and then begin involving parents; or (b) to organize a small committee to act as a study, planning, and support group before initiating curriculum into the classroom; or (c) to inform and involve all the parents simultaneously in beginning anti-bias activities with children.

4. *What are the most effective methods for educating and involving your parents throughout the year?*

The traditional method of parent meetings, held during the day or evening, may work well for you. However, if attendance is low, don't automatically assume it is lack of interest. Talk to parents about why they do not come. Adapt to their needs. For example, some child care centers combine dinner with a parent meeting at the time most parents pick up their children. Work with parents who can and do come to meetings, and keep the rest informed through other means (Stone, 1987).

Use a variety of methods for informing parents: newsletters (translated into all the languages represented in your parent group), a parent bulletin board, individual letters, and phone calls. Brief discussions when parents bring and pick up children are very useful. It helps to have a place for drinking a cup of coffee or tea and a teacher assigned to being with parents at these times. Use interested parents to help involve "hard to reach" parents.

In sum, a carefully thought-through, varied, and ongoing parent program is a vital component of implementing anti-bias curriculum with children. Not engaging in a thorough parent program guarantees that the anti-bias curriculum will upset both teachers and parents and will not succeed. The more fully teachers do anti-bias work with parents, the longer lasting will be their work with children.

References

Derman-Sparks, L., & Atkinson, B. (Producers). (1988). *Anti-bias curriculum* [video]. Pasadena, CA: Pacific Oaks College.

Piaget, J. (1973). *To understand is to invent* (G. Roberts, Trans.). New York: Grossman. (Original work published 1948)

Council on Interracial Books for Children. (1980). *Selecting bias-free textbooks and storybooks*. New York: Author.

Council on Interracial Books for Children. (undated). *Sexism in children's books* [filmstrip]. New York: Author.

Council on Interracial Books for Children. (undated). *Racism in children's books* [filmstrip]. New York: Author.

Stone, J.G. (1987). *Teacher-parent relationships*. Washington, DC: NAEYC.

GETTING STARTED: A SELF-EDUCATION GUIDE

12

GOALS

1. To increase awareness of your attitudes about gender, race, ethnicity, and different physical abilities
2. To learn to identify ways that institutional racism, sexism, and handicappism affect your program
3. To gain an understanding of how young children develop identity and attitudes
4. To plan ways to introduce anti-bias curriculum into your setting

---

Step One: Make a Personal Commitment

Learning to integrate anti-bias curriculum into your class takes energy and time. It means making this a priority—and working on it, bit by bit, over a whole school year.

Step Two: Organize a Support Group

A support group is essential for preparing for and implementing anti-bias curriculum. Cooperative learning is the best method for developing anti-bias awareness and knowledge. We need the diverse perspectives and honest feedback of peers to develop the insights for rethinking how we teach. Ongoing support while we try out anti-bias activities is also essential: to share the successes, evaluate the mistakes, provide encouragement, and plan strategies to get past the hard spots.

A support group can consist of coteachers and staff in your class, other teachers in your school or center, teachers from other schools in your community, and parents from your school or center. It can be as small as two people, or as big as eight.

Step Three: Do Consciousness-Raising Activities

It is not necessary to know all the answers before you get started in the classroom. No one does; everyone using an anti-bias curriculum approach is continually learning. All you need is a beginning foundation upon which you will build, as you gain experience and reflect on your experiences with your support group.

Select activities from each of these three categories: self-awareness, institutional "isms," and children's development.

Activities for increasing self-awareness

Integrating an anti-bias curriculum into your class takes thoughtful personal work. No one escapes learning and believing some of the stereotypes and biases that undergird sexism, racism, and handicappism. We all carry scars, whether as initiator or target of unjust acts. Many of us have been both at different times. Few of us have had the opportunity or taken the time to examine deeply and openly the impact on us of these experiences. Instead, we keep them hidden and are reluctant to expose our confusions, frustrations, hurt, anger, and guilt. These experiences and feelings daily influence our interactions with children, even if we are not aware of it.

The self-awareness exercises will help you clarify your thinking and identify discomforts and prejudices that would interfere with doing anti-bias work with children. For these exercises to be useful, allow each member to reveal her or his feelings in safety. Do not judge each other. Help each other examine the attitudes which emerge.

As you do the self-awareness activities you may feel pain. Racism, sexism, and handicappism are ugly, so it can hurt as we face their negative image of us. Don't let the pain stop you. Acknowledge it, and then figure out how to turn pain into energy for acting to implement anti-bias curriculum.

Begin with the following:

- Share with your group how you describe or define your racial/ethnic identity. What is important and not important to you about this aspect of yourself? If it is important, why? If not, why not? How do you feel about your racial/ethnic identity? Repeat this exercise two more times, the second talking about gender identity, and the third about differences in physical abilities.

- Share how you learned about your racial/ethnic identity, your gender identity, and your physical abilities and limitations. What are your earliest memories? What was fun or painful as you learned about these aspects of your identity?

- Share how you agree or disagree with your parents' views about race, ethnicity, gender, and abledness. If you disagree, how did you develop your own ideas? What and who were significant influences on you? If you are a parent (or plan to be one), what do you want to teach your own children?

- Write down your list of acceptable and nonacceptable behaviors for girls and boys, men and women. Compare lists with support group members. Discuss what range of sex-role behaviors you accept in the children you teach.

- Make a list of what you want other people to know about and what you don't want people to say about your racial and ethnic identity. Share with the group. Discuss how you want a person who knows very little about your group to learn.

- Able-bodied group members, share a time when you were temporarily disabled. What did you learn about other people's attitudes, environmental limitations, and your feelings about asking for and accepting help? Differently abled group members, share how able-bodied people's attitudes, environmental lack of accessibility, and your feelings about asking for and accepting help affect you.

Supplementary activities

- Take one of the popular European fairy tales (Sleeping Beauty, Cinderella, Snow White) and rewrite it, switching genders of the characters. Read your new version to each other. What are your responses to the role reversals?

- Read the chapter, "Homosexuality, Hysteria and Children Growing Up Free" (Pogrebin, 1980). Discuss the feelings that emerge as you read. With what do you agree? Disagree? Why?

- Read the children's books *What Is a Girl? What Is a Boy?* (Waxman, 1976), and *Bodies* (Brenner, 1973). Both show photos of nude children. Discuss if you would be comfortable reading these books to children. Why? Why not?

- Write down what you know about your family's cultural background, experiences with discrimination, and involvement in activism (women's movement, labor, civil rights, disabled rights). Interview parents, grandparents, and other relatives to get more information. Share the results of your investigations with your support group.

- Experience a day being differently abled (using a wheelchair, having the use of only one arm), going through a typical routine. Pay attention to what modifications in your environment would enable you to be more independent. Pay attention to how other people respond to you. Share the experiences in your support group.

- Write down the kinds of disabilities with which you feel comfortable and uncomfortable. In the group, explore the sources of your comfort and discomfort.

Activities for learning about institutional "isms"

In Chapter 1, *sexism, racism, handicappism,* and *homophobia* are defined as any attitude, action, or institutional practice, *backed up by institutional power,* that subordinates people because of their color, ethnicity, gender, disability, or sexual preference. The institutional forms of the "isms" are broader and more encompassing than individual prejudice and discriminatory behaviors. They may be overt and obvious—refusing people of color admittance to schools or housing, prohibiting homosexuals from housing or jobs. They may also be covert—cutting funds for health and nutrition programs for pregnant women in order "to balance the budget" is one example. Although no obvious words of prejudice are stated, the consequence of the institutional act is oppressive to low-income women. Another example is lack of accessibility to public buildings. The reason may be that "the building was constructed before laws requiring ramps," but the consequences are the same as if a sign openly read, "No wheelchairs."

Institutional "isms" have a profound impact on the quality of education provided for young children. The number of young children lacking needed child care programs is an example of institutional sexism. Lack of quality in-service training for working with differently abled children in many settings is an example of handicappism. The paucity of nonstereotypic children's books about Native Americans, Asian Americans, and Latinos is a consequence of institutional racism.

As individuals, teachers may participate in institutional "isms" even if they do not agree with them, unless they actively counter specific practices. If a preschool teacher does not read numerous books to her children that depict diversity because "there aren't any available books in my school (bookstores, approved educational supply companies)," then she is participating in institutional racism because her children learn only a White-centered view of life. To be anti-racist in this example requires the teacher to actively and persistently find ways to include diversity in children's books.

Do the following exercises to deepen your awareness of how institutional "isms" operate:

- Read "Nurturing Diversity for Today's Children and Tomorrow's Leaders" (Phillips, 1988).

- Tell about an incident in which you experienced prejudice or discrimination against yourself. What did you do? Next, tell about an incident in which you observed prejudice or discrimination directed at someone else by a third party. What did you do? Are you satisfied with the strategies you used? If not, what do you wish that you had done?

With the group, share your experiences. Make a list of the strategies you all used to respond to prejudice against yourselves and against someone else. Discuss what supported you to act and what held you back from acting or acting satisfactorily. The difficulties adults often experience in challenging biased behavior reflect the impact of institutional "isms" on individual behavior. In order to challenge bias, adults have to overcome the personal obstacles that interfere with acting.

- Take your "Anti-Bias Awareness IQ": How do you keep up with what people are currently saying and doing about eliminating bias against women, people of color, differently abled people, and homosexuals? List television programs, public radio programs, movies, magazines, novels, nonfiction books, journals, plays, and art exhibits dealing with these issues you have seen or read in the past year. What are local civil rights and community organizing groups in your city working on? Give yourself one point for each item.

  Score yourself: 0–2 very low ABA IQ, 3–5 low ABA IQ, 6–8 medium, 9–12 medium high, 12 and above high ABA IQ.

  A low score is not uncommon: It reflects the impact of institutional "isms" on our education, the media, publishers, and bookstores. However, to do anti-bias work it is necessary to overcome the limits on our knowledge caused by institutional "isms."

- Survey your local book, toy, and greeting card stores. Do they carry products that depict a diversity of gender roles, racial and ethnic identities, and physical abilities? The lack of diversity is another consequence of institutional "isms."

  Find out what stores do carry material that reflects diversity. Locate organizations that work on community and civil rights issues. Develop a resource list with your support group.

- Survey your school, neighborhood supermarket, movie theater, restaurants, park, YMCA/YWCA, church, government buildings (city hall, court, welfare office, Social Security), public transportation. What provisions are there for people with different kinds of disabilities? Are there ramps, doorways wide enough for wheelchairs, Braille signs, lower counters, people who know sign language, and so on?

- Choose five children's picture books you like to use in your class and five books you liked as a child. Evaluate each group member's choices, using "Ten Quick Ways" (p. 143) and the common stereotypes worksheet (p. 141). Discuss what to do with books that are stereotypic.

Here is an example of how the teachers at Pacific Oaks Children's School dealt with this issue. As teachers evaluated the environment, they became increasingly concerned about the stereotyping in many of the children's books in the school library. Teachers wanted to establish a method for evaluating books that would be educational, rather than censorship. The solution, after considerable discussion, was the "dialogue process": Every book in the Children's School library has a 5″ x 8″ dialogue card in a pocket at the front with the message:

This dialogue card is for all members of the comunity to share critical evaluations and techniques for use of this book; to become more aware of both discriminatory and authentic messages and images.

The whole community (college and Children's School teachers, students big and little, parents, visitors) may participate in the dialogue process. Here is an example of comments from three people about the book, *Harry the Dirty Dog* (Zion, 1956):

Person 1: "The message of this book is definitely racist. A white dog becomes unrecognizable to his owners when he gets covered with coal and turns "black." After he is washed and looks white again, he is reclaimed by his owners. I think this book should not be used with young children.

Person 2: "I disagree. I have read this book to children many times. It is a favorite story because they love Harry's getting dirty and then getting clean. This is an issue they have to deal with themselves a lot. I do not see that it is racist. Surely, the author had no such intention. After all, Harry is just a dog."

Person 3: "Whatever the author's interest, the story does play into "pre-prejudice" and misconceptions of young children. Two common questions from White 3- and 4-year-olds is whether Black skin is dirty and whether Black skin color comes off in the bathtub. *Harry the Dirty Dog* reinforces these ideas and adds the further message that the black-colored dog is not only dirty, but unwanted until he is white. Imagine reversing the situation. A black dog gets covered with white flour and is unrecognized and unwanted until he gets black again. Perhaps if we had a story with that plot, then we could read the two books side by side without a negative impact."

- Read *Blaming the Victim* (Ryan, 1976) together. Share examples of victim blaming you have participated in or seen in educational settings. Discuss ways to eliminate victim-blaming practices in your program.

Activities for learning about children's development

Knowing the specific tasks involved in children's constructing their identity and attitudes, and how to identify signs of pre-prejudice, enables you to provide developmentally appropriate environments and activities. Understanding children's issues also frees you to adapt and create new anti-bias activities to supplement those suggested in this book.

- Carefully read the research review in Chapter 1 and the developmental tasks and guidelines in Chapters 3 through 8. Discuss with the group what you learned. Have you seen similar behaviors or heard similar comments in your teaching and parenting experiences?

- For the next month, compile a list of questions, comments, and behaviors you hear and see about race and ethnicity, gender, and different physical abilities in your classroom. Share your data with each other. How do they fit into the developmental tasks reported in this book?

- When you begin doing anti-bias activities in your classroom, keep notes about children's responses and periodically share your anecdotes to increase your understanding of children's thinking.

Supplementary activities

- Read and discuss some of the following books and articles:

Different physical abilities—Brightman (1983), Women and Disability Awareness Project (1984)

Gender—Pogrebin (1980), Honig (1983)

Race/ethnicity—Cross (1985), Dennis (1981), Katz (1982), Saracho & Spodek (1983), Semaj (1985), Tinney (1983)

Step Four: Plan How To Introduce Anti-Bias Curriculum Into Your Program

Evaluate your material environment. Use the questions in Chapter 2 to evaluate every aspect of your material environment. Set up a checklist form with the questions and the headings: *have enough/ need more/have none.* For example, one question is "Do you have brown and black paint, paper, play dough, 'flesh-colored' crayons in your art area?" You check whether you have enough, need more, or have none.

Make a plan for increasing the diversity of your environment. Reread those sections in Chapter 2 about selecting, eliminating, purchasing, and making new materials. Make a shopping list with columns titled *to eliminate* and *to buy/to make.* Prioritize the items and make a time line for each task.

Evaluate your current activity. Make a chart about approaches to diversity with the headings: *Color-denial; "Tourist" multicultural;* and *Anti-Bias.* With your support group, brainstorm the key words that describe the characteristics of each approach. Review the common questions section in Chapter 1 that discusses differences among the approaches. Use your chart to help evaluate how you are addressing diversity in your classroom.

Observe your children's play and interaction patterns over a two-week period. What do girls/ boys not play with? Are there indicators of any children being excluded in play because of their identity? If you have physically challenged children, are their environments obstacles to their full participation in activities?

Based on your observations, brainstorm ideas for increasing children's use of all materials, for improving social interactions, and for improving environment accessibility.

Evaluate your own interactions with children. Work together with your support group members to get data: Observe each other or videotape each other. Use the questions in the "Interactions" section of Chapter 2 to guide your observations. Make columns headed *frequently/ sometimes/never* to keep track of the observations.

Discuss your "Interaction Profiles" in your support group. Brainstorm ways you want to change your interactions to make them more reflective of an anti-bias approach.

Evalute your current curriculum. Make a list of "What I am already doing in my current curriculum about gender/race/culture/different physical abilities/stereotyping and discriminatory behaviors/activism." Write down every activity you usually do.

Thoughtfully evaluate the activities: Are you using a "color-denial" or "tourist" approach to learning about diversity? Are you doing nothing or little in some areas? Which activities do you want to keep or discard?

Make a sample weekly plan for integrating anti-bias content into your present weekly schedule. Think of everything you *might* do. (See Figure 12.1.)

Consider how to incorporate anti-bias activities into your present curriculum model.

- If you use an *emergent* model, curriculum planning flows out of the interests and contexts of the children, the teacher, the parents, and the community. Any one of these four sources of curriculum can spark a series of interrelating activities. Planning is cyclical rather than linear, as one activity opens up further interests and as the teacher "weaves" a web of interconnecting activities. Anti-bias activities are a natural part of this webbing, if you keep anti-bias issues in mind. Asking children about their thoughts on a subject also opens up ideas for activities.

  For example, asking children what they know about "Indians" will let you in on what specific misconceptions you want to challenge through the activities you do. Make a "webbing" chart, beginning with children's questions about Native Americans in circles in the middle of the page. Draw lines from each question and write down possible activities that address each question. See how these activities interconnect and draw lines between them. Decide which activity you will use first.

- If you use a *unit* or *theme* model, planning involves creating a number of activities to be carried out over a designated period of time (a week, a month) around a specific topic. Common preschool and kindergarten units are: "Ourselves," "Our Families," "Community Helpers," "Our Neighborhood," "Transportation," "Work." All of these units lend themselves to anti-bias content. The guidelines and activities for learning about differences and similarities of race, physical abilities, gender, and culture can easily be integrated into your activities.

- If you use a *skill-based* model, where activities are organized around specific cognitive and social objectives, select anti-bias activities that require the use of specific skills. For example, if you are planning activities for fostering "classification," include objects and pictures that depict diversity in your classification games. All of the suggested activities for making posters, books, or charts about children's families can open up classification questions of what's the same?/ what's different?

Choose the anti-bias area to be tackled first. Consider these questions as you make a choice appropriate to your setting:

1. What are you most interested in? Comfortable with? Knowledgeable about?

2. Who are your children: their background, developmental levels, interests, needs?

3. What would your parents be most interested in? Comfortable with? What would they find most uncomfortable?

4. What are current issues in your community directly affecting your children's lives? What resources—materials and people—are there in your community for doing specific anti-bias activities?

Consider supports and obstacles to doing anti-bias curriculum in your program. Make a chart about "Obstacles to implementing anti-bias curriculum in my program/classroom." Under the headings *parents, other teachers, administrators,* and *myself,* list potential problems. Second, make a chart about "Strategies for overcoming obstacles" under the same headings. Third, make a chart about "Sources of support" for implementing anti-bias curriculum. Use your charts to help make a plan for addressing obstacles that includes ways to use your sources of support, a time line for achieving results, and thoughts on how you will know when a particular obstacle has been overcome.

Plan how you will work with parents. Use Chapter 11, "Working With Parents," to develop an initial plan, which you will evaluate and modify as you actually begin work.

Figure 12.1

Daily Schedule		Days of the Week				
Times/Structures		Monday	Tuesday	Wednesday	Thursday	Friday
8:45–9:45	*Choice Time* Art					
	Dramatic Play					
	Manipulatives					
	Blocks					
	Water Table					
	Sand Table					
	Books					
9:45–10:00	Cleanup					
10:00–10:45	Snack and Small-Group Activity					
10:45–11:30	Outside					
11:30–Noon	Large-Group Activity					
In this column: Write down *your* schedule		In these boxes fill in possible anti-bias activities for each part of your daily schedule				

Step Five: Hasten Slowly

Slowly begin to implement activities in the area you have chosen. It is fine to focus on one subject area (e.g., gender or different abilities) at first, and then gradually introduce other areas. Or you may prefer to work with several areas simultaneously (e.g., exploring physical differences and similarities in gender, race, and physical abilities).

Keep notes on how children respond to activities. Share your observations with your support group, and get ideas for further activities. Bring problems that arise to your support group and brainstorm together how to solve them.

As we become aware of all the *nos* people have imposed on those they fear because they're different, we who have devoted our lives to enabling children to grow as freely and as fully as possible continue to seek alternative ways of relating to each other that promote understanding rather than fear, opportunities rather than restrictions. Anti-bias is not a subject you can teach and be done with; it's a way of life. You teach anti-bias by living it, by helping children to say *yes* as often and as loudly as possible, both for themselves and for each other.

ADAPTATION

- If you are a director of a preschool or child care center and want to introduce anti-bias curriculum with your staff, then you and your staff (and parents if you wish) constitute the "support group." Make sure you work together as a cooperative group: Do not go faster than the group—but also provide leadership so that the group keeps moving. Remember that imposing anti-bias activities on teachers without their interest or participation is antiethical to an anti-bias approach.

- If you work in a college preparing teachers, or as an educational coordinator/consultant doing in-services, use and adapt the activities in this chapter to develop your class syllabus. Select additional readings from the resource section in the appendix.

References

Brenner, B. (1973). *Bodies.* New York: Dutton.

Brightman, A. (1983). *Ordinary moments: The disabled experience.* Baltimore: University Park Press.

Cross, W.E. (1985). Black identity: Rediscovering the distinction between personal identity and reference group orientations. In M.B. Spencer, G.K. Brookins, & W.R. Allen (Eds.), *Beginnings: The social and affective development of Black children* (pp. 155–172). Hillsdale, NJ: Erlbaum.

Dennis, R. (1981). Socialization and racism: The White experience. In B.P. Bowser & R.G. Hunt (Eds.), *Impact of racism on White Americans* (pp. 71–86). Beverly Hills, CA: Sage Publications.

Honig, A.S. (1983). Research in review. Sex role socialization in early childhood. *Young Children, 38*(6), 57–70.

Katz, P. (1982). Development of children's racial awareness and intergroup attitudes. In L. G. Katz (Ed.), *Current topics in early childhood education* (Vol. 4, pp. 17–54). Norwood, NJ: Ablex.

Phillips, C.B. (1988). Nurturing diversity for today's children and tomorrow's leaders. *Young Children, 43*(2), 42–47.

Pogrebin, L. (1980). *Growing up free: Raising your child in the 80's.* New York: McGraw-Hill.

Ryan, W. (1976). *Blaming the victim.* New York: Random House.

Saracho, O.N., & Spodek, B. (Eds.). (1983). *Understanding the multicultural experience in early childhood education.* Washington, DC: NAEYC.

Semaj, L.T. (1985). Africanity, cognition and extended self. In M.B. Spencer, G.K. Brookins, & W.R. Allen (Eds.), *Beginnings: The social and affective development of Black children* (pp. 173–184). Hillsdale, NJ: Erlbaum.

Tinney, J. (1983). Interconnections: Racism, sexism, heterosexism and homophobia. *Interracial Books for Children Bulletin, 12*(3 & 4), 4–6.

Waxman, S. (1076). *What is a girl? What is a boy?* Los Angeles: Peace Press.

Women and Disability Awareness Project. (1984). *Building community: A manual exploring issues of women and disability.* New York: Educational Equity Concepts.

Zion, G. (1956). *Harry the dirty dog.* New York: Harper & Row

RESOURCES

Children's Books

Here is a list of children's books that address diversity in families, gender roles, racial and ethnic identity, disabilities, and work; prejudice; and activism. Some of the books are good literature; some are not but are useful for our purposes. Some topics are covered better than others. More books are needed about Asian-Pacific Americans, Latinos, Native American families and children, gay and lesbian families, interracial/ethnic marriages and adoptions, stepparents and blended families. Getting a comprehensive selection of anti-bias books still requires activism from early childhood educators. For the time being, teacher-made books and stories will have to supplement the commercially available books.

We listed books in two ways:

1. A chart that indicates suggested ages and specific topics. The final column, "comments," briefly indicates the subject of each book and occasionally points out specific ideas for using it. (Ages give you a general idea of the population a book is for, but don't be constrained by the ages—children like a variety of books.)

2. An alphabetical list by author, with title, publisher, and date.

Some categories of books usually mentioned in multicultural bibliographies are missing. Books of folktales from different cultures and countries are not listed. These books are wonderful to use with young children to stretch their imaginations and awareness of human behavior and feelings; they are not useful for teaching young children about someone's culture—especially if the cultures are from other countries. Imagine teaching young children in Africa about the U.S.A. by reading Appalachian folktales as the source of information.

The tales are wonderful, but they hardly represent a complete or accurate picture of life in contemporary American society. Books about famous people are also not on the list (with a few exceptions). For the most part, these books are more appropriate to use with children 6 years old and older.

When selecting from the chart, look for:

- books that represent children in your class;
- books that open up new images, ideas, and information to your children; and
- a balance of books addressing each topic on the chart. Many of the books address more than one issue.

As you build your library with anti-bias books, keep some of your old books that you now realize are stereotypic to teach 4- and 5-year-olds critical thinking.

A number of books on the list come from small, alternative presses, and many are only sold in alternative bookstores—not in well-known, large bookstores. The resource list that follows provides names and addresses of these presses and some of the bookstores from which you can order.

New books keep appearing, so it is very helpful to locate a bookstore or children's librarian in your city or town who supports your efforts. Work with them to locate, review, and get good anti-bias books. "Ten Quick Ways," the guidelines from the Council on Interracial Books for Children (p. 143), will help you evaluate books you already have in your classroom and school library and guide your selection of new books not listed here. Read a new book to yourself a few times before you read it to children, so that you are familiar with the content and are prepared to respond to children's questions and comments.

119

Author	Title	2s	3s	4s	5s	Family	Gender	People of Color	Disabilities
Adoff	Black Is Brown Is Tan		•	•		•	•	•	
Anders	A Look at Prejudice and Understanding				•				
Aseltine	I'm Deaf and It's Okay		•	•	•				•
Atkinson	Maria Teresa			•	•	•	•	•	
Bales	Kevin Cloud: Chippewa Boy in the City				•	•		•	
Bang	Ten, Nine, Eight	•	•			•	•	•	
Bang	The Paper Crane			•	•			•	
Baylor	Hawk, I'm Your Brother			•	•			•	
Behrens	I Can Be a Truck Driver	•	•	•			•		
Beim & Beim	Two Is a Team		•					•	
Beim & Beim	The Swimming Hole			•	•			•	
Bellet	A-B-C-ing: An Action Alphabet	•	•	•					•
Bethel	Three Cheers for Mother Jones				•		•		
Blood & Link	The Goat in the Rug			•	•			•	
Blue	I Am Here/Yo Estoy Aqui			•	•	•		•	
Boone-Jones	Martin Luther King, Jr.: A Picture Story			•	•			•	
Bosche	Jenny Lives With Eric and Martin					•	•		
Bourke	Handmade ABC Reading		•	•	•				•
Brenner	Bodies	•	•	•			•	•	
Brenner	Wagon Wheels			•	•	•		•	
Brightman	Like Me			•	•				•
Brown	Someone Special, Just Like You		•	•	•		•		•
Bunin & Bunin	Is That Your Sister?			•	•	•		•	
Caines	Abby		•	•		•		•	
Caines	Daddy		•	•	•	•	•	•	
Caines	Just Us Women		•	•	•	•	•	•	
Cairo	Our Brother Has Down's Syndrome			•	•	•			•
Cameron	Spider Woman				•		•	•	
Chang	The Iron Moonhunter				•			•	
Children's Television Workshop	Sign Language Fun		•	•	•				•
Church	Colors Around Me	•	•	•	•			•	
Clifton	Don't You Remember?			•	•		•	•	
Clifton	Everett Anderson's Friend			•	•	•		•	

Work	Preju-dice	Acti-vism	Comments
			Interracial Black-White family
	•	•	Discussion about different forms of prejudice
	•	•	Hearing-impaired teenager helps a hearing-impaired child
	•	•	Hispanic child in Midwest encounters and handles discrimination
•			Photo story of a Native American child who lives in Chicago
			Black father puts his daughter to bed
			Poor stranger (Japanese-American) brings special gifts to a multiethnic group in a working-class community. Raises anti-materialism
			Native-American boy befriends a hawk and flies in spirit with him
			Men and women can be truck drivers
			Interracial friendship
	•		Two Black and White friends cope with prejudice from other 6-year-olds
			Children with various disabilities being active
•		•	Story about children in cotton mills and a children's strike
•			About a Navajo woman
			Puerto Rican 5-year-old begins kindergarten speaking only Spanish
	•	•	A picture book appropriate for young children
	•		A gay family sensitively portrayed discuss feelings that arise when encountering prejudice
			Sign language for each letter of the alphabet
			Photos
	•		A true story of a Black pioneer family. Challenges stereotypes about Native Americans
			Written from the viewpoint of a developmentally delayed child
			Photos depicting children with disabilities doing a variety of activities
			Interracial adoption: White family/Black child
			Black family explains adoption to their young adopted child
			Black father and daughter
			Black aunt and niece—the aunt is a strong role model of active woman
			Sensitively discusses a disability usually not addressed in children's books
			Story of an important figure in the Navajo belief system
•	•	•	Story of prejudice against Chinese workers who built the TransAtlantic Railroad
			Signing for words children commonly use
			Creatively describes varieties of skin tone among Afro-Americans—good for all children
•			Working-class Black family. Mother and father work
•			Single-parent family; latchkey child. Friendship between a Black boy and Mexican-American girl

Author	Title	2s	3s	4s	5s	Family	Gender	People of Color	Disabil- ities
Clifton	Everett Anderson's Goodbye			•	•	•		•	
Clifton	My Friend Jacob			•	•				•
Cole	How You Were Born			•	•	•	•		
Constant	First Snow			•	•	•		•	
Corey	You Go Away	•	•				•	•	
Crowder	Stephanie and the Coyote		•	•	•	•		•	
DeGrosbois et al.	Mommy Works on Dresses			•	•	•	•		
dePaola	Now One Foot, Now the Other			•	•	•			•
dePaola	The Legend of the Bluebonnet				•			•	
DePoix	Jo, Flo and Yolanda			•	•			•	•
Detton	My Mother Lost Her Job Today			•	•	•	•		
Dragonwagon	Wind Rose			•	•	•	•		
Dragonwagon	Always, Always			•	•	•			
Drescher	Your Family, My Family			•	•		•	•	
Epstein	History of Women for Children				•		•		
Fagerstrom & Hanson	Our New Baby				•	•	•		
Fassler	Howie Helps Himself		•	•	•				•
Fassler	My Grandpa Died Today			•	•	•			
Feelings & Greenfield	Daydreamers				•		•	•	
Feeney	A Is for Aloha	•	•	•				•	
Feeney	Hawaii Is a Rainbow	•	•	•				•	
Flournoy	The Twins Strike Back			•	•	•	•	•	
Fogel	Wesley Paul: Marathon Runner				•			•	
Frank	About Handicaps		•	•	•				•
Friedman	How My Parents Learned To Eat			•	•	•		•	
Goldin	Straight Hair, Curly Hair				•			•	
Greenberg	People Aren't Potatoes				•			•	•
Greenberg	I Know I'm Myself Because	•	•	•	•	•	•		
Greenberg	Rosie and Roo	•	•	•	•	•			
Greenfield	Rosa Parks				•		•	•	
Greenfield	Me and Nessie			•			•	•	
Greenfield	Honey, I Love	•	•	•			•	•	
Greenfield	Darlene			•	•	•		•	•
Grimes	Something on My Mind		•	•	•		•	•	
Hazen, B.S.	Tight Times			•	•	•	•		

Work	Preju-dice	Acti-vism	Comments
			A child deals with the death of his father
	•		Young child tells about his best friend who is developmentally delayed
			Explains process of birth
			Vietnamese-American family
			Multiracial child care. Both parents shown in nurturing role. Deals with separation
•			Contemporary Navajo girl helps take care of family's sheep. Bilingual
•			Mother works in a factory
			When his grandfather has a stroke, boy helps him relearn how to walk
		•	Story of a Native American girl who gives up her most precious possession to help bring the rain. Help children realize that story is set in the past
			Explores similarities and differences among friends
•			Single parent. Tensions over the loss of a job
			Mother tells daughter about excitement of waiting for her to be born. Discusses birth
			About divorce and shared custody
			Shows a lesbian family among many kinds of family. Substitute "birth parents" for "real parents" in discussing adopting families
•	•	•	Difficulties and successes of women's search for equality
			A picture book about birth for parents and children
			A child with cerebral palsy learns to move his wheelchair by himself. Has a stereotypic picture of a child playing "Indian"—Raise this critically with children
			Jewish family
			Black children beautifully illustrated daydreaming their dreams of growth
			Diverse ethnic groups in Hawaii depicted through photographs
			A multicultural book about colors
		•	Girl twins find a way to teach their family to treat them as individuals
	•		Asian-American boy who becomes a long-distance runner
			Father talking with his son about different disabilities
			How a Japanese woman and White American man meet and learn about each other's cultures
			A scientific explanation of different hair types
	•		Simple cultural anthropology: how people are alike and unique
			Independent little girl with great self-image; happy mother but no father mentioned
			A happy interracial family: two mothers, two babies, and a grandmother; no father mentioned
	•	•	Story of the Montgomery Bus Boycott for young children
			Black girl and her invisible friend
			Wonderful, loving poems
			Black girl in a wheelchair faces her disability with the help of her cousin and uncle
			Poetry. Children in diverse cultural settings
•			Working class family copes with the father's unemployment (one scene shows father crying)

Author	Title	2s	3s	4s	5s	Family	Gender	People of Color	Disabil- ities
Hazen, B.S.	Why Are People Different? A Book About Prejudice			•	•				
Hazen, N.	Grown-Ups Cry Too		•	•	•	•	•		
Heide	Sound of Sunshine, Sound of Rain			•	•	•		•	
Henriod	Grandma's Wheelchair		•	•	•	•			•
Hirsh	I Love Hanukkah		•	•	•	•			
Jensen	Catching		•	•	•				•
Jonas	When You Were a Baby	•					•	•	
Jordan	New Life: New Room		•	•	•	•		•	
Kempler	A Man Can Be . . .	•	•	•	•	•	•	•	
Klein	Girls Can Be Anything			•	•		•		
Larch	Father Gander Nursery Rhymes		•	•	•		•	•	•
Larson	Don't Forget Tom			•	•				•
Lasker	Mothers Can Do Anything		•	•	•	•	•		
Lasker	He's My Brother			•	•	•			•
Lionni	Swimmy		•	•	•				
Litchfield	A Button in Her Ear		•	•	•			•	•
Litchfield	A Cane in Her Hand		•	•	•				•
Litchfield	Words in Our Hands			•	•	•			•
Little & Greenfield	I Can Do It by Myself			•	•	•		•	
Mack	Jessie's Dream Skirt			•	•		•		
Macmillan & Freeman	My Best Friend Martha Rodriguez			•	•	•		•	
Mann	The Street of the Flower Boxes			•	•		•	•	
Manry	My Mother and I Are Growing Strong			•	•	•			
Martel	Yagua Days				•	•		•	
Martin	Brown Bear, Brown Bear, What Do You See?	•	•					•	
Martin	I Am Freedom's Child	•	•					•	
Maurey	My Mother the Mail Carrier			•	•	•	•	•	
McGovern	Black Is Beautiful	•	•	•	•				
McKee	Snow Woman		•	•			•		
Merriman	Boys and Girls, Girls and Boys		•	•	•		•	•	
Monjo	The Drinking Gourd				•				
Mower	I Visit My Tutu and Grandma		•	•		•		•	

Work	Preju-dice	Acti-vism	Comments
	•		Child discusses prejudice with a grandparent
			Good discussion of why grown-up men and women sometimes cry. Bilingual
	•		A blind Black boy deals with racism and friendship
			An active, involved grandma with a disability
			Jewish family
			A book for blind and sighted children with pictures to feel and see
			Multicultural images
			A low-income family has a new child
			Two fathers, Black and White, shown in varying moods and activities
	•	•	Girl challenges her friend Adam's ideas about gender roles
•	•		Mother Goose rewritten and reillustrated to reflect diversity
			Story about a developmentally delayed child
•			Good photos depicting mothers in a variety of roles and jobs
			An older brother tells about his younger developmentally delayed brother
		•	A fish organizes a school of small fish so they can outwit a big bully fish
•			Includes a Black woman doctor
			Visually impaired child. May need paraphrasing for younger children
			Hearing-impaired parents. May need paraphrasing for younger children
			A Black youngster decides to buy his mother's present by himself
	•	•	A preschool boy dresses up in a skirt and faces teasing from classmates; is helped by a supportive teacher who is male and Black
			A White American girl becomes friends with a Mexican-American girl; they learn about each other
		•	Children cooperate to make change in their neighborhood
•	•		Mother and daughter learn to cope alone after father is sent to jail
			Puerto Rican family in U.S. visits Puerto Rico
			Encourages discussion about color
			Wonderful, rhymed story about embracing differences
•			Bilingual
			Photos of Black animals, plants, people, objects
			Children make snow women instead of snow men
			Opens up gender behavior options
	•	•	White child helps free slaves in the underground railroad
			Hawaiian-White child learns culture from two different grandmothers

Author	Title	2s	3s	4s	5s	Family	Gender	People of Color	Disabilities
New Mexico People and Energy Collective	Red Ribbons for Emma				•	•	•	•	
Nolan	My Daddy Don't Go to Work			•	•	•		•	
Ormerod	Sunshine	•	•			•	•		
Pack	Aekyung's Dream			•	•	•	•	•	
Parish	I Can, Can You?	•					•	•	
Pearson	Everybody Knows That			•	•			•	
Peterson	I Have a Sister, My Sister Is Deaf		•	•	•				•
Pinkwater	Wingman				•				
Pogrebin	Stories for Free Children			•	•		•		
Powers	Our Teacher's in a Wheelchair		•	•	•				•
Quinlan	My Dad Takes Care of Me			•	•	•	•		
Quinsey	Why Does That Man Have Such a Big Nose?			•	•				•
Robinson	An Eskimo Birthday			•	•	•		•	
Rockwell, A.	When We Grow Up		•	•	•		•	•	
Rockwell, H.	My Nursery School	•	•				•	•	
Rosario	Idalia's Project ABC		•	•	•			•	
Rosenberg	Being Adopted			•	•	•		•	
Rosenberg	Living in Two Worlds			•	•	•		•	
Rosenberg	My Friend Leslie		•	•	•				•
Sargent & Wirt	My Favorite Place		•	•	•				•
Schaffer	How Babies and Families Are Made			•	•	•	•		
Scott	On Mother's Lap		•	•	•	•		•	
Seuss	The Sneetches			•	•				
Severance	Lots of Mommies			•	•	•	•		
Shor	When the Corn Is Red				•			•	
Showers	Look at Your Eyes				•			•	
Showers	Your Skin and Mine				•			•	
Simon	What Do I Do? Que Hago?		•	•	•			•	
Simon	All Kinds of Families			•	•	•		•	
Simon	Why Am I Different?		•	•	•	•	•		

Work	Preju-dice	Acti-vism	Comments
		•	Contemporary Navajo girl takes action to help her family and herself
•			An urban Black family deals with the father's unemployment
			Nonsexist gender roles in family. No words
			Story about a Korean-American girl
			Four "first" books—levels 1, 2, 3, and 4. Includes Black children
	•		Challenges children's sex role stereotypes
			Explores sibling relationship and being deaf
	•		Chinese-American boy faces racism in his school. May need to shorten for 5s
•			Collection of nonsexist stories
•			Male teacher who uses a wheelchair. Photos depict his day at school
•			Unemployed father in White, middle-class family takes care of his son while looking for work
	•		Excellent model of how to answer children's questions about disabilities
			Explores similarities and differences in a concrete activity meaningful to young children
			Diversity of gender roles
			Diversity of ethnic backgrounds and gender behavior
			English and Spanish alphabet with urban scenes
			Interracial/intercultural adoptions. Photos. Will need paraphrasing for 3s and 4s
			Biracial children, photos. Addresses what it means to be biracial/bicultural
			Mainstreaming
			Blind child running and swimming in waves
			Shows variety of ways a family comes into being: birth, adoption
			Eskimo family. A new baby arrives
	•		One of very few books for young children exploring prejudice
			A young girl lives with three women who share a home and child care and do nontraditional work
	•	•	Portrays the clash between Native Americans and Whites honestly. Read carefully before reading to children
	•		A scientific explanation of why eyes differ
			A scientific explanation for children about why skin colors differ
			Bilingual—Spanish and English
•			Diverse ways families live, including a family with a father in prison
			Depicts people of varying ages active in the community

Author	Title	2s	3s	4s	5s	Family	Gender	People of Color	Disabil-ities
Sonneborn	Friday Night Is Papa's Night			•	•	•		•	
Stein	About Handicaps			•	•				•
Steptoe	Stevie			•	•	•		•	
Steptoe	My Special Best Words	•	•					•	
Steltzer	A Haida Potlatch			•	•	•		•	
Stinson	Mom and Dad Don't Live Together Anymore		•	•	•	•			
Surowrecki	Joshua's Day		•	•		•			
Tax	Families		•	•	•	•			
United Indians of All Tribes Foundation	Interviews With Native American Men and Women in Various Jobs			•	•			•	
United Indians of All Tribes Foundation	Sharing Our Worlds			•	•			•	
Waber	Ira Sleeps Over		•	•			•		
Waber	You Look Ridiculous			•	•				
Walter	My Mother Needs Me		•	•	•	•			
Walton	What Color Are You?				•			•	
Wandro	My Daddy Is a Nurse		•	•	•		•		
Waterton	A Salmon for Simon		•	•	•			•	
Waxman	What Is a Girl? What Is a Boy?		•	•	•		•		
Weissman	All About Me/Let's Be Friends	•	•				•	•	•
Welber	The Train			•	•	•		•	
Williams	A Chair for My Mother		•	•	•	•	•		
Williams	Something Special for Me		•	•	•	•	•		
Wolf	Don't Feel Sorry for Paul			•	•				•
Yarbrough	Cornrows		•	•	•			•	
Yashima	Umbrella		•	•	•			•	
Yee & Kokin	Got Me a Story			•	•			•	
Zolotow	William's Doll		•	•			•		

Work	Preju-dice	Acti-vism	Comments
			Latino family. Father works at two jobs—comes home on weekends
	•		A nondisabled child faces his fears about a disabled friend
			About a child in a foster family and sibling relationships. Raise unfair "Cowboys and Indians" play with children
			Toilet training. Black family depicted
•			Photos. Contemporary Haida Native Americans prepare for a potlach. Family relationships. Daily and ritual dress
			Divorce
•			Single, working mom
			Single mothers and fathers, stepmother, extended family. Images of Latino and Black families must supplemented with other books
•			Good photos and information. Text is long and will need paraphrasing
			Shows Native American children today
			Addresses a young boy's fears and how he copes
	•		A hippopotamus wants to look different; finds out it is best to be himself
			Mother comes home with a new baby sister and Jason helps out
	•		Explains skin color differences and explores people's similarities
•			Expanding gender roles of men
			Simon is a Northwest Coast Native American child. Contemporary
			Explains the anatomy of gender and challenges sex gender stereotyping
			Nonsexist, multiethnic; children with disabilities shown
			One of the few books depicting an interracial family
•			An extended working-class family. Strong girl and women
•			Continues the story of the child and family in *A Chair for My Mother*
			Child with a prosthesis. Great photos. Story of child's daily life. Paraphrase for preschoolers
			Meaning of cornrows in the Black tradition discussed while Mother braids a child's hair
			Japanese-American girl's adventures
			Black, Hindi, Latino, Chinese, Salvadorian, and Filipino families represented
	•		William wants and gets a doll; some family members disapprove

Adoff, A. (1973). *Black is brown is tan*. New York: Harper & Row.

Anders, R. (1976). *A look at prejudice and understanding*. Minneapolis: Lerner.

Aseltine, L., & Mueller, E. (1986). *I'm deaf and it's okay*. Niles, IL: Whitman.

Atkinson, M. (1979). *Maria Teresa*. Carrboro, NC: Lollipop Power.

Bales, C.A. (1972). *Kevin Cloud: Chippewa boy in the city*. Chicago: Reilly & Lee.

Bang, M. (1983). *Ten, nine, eight*. New York: Greenwillow.

Bang, M. (1985). *The paper crane*. New York: Morrow.

Baylor, B. (1976). *Hawk, I'm your brother*. New York: Scribner's.

Behrens, J. (1985). *I can be a truck driver*. Chicago: Childrens.

Beim, J., & Beim, J. (1945). *Two is a team*. New York: Harcourt Brace Jovanovich.

Beim, L., & Beim, J. (1947). *The swimming hole*. New York: Morrow.

Bellet, J. (1984). *A-B-C-ing: An action alphabet*. New York: Crown.

Bethel, J. (1970). *Three cheers for Mother Jones*. New York: Holt, Rinehart & Winston.

Blood, C., & Link, M. (1980). *The goat in the rug*. New York: Macmillan.

Blue, R. (1971). *I am here/Yo estoy aqui*. New York: Franklin Watts.

Boone-Jones, M. (1968). *Martin Luther King, Jr.: A picture story*. Chicago: Childrens.

Bosche, S. (1983). *Jenny lives with Eric and Martin*. Gay Men's Press, P.O. Box 247, London N15 GRW, England.

Bourke, L. (1981). *Handmade ABC reading*. Reading, MA: Addison-Wesley.

Brenner, B. (1973). *Bodies*. New York: Dutton.

Brenner, B. (1978). *Wagon wheels*. New York: Harper & Row.

Brightman, A. (1976). *Like me*. Boston: Little, Brown.

Brown, T. (1984). *Someone special, just like you*. New York: Holt, Rinehart & Winston.

Bunin, C., & Bunin, S. (1976). *Is that your sister?* New York: Pantheon.

Caines, J. (1973). *Abby*. New York: Harper & Row.

Caines, J. (1977). *Daddy*. New York: Harper & Row.

Caines, J. (1982). *Just us women*. New York: Harper & Row.

Cairo, S. (1985). *Our brother has Down's syndrome*. Willowdale, ON: Annick Press.

Cameron, A. (1988). *Spider woman*. Madeira Park, BC: Harbour Publishing Co.

Chang, K. (1977). *The iron moonhunter*. San Francisco: Children's Book Press.

Children's Television Workshop. (1980). *Sign language fun*. New York: Random House.

Church, V. (1971). *Colors around me*. Chicago: Afro-American Publishing.

Clifton, L. (1973). *Don't you remember?* New York: Dalton.

Clifton, L. (1976). *Everett Anderson's friend*. New York: Holt, Rinehart & Winston.

Clifton, L. (1983). *Everett Anderson's goodbye*. New York: Holt.

Clifton, L. (1980). *My friend Jacob*. New York: Elsevier/Dutton.

Cole, J. (1985). *How you were born*. New York: Morrow.

Constant, H. (1974). *First snow*. New York: Knopf.

Corey, D. (1983). *You go away*. New York: Greenwillow.

Crowder, J. (1969). *Stephanie and the coyote*. Upper Strata, Box 278, Bernalillow, NM 87004.

DeGrosbois, L., Lacelle, N., LaMothe, R., & Nantel, L. (1976). *Mommy works on dresses* (C. Bayard, Trans.). Toronto: Women's Press.

dePaola, T. (1981). *Now one foot, now the other*. New York: Putnam.

dePaola, T. (1983). *The legend of the bluebonnet*. New York: Putnam.

DePoix, C. (1973). *Jo, Flo and Yolanda*. Carrboro, NC: Lollipop Power.

Delton, J. (1980). *My mother lost her job today*. Niles, IL: Whitman.

Dragonwagon, C. (1976). *Wind rose*. New York: Harper.

Dragonwagon, C. (1984). *Always, always*. New York: Macmillan.

Drescher, J. (1980). *Your family, my family*. New York: Walker.

Epstein, V.S. (1984). *History of women for children*. Milwaukee: Quality Press.

Fagerstrom, G., & Hanson, G. (1982). *Our new baby: A picture story about birth for parents and children*. Woodbury, NY: Barron's.

Fassler, J. (1975). *Howie helps himself*. Niles, IL: Whitman.

Fassler, J. (1983). *My grandpa died today*. New York: Human Sciences Press.

Feelings, T., & Greenfield, E. (1981). *Daydreamers*. New York: Dial.

Feeney, S. (1980). *A is for Aloha*. Honolulu: The University Press of Hawaii.

Feeney, S. (1985). *Hawaii is a rainbow*. Honolulu: The University of Hawaii Press.

Flournoy, V. (1980). *The twins strike back*. New York: Dial.

Fogel, J. (1979). *Wesley Paul: Marathon runner*. New York: Lippincott.

Frank, D. (1974). *About handicaps: An open family book for parents and children together*. New York: Walker.

Friedman, I. (1987). *How my parents learned to eat*. Boston: Houghton Mifflin.

Goldin, A. (1965). *Straight hair, curly hair*. New York: Harper & Row.

Greenberg, P. (1954). *People aren't potatoes*. The Growth Program Press, 4914 Ashby St., N.W., Washington, DC 20007.

Greenberg, P. (1981). *I know I'm myself because*. New York: Human Sciences Press.

Greenberg, P. (1988). *Rosie and Roo*. The Growth Program Press, 4914 Ashby St., N.W., Washington, DC 20007.

Greenfield, E. (1973). *Rosa Parks*. New York: Harper.

Greenfield, E. (1975). *Me and Nessie*. New York: Harper & Row.

Greenfield, E. (1978). *Honey, I love and other love poems*. New York: Crowell.

Greenfield, E. (1980). *Darlene*. New York: Methuen.

Grimes, N. (1986). *Something on my mind*. New York: Dial.

Hazen, B.S. (1983). *Tight times*. New York: Penguin.

Hazen, B.S. (1985). *Why are people different? A book about prejudice*. New York: Golden Books.

Hazen, N. (1973). *Grown-ups cry too*. Carrboro, NC: Lollipop Power. English-Spanish text, 1978.

Heide, F. (1979). *Sound of sunshine, sound of rain*. New York: Scholastic.

Henriod, L. (1982). *Grandma's wheelchair*. Niles, IL: Whitman.

Hirsh, M. (1984). *I love Hanukkah*. New York: Holiday House.

Jensen, V.A. (1983). *Catching*. New York: Putnam.

Jonas, A. (1982). *When you were a baby*. New York: Greenwillow.

Jordan, J. (1975). *New life: New room*. New York: Crowell.

Kempler, S. (1981). *A man can be . . . .* New York: Human Sciences Press.

Klein, N. (1973). *Girls can be anything*. New York: Dutton.

Larch, D.W. (1986). *Father Gander nursery rhymes*. Advocacy Press, P.O. Box 236, Santa Barbara, CA 93102.

Larson, H. (1978). *Don't forget Tom*. New York: Crowell.

Lasker, J. (1972). *Mothers can do anything*. Niles, IL: Whitman.

Lasker, J. (1974). *He's my brother*. Niles, IL: Whitman.

Lionni, L. (1973). *Swimmy*. New York: Knopf.

Litchfield, A. (1976). *A button in her ear*. Niles, IL: Whitman.

Litchfield, A. (1977). *A cane in her hand*. Niles, IL: Whitman.

Litchfield, A. (1980). *Words in our hands*. Niles, IL: Whitman.

Little, L.J., & Greenfield, E. (1978). *I can do it by myself*. New York: Crowell.

Mack, B. (1979). *Jessie's dream skirt*. Carrboro, NC: Lollipop Power.

Macmillan, D., & Freeman, D. (1987). *My best friend Martha Rodriquez*. New York: Julian Messner.

Mann, P. (1966). *The street of the flower boxes*. New York: Coward, McCann & Geoghegan.

Manry, I. (1979). *My mother and I are growing strong*. Berkeley, CA: New Seeds Press.

Martel, C. (1976). *Yagua days*. New York: Dial.

Martin, B., Jr. (1983). *Brown bear, brown bear, what do you see?* New York: Holt, Rinehart & Winston.

Martin, B., Jr. (1970). *I am freedom's child*. Oklahoma City: Bowmar.

Maurey, I. (1976). *My mother the mail carrier*. New York: Feminist Press.

McGovern, A. (1969). *Black is beautiful*. New York: Scholastic.

McKee, D. (1987). *Snow woman*. New York: Lothrop, Lee & Shepard.

Merriman, E. (1972). *Boys and girls, girls and boys*. New York: Holt, Rinehart & Winston.

Monjo, F.N. (1970). *The drinking gourd*. New York: Harper & Row.

Mower, N. (1984). *I visit my Tutu and Grandma*. Kailua, HI: Press Pacifica.

New Mexico People and Energy Collective et al. (1981). *Red ribbons for Emma*. Berkeley, CA: New Seeds Press.

Nolan, M. (1978). *My daddy don't go to work*. Minneapolis: Carolrhoda.

Ormerod, J. (1981). *Sunshine*. New York: Lothrop, Lee & Shepard.

Pack, M. (1978). *Aekyung's dream*. Chicago: Childrens Press.

Parish, P. (1984) *I can, can you?* New York: Greenwillow.

Parish, P. (1984). *Everybody knows that*. New York: Dial.

Peterson, J. (1977). *I have a sister, my sister is deaf*. New York: Harper & Row.

Pinkwater, M. (1975). *Wingman*. New York: Dodd, Mead.

Pogrebin, L.C. (Ed.). (1983). *Stories for free children*. New York: McGraw-Hill.

Powers, M.E. (1986). *Our teacher's in a wheelchair*. Niles, IL: Whitman.

Quinlan, P. (1987). *My dad takes care of me*. Willowdale, ON: Annick Press.

Quinsey, M.B. (1986). *Why does that man have such a big nose?* Seattle: Parenting Press.

Robinson, T. (1975). *An Eskimo birthday*. New York: Dodd, Mead.

Rockwell, A. (1981). *When we grow up*. New York: Dutton.

Rockwell, H. (1976). *My nursery school*. New York: Greenwillow.

Rosario, I. (1987). *Idalia's project ABC: An urban alphabet book in English and Spanish*. New York: Holt, Rinehart & Winston.

Rosenberg, M. (1984). *Being adopted*. New York: Lothrop, Lee & Shepard.

Rosenberg, M. (1986). *Living in two worlds*. New York: Lothrop, Lee & Shepard.

Rosenberg, M. (1983). *My friend Leslie*. New York: Lothrop, Lee & Shepard.

Sargent, S., & Wirt, D. A. (1983). *My favorite place*. New York: Abingdon.

Schaffer, P. (1988). *How babies and families are made*. Berkeley, CA: Taber Sarah Books.

Scott, A. (1972). *On Mother's lap*. New York: McGraw-Hill.

Seuss, Dr. (1961). *The sneetches*. New York: Random House.

Severance, J. (1983). *Lots of mommies*. Carrboro, NC: Lollipop Power.

Shor, P. (1973). *When the corn is red*. New York: Abingdon.

Showers, P. (1962). *Look at your eyes*. New York: Crowell.

Showers, P. (1965). *Your skin and mine*. New York: Crowell.

Simon, N. (1974). *What do I do? Que hago?* Niles, IL: Whitman.

Simon, N. (1975). *All kinds of families*. Niles, IL: Whitman.

Simon, N. (1976). *Why am I different?* Niles, IL: Whitman.

Sonneborn, R. (1987). *Friday night is Papa's night*. New York: Puffin.

Stein, S.B. (1974). *About handicaps*. New York: Walker.

Steptoe, J. (1969). *Stevie*. New York: Harper & Row.

Steptoe, J. (1974). *My special best words*. New York: Viking.

Steltzer, U. (1984). *A Haida potlatch*. Seattle: University of Washington Press.

Stinson, K. (1985). *Mom and Dad don't live together any more*. Willowdale, ON: Annick Press.

Surowrecki, S. (1977). *Joshua's day*. Carrboro, NC: Lollipop Power.

Tax, M. (1981). *Families*. Boston: Little, Brown.

United Indians of All Tribes Foundation. (1979). *Interviews with Native American men and women in various jobs*. Seattle: Author.

United Indians of All Tribes Foundation. (1980). *Sharing our worlds: Native American children today*. Seattle: Author.

Waber, B. (1972). *Ira sleeps over*. Boston: Houghton Mifflin.

Waber, B. (1966). *You look ridiculous*. Boston: Houghton Mifflin.

Walter, M.P. (1983). *My mother needs me*. New York: Lothrop, Lee & Shepard.

Walton, D. (1973). *What color are you?* Boulder, CO: Johnson.

Wandro, M. (1981). *My daddy is a nurse*. Reading, MA: Addison Wesley.

Waterton, B. (1978). *A salmon for Simon*. Vancouver: Douglas

& McIntyre. (Distributed by Salem House, 462 Boston St., Topsfield, MA 01983.)

Waxman, S. (1989). *What is a girl? What is a boy?* New York: Harper & Row.

Weissman, J. (1981). *All about me/Let's be friends.* Gryphon House, 3706 Otis St., Mt. Rainier, MD 20712. Book and record available.

Welber, R. (1972). *The train.* New York: Pantheon.

Williams, V. (1982). *A chair for my mother.* New York: Greenwillow.

Williams, V. (1983). *Something special for me.* New York: Greenwillow.

Wolf, B. (1974). *Don't feel sorry for Paul.* New York: Harper & Row.

Yarbrough, C. (1979). *Cornrows.* New York: Putnam.

Yashima, T. (1958). *Umbrella.* New York: Viking.

Yee, S., & Kokin, L. (1978). *Got me a story.* San Francisco: St. John's Educational Threshold Center.

Zolotow, C. (1972). *William's doll.* New York: Harper & Row.

Animal Stories and Anti-Bias Themes

Here is an additional list of children's books that address themes related to anti-bias interactions between animals. They are fun supplements to the books that more directly address anti-bias issues with people.

Alexander, M. (1976). *I sure am glad to see you, Blackboard Bear*. New York: Dial. (Ages 3–4)
Friendship: An imaginary bear helps a child solve problems with playmates. Sharing and caring discussed.

Burningham, J. (1973). *Mr. Gumpy's motor car*. New York: Crowell. (Ages 2–4)
Cooperation: When a car gets stuck in the mud, everyone has to help push.

dePaola, T. (1981). *The hunter and the animals*. New York: Holiday House. (Ages 4–7)
Activism: A hunter changes his relationship toward the animals by breaking his gun.

Galdone, P. (1973). *The Little Red Hen*. Boston: Houghton Mifflin. (Ages 3–5)
Being fair and Activism: Animals who don't help do the work don't get to share the fruits of the work.

Hadithij, M., & Kennaway, A. (1983). *Crafty Chameleon*. Boston: Little, Brown. (Ages 3–5)
Being fair and Activism: A small animal teaches two big animals a lesson about being bullies.

Henkes, K. (1987). *Sheila Rae, the brave*. New York: Greenwillow. (Ages 4–5)
Courage and Friendship: About being brave and about when you need support.

Hoban, R., & Hoban, L. (1969). *Best friends for Frances*. New York: Scholastic. (Ages 4–5)
Friendship: How a threesome can be best friends.

Iwamura, K. (1984). *Ton and Pon*. New York: Bradbury. (Ages 2–4)
Cooperation: Two different-sized friends figure out how to do a job together.

Lionni, L. (1967). *Frederick*. New York: Pantheon. (Ages 3–5)
Appreciating differences: The value of the mouse who is an artist to the mouse community.

Lionni, L. (1968). *The biggest house in the world*. New York: Pantheon. (Ages 3–5)
Materialism: A snail learns that bigger and more is not always best.

Lionni, L. (1970). *Fish is fish*. New York: Pantheon. (Ages 3–5)
Appreciating differences and Friendship: Fish and frog learn important lessons about the value of each one's way of life.

Lionni, L. (1973). *Swimmy*. New York: Knopf. (Ages 3–5)
Cooperation and Activism: Little fish learn to stop a bully by working together.

Lionni, L. (1983). *Cornelius*. New York: Pantheon. (Ages 3–5)
Appreciating differences: A crocodile learns about the problems and values of being different.

Martin, J. B. (1984). *Bizzy Bones and Uncle Ezra*. New York: Lothrop, Lee & Shepard. (Ages 3–5)
Activism: Uncle Ezra acts on his environment to make it work for Bizzy and himself.

Pelt, B. (1986). *Zeila Zorek and Zodiak*. Boston: Houghton Mifflin. (Ages 4–5)
Appreciating differences and Friendship: A zebra and ostrich learn the value of friendship and differences.

Steig, W. (1971). *Amos and Boris*. New York: Puffin. (Ages 4–5)
Appreciating differences and Friendship: The mutual respect, help, and friendship of a mouse and a whale.

Seuss, Dr. (1950). *Yertle the Turtle and other stories*. New York: Random House. (Ages 4–5)
Self appreciation; Misuses of power: Yertle the Turtle learns about the importance of the turtles "on the bottom." Gertrude McFuzz learns about liking herself as he is. In "The Big Brag," a rabbit and a bear learn about the foolishness of competition.

Vincent, G. (1982). *Ernest and Celestine*. New York: Greenwillow. (Ages 2–3)
Friendship: A bear and a mouse live together and learn an important lesson about caring for each other.

Waber, B. (1966). *You look ridiculous*. Boston: Houghton Mifflin. (Ages 3–5)
Self-appreciation: A hippopotamus learns about accepting oneself.

Curriculum Materials

Some anti-bias materials are found in established commercial educational supply catalogues and stores. However, many are not. Knowing how to locate alternative sources is an important skill. Alternative presses, bookstores, and educational supply stores come and go. Don't get discouraged; look for another one. Often, they do not have the financial resources to advertise widely, so becoming aware of them requires getting into the networks of people involved in anti-bias issues. Most communities have some such network. In large cities there may be different, although overlapping, networks.

The list of resources here is a starting place. Once you have begun using a few of them you will also discover other sources of materials and people with whom to network. Doing your own community survey to identify local organizations and stores that have anti-bias curriculum supplies is key. There are several ways to do this:

- Check the telephone book for alternative bookstores, women's bookstores, "ethnic" bookstores, and college bookstores. If your community doesn't have any, check if the biggest city in your state does (phone directories are in public libraries).

- Check if there are women's centers, ethnic cultural centers, gay/lesbian centers, and regional centers for the disabled in your city and at local colleges, state colleges, or a large university in your state. Contact your state department of health for regional centers for the disabled.

- Contact support/advocacy groups in your community that address anti-bias issues. They may know of places to purchase curriculum supplies and books. Possibilities are: church social action committees, local or state chapters of NOW (National Organization for Women), peace groups, groups for disabled rights (these include organization for specific disabilities, parents' groups, legal centers), American Friends Service Committee, and gay/lesbian rights groups. People who work in these groups want to share their information, so ask!

- Contact crafts people in your community who may be able to help you make curriculum materials (posters, puzzles, dolls, books).

- Be persistent!

Afro-Am Education Materials, 819 S. Wabash Ave., Chicago, IL 60605. 312-791-1611.
Catalogue of books, records, dolls, posters, and puzzles.

American Brotherhood for the Blind, Twin Vision Books, 18440 Oxnard St., Tarzana, CA 91356. 818-343-2022.
This organization has a lending library of children's books that are in both print and Braille.

American Indian Resource Center, Huntington Park Library, 6518 Miles Ave., Huntington Park, CA 90255. 213-583-1461.
Books and curriculum ideas about Native Americans.

Bilingual Publicatons Co., 1996 Broadway, New York, NY 10023. 212-873-2067.
Books in Spanish for all grade levels; many about Puerto Rican and Mexican-American people.

Chapel Hill Training Outreach Project, Merritt Mill Rd., Lincoln Center, Chapel Hill, NC 27514. 919-967-8295.
Easy-to-follow patterns for making dolls, including those with disabilities.

Children's Book and Music Center, 2500 Santa Monica Blvd., Santa Monica, CA 90406-1130. 800-443-1856 (in California, 213-829-0215).
Books and records for children; some teacher resources.

Children's Book Press, 5925 Doyle St., Suite U, Emeryville, CA 94608. 415-428-1991.
Stories about children of color living in North America.

Choice Puzzles—Non-Sexist Puzzles for Children, 1608 E. Republican, #1, Seattle, WA 98112. 206-325-4882.
Quality puzzles handcrafted from color photographs of women (carpenter, electrician, welder, bicycle racers) and men (folk dancer, hairdresser, early childhood teacher, and quiltmaker).

Claudia's Caravan, P.O. Box 1582, Alameda, CA 94501. 415-521-7871.
Extensive collection of multilingual, multicultural materials.

Community Playthings and *Equipment for the Handicapped*, Route 213, Rifton, NY 12471. 914-658-3141.
Quality equipment for children who are disabled.

Council on Interracial Books for Children, 1841 Broadway, New York, NY 10023. 212-757-5339.
Educational materials for adults and children (filmstrips, articles, curriculum, books on many anti-bias issues).

Creative Concepts for Children, P.O. Box 8697, Scottsdale, AZ 85252-8697. 602-483-9274.
Nonsexist, multicultural puppets. Also made to order and personalized.

Disability Rights Education and Defense Fund, 2212 Sixth St., Berkeley, CA 94710. 415-644-2555.
Materials about legal rights of people with disabilities, current struggles, posters.

Education Development Center, Inc., 55 Chapel St., Newton, MA 02160. 617-969-7100.
"We are family," black-and-white poster displaying a collection of 32 photographs of a variety of families. Multiracial and multigenerational. Also location of the Women's Educational Equity Act Publishing Center, which has curriculum

and teacher in-service materials about sex inequities in education.

Educational Equity Concepts, 114 E. 32nd St., 3rd Floor, Room 306, New York, NY 10016. 212-725-1803.

Early childhood curriculum guides and resource materials.

Faces: The Magazine About People, Cobblestone Publishing, 20 Grove St., Peterborough, NH 03458. 603-924-7209.

Source for photos showing diversity.

Feminist Press, Talman Co., 150 Fifth Ave., Suite 514, New York, NY 10011. 800-537-8894.

Children's and adult books, in-service materials about women and sexism.

Firefly Books, Ltd., 3520 Pharmacy Ave., Unit 1-C, Scarborough, Ontario M1W 2T8, Canada. 416-499-8412.

Distributes Annick Press books.

Gallaudet College for the Deaf, Office of Public Relations, 800 Florida Ave., N.E., T-6, Washington, DC 20002. 202-651-5505 (voice and TTY).

The college issues a list of organizations and programs serving people who are hearing impaired. From this list you may find hearing aid dealers and/or people who are hearing impaired who would talk in your classroom.

Global Village Toys, 2210 Wiltshire Blvd., Suite 262, Santa Monica, CA 90403. 213-459-5188.

Excellent early childhood books and materials for implementing anti-bias curriculum.

Gryphon House, Inc., Early Childhood Books, 3706 Otis St., P.O. Box 275, Mt. Rainier, MD 20712. 800-638-0928.

Nonsexist, multiracial books that are inclusive of people who are differently abled.

Hal's Pals, P.O. Box 3490, Winter Park, CO 80482.

Soft sculpture dolls depicting children with disabilities. Will custom make dolls.

Howe Press, Perkins School for the Blind, 175 N. Beacon St., Watertown, MA 02172. 617-924-3434.

Books in both print and Braille.

Interracial Family Alliance, P.O. Box 16248, Houston, TX 77222. 713-454-5018.

This organization will provide you with addresses for local interracial family organizations.

Institute for Peace and Justice, 4144 Lindell, Room 122, St. Louis, MO 63108. 314-533-4445.

Curriculum and media about racism, sexism, and peace education for children, teachers, and parents.

Japanese American Curriculum Project, 414 Third St., San Mateo, CA 94401. 415-343-9408.

Japanese-American and other Asian-American curriculum materials.

Kar-Ben Copies, Inc., 6800 Tildenwood Lane, Rockville, MD 20852. 301-984-8733.

Books reflecting the Jewish tradition.

Lakeshore Curriculum Materials, 2695 E. Domingues St., Carson, CA 90749. 213-537-8600.

Multicultural materials including Native American, Asian, Latino, and Black dolls of both sexes, excellent puzzles, doll families (Black, Latino, White).

Liberation Bookstore, 421 Lenox Ave., New York, NY 10037. 212-281-4615.

Adult and children's books on Afro-Americans.

Lollipop Power, Carolina Wren Press, P.O. Box 277, Carrboro, NC 27510.

Free catalogue listing antisexist, nonracist children's books.

National Association for Hearing and Speech Action, 10801 Rockville Pike, Rockville, MD 20852. 800-638-8255 or 301-897-8682 (voice and TTY).

Will send one copy of the manual alphabet (finger spelling) on request.

National Association for the Deaf, 814 Thayer Ave., Silver Spring, MD 20910. 301-587-1788 (office, voice and TTY); 301-587-6262 (bookstore, voice and TTY).

Pamphlets and bookstore catalogue; information about local chapters.

Navajo Curriculum Center Press, Rough Rock Demonstration School, P.O. Box 217, Chinle, AZ 86503. 602-728-3311.

Wonderful source for materials on Navajo culture.

New Seeds Press, P.O. Box 9488, Berkeley, CA 94709. 415-540-7576.

Nonsexist children's books.

Office for Civil Rights, Office for Special Concerns, U.S. Department of Education, 330 C St., S.W., Washington, DC 20202. 202-732-1213.

Materials about civil rights.

Organization for Equal Education of the Sexes, 808 Union St., Brooklyn, NY 11215. 718-783-0332.

Posters of women of all cultures. "Men Working . . . Helping People" poster.

Puerto Rican Resource Units, State Education Department, Bureau of Bilingual Education, Albany, NY 12234. 518-474-2121.

Curriculum materials and comprehensive bibliography.

Red & Black Books, 430 15th Ave. E., Seattle, WA 98112. 206-322-7323.

Books covering women's issues, minorities, gays and lesbians; children's books.

Regional Centers (for the disabled).

Called by different names in different states and cities. Call your State Department of Health for information about regional centers in your state.

Resource Access Group, Administration for Children, Youth and Families (ACYF), U.S. Department of Health and Human Services, Sixth & D Streets, S.W., Donohue Bldg., Washington, DC 20201. 202-755-7762.

Curriculum and teacher training materials about disability issues.

Resource Center for Nonviolence, 515 Broadway, Santa Cruz, CA 95060. 408-423-1626.

Materials on conflict resolution and peace education.

Sports and Spokes, 5201 N. 19th Ave., Suite 111, Phoenix, AZ 85015. 602-246-9426.

This magazine provides information on wheelchair sports and recreation. Multiracial photographs of athletes who use wheelchairs are available on loan or to be purchased.

Syracuse Cultural Workers, Box 6367, Syracuse, NY 13217. 315-474-1132.

Excellent posters, pictures in many aspects of anti-bias curriculum. Catalogue.

The 52 Association, Inc., 441 Lexington Ave., New York, NY 10017.

Pictures of people who are differently abled participating in sports activities are available free of charge upon request.

United Indians of All Tribes Foundation, P.O. Box 99100, Seattle, WA 98199. 206-285-4425.

Curriculum and books about Northwest and Alaskan Native Americans.

University Bookstore, 4326 University Way, N.E., Seattle, WA 98105. 206-634-3400.

Good anti-bias materials; will do mail orders.

Women's Action Alliance, Inc., 370 Lexington Ave., New York, NY 10017. 212-532-8330.

Men in the Nurturing Role. A series of eight black-and-white photographs of men in nurturing roles. Multiracial and intergenerational.

People at Work. Twenty-four multiethnic pictures of women and men working at a wide variety of jobs, some nontraditional for the sex shown. Complete teaching guide included.

Equal Play. Twice-a-year journal with articles about anti-bias issues.

Other nonsexist, multiracial materials available.

Adult Books

How Children Develop Identity and Attitudes

Disabilities

Adams, B. (1979). *Like it is: Facts and feelings about handicaps from kids who know.* New York: Walker.

Conant, S., & Budoff, M. (1983). Patterns of awareness in children's understanding of disabilities. *Mental Retardation, 21,* 119–125.

Eggers, N. (1983). Influencing preschoolers' awareness and feelings regarding depicted physical disability. *Early Childhood Development and Care, 12*(2), 199–206.

Roth, W. (1981). *The handicapped speak.* Jefferson, NC: McFarland.

Gender

Booth-Butterfield, M. (1981). The cues we don't question: Unintentional gender socialization in the day care. *Day Care and Early Education, 8*(4), 20–22.

Dweck, C. S., & Dweck, A. L. (1980). Sex differences in learned helplessness. *Developmental Psychology, 14,* 268–276.

Fairchild, B. & Haywood, N. (1981). *Now that you know: What every parent should know about homosexuality.* New York: Harcourt Brace & Jovanovich.

Heron, A. (Ed.). (1983). *One teenager in ten: Testimony by gay and lesbian youth.* New York: Warner.

Homophobia and education [special issue]. (1983). *Interracial Books for Children Bulletin, 14*(3 &4).

Honig, A. S. (1983). Sex role socialization in early childhood. *Young Children, 38*(6), 57–80.

Pogrebin, L. C. (1980). *Growing up free: Raising your child in the 80's.* New York: McGraw-Hill.

Serbin, L., & Connor, (1974). Sex-typing of children's play preferences and patterns of cognitive performance. *Journal of Genetic Psychology, 134,* 310–316.

Serbin, L., & O'Leary, D. (1975, December). How nursery schools teach girls to shut up. *Psychology Today,* pp. 56–58, 102–103.

Serbin, L. (1980). Play activities and the development of visual spatial skills. *Equal Play, 1*(4), 5.

Race and ethnicity

Barnes, E. (1980). The Black community as the source of positive self-concept for Black children. In R. L. Jones (Ed.), *Black psychology* (pp. 106–130). New York: Harper & Row.

Beuf, A. (1977). *Red children in White America.* Philadelphia: University of Pennsylvania Press.

Citron, A. (1969). *The rightness of Whiteness: The world of the White child in a segregated society.* Office of Urban Education, College of Education, Wayne State University, Detroit, MI 48202.

Dennis, R. (1981). Socialization and racism: The White experience. In B. P. Bowser & R. G. Hunt (Eds.), *Impact of racism on White Americans* (pp. 71–86). Beverly Hills, CA: Sage Publications.

Derman-Sparks, L., Higa, C. T., & Sparks, W. (1980). Children, race and racism: How race awareness develops. *Interracial Books for Children Bulletin, 11*(3 & 4), 3–9.

Garcia, E. (1980). Bilingualism in early childhood. *Young Children, 35*(4), 52–66.

Gay, K. (1987). *The rainbow effect: Interracial families.* New York: Franklin Watts.

Gutierrez, M. (1982). *Chicano parents' perceptions of their children's racial/cultural awareness.* Unpublished master's thesis, Pacific Oaks College, Pasadena, CA.

Katz, P. (1982). Development of children's racial awareness and intergroup attitudes. In L. G. Katz (Ed.), *Current topics in early childhood education* (Vol. 4, pp. 17–54). Norwood, NJ: Ablex.

Milner, D. (1983). *Children and race.* London: Ward Lock Educational.

Nobles, W. W. (1980). Extended self: Rethinking the so-called Negro self-concept. In R. L. Jones (Ed.), *Black psychology* (pp. 99–105). New York: Harper & Row.

Phinney, J., & Rotherman, M. (Eds.). (1987). *Children's ethnic socialization: Pluralism and development.* Beverly Hills, CA: Sage Publications.

Shackford, K. (1984). Interracial children: Growing up healthy in an unhealthy society. *Interracial Books for Children Bulletin, 15*(6), 4–6.

Spencer, M. B., Brookins, G. K., & Allen, W. R. (Eds.). (1985). *Beginnings: The social and affective development of Black children.* Hillsdale, NJ: Erlbaum.

Wardle, F. (1987). Are you sensitive to interracial children's special identity needs? *Young Children, 42*(2), 53–59.

Class

Coles, R. (1977). *Privileged ones: The well-off and the rich in America.* Boston: Little, Brown.

Draper, G. (1985). A child's eye view of the U.S. economy: Some interviews. *Interracial Books for Children Bulletin, 16*(2–3), 17–21.

Leahy, R. (Ed.). (1983). *The child's construction of inequality.* New York: Academic.

Additional Curriculum Resources

Disabilities

Froschl, M., Colon, L., Rubin, E., & Sprung, B. (1984). *Including all of us: An early childhood curriculum about disabilities.* New York: Educational Equity Concepts.

Project Head Start. (undated). *Mainstreaming preschoolers:*

Eight manuals. Washington, DC: Head Start Bureau, Administration for Children, Youth and Families.

Souweine, J., Crimmins, S., & Mazel, C. (1981). *Mainstreaming: Ideas for teaching young children.* Washington, DC: NAEYC.

Gender

Beaglehole, R. (1983). Validating all families. *Interracial Books for Children Bulletin, 14*(7 & 8), 24–26.

Beginning Equal Project. (1983). *Beginning equal: A manual about non-sexist childrearing for infants and toddlers.* New York: Women's Action Alliance and Pre-School Associaton.

Jenkins, J. (1979). *Growing up equal: Activities and resources for parents and teachers of young children.* Englewood Cliffs, NJ: Prentice-Hall.

Sprung, B. (1975). *Non-sexist education for young children.* New York: Citation.

Race and ethnicity

Council on Interracial Books for Children. (undated). *Unlearning "Indian" stereotypes.* New York: Author.

Kendall, F. (1983). *Diversity in the classroom: A multicultural approach to the education of young children.* New York: Teachers College Press, Columbia University.

Ramsey, P. G. (1987). *Teaching and learning in a diverse world.* New York: Teacher's College Press, Columbia University.

Saracho, O., & Spodek, B. (Eds.). (1983). *Understanding the multicultural experience in early childhood education.* Washington, DC: NAEYC.

Shannon-Thornberry, M. (1982). *The alternative celebrations catalogue.* New York: Pilgrim Press.

Wardle, F. (1987). Building positive images: Interracial children and their families. In B. Neugebauer (Ed.), *Alike and different: Exploring our humanity with young children.* (pp. 97–105). Redmond, WA: Exchange Press.

Culture, learning styles, and curriculum

Ashton-Warner, S. (1986). *Teacher.* New York: Simon & Schuster.

Cazden, C. B. (1981). *Language in early childhood education* (rev. ed.). Washington, DC: NAEYC.

France, P. (1983). Working with young bilingual children. *Early Child Development and Care, 10,* 283–292.

Kitano, M. (1980). Early childhood education for Asian American children. *Young Children, 35*(2), 13–26.

Rashid, H. M. (1984). Promoting biculturalism in young African-American children. *Young Children, 39*(2), 12–23.

Williams, L., De Gaetano, Y., Sutherland, I., & Harrington, C. (1985). *Alerta: A multicultural-bilingual approach to teaching young children.* Reading, MA: Addison-Wesley.

Multiple issues

Banfield, B., Moore, R., Califf, J., Knox, C., & Hoffman, L. (1980). *Winning justice for all.* New York: Council on Interracial Books for Children.

Edicot, F., & Thomas, B. (1979). *The city kids teacher's book.* Toronto: Ontario Institute for Studies in Education.

Fiarotta, P., & Fiarotta, N. (1977). *Be what you want to be!* New York: Workman.

Guidelines for Selecting Bias-Free Textbooks and Storybooks. (1980). New York: Council on Interracial Books for Children.

Multicultural Project for Communication and Education. (1981). *Caring for children in a social context.* Cambridge, MA: Author.

Neugebauer, B. (Ed.). (1987). *Alike and different: Exploring our common humanity with young children.* Redmond, WA: Exchange Press.

Schniedewind, N., & Davidson, E. (1983). *Open minds to equality: A source book of learning activities to promote race, sex, class and age equity.* Englewood Cliffs, NJ: Prentice-Hall.

Sprung, B., Froschl, M., & Campbell, P. (1985). *Young children and the scientific method.* New York: Educational Equity Concepts.

Stein, S. (1988). Shipboard reflections—When the chosen journey is rough. *Child Care Information Exchange, 59,* 39–42.

Wenning, J., & Wortis, S. (1986). *Made by human hands: A curriculum for teaching young children about work and working people.* Cambridge, MA: The Multicultural Project for Communication and Education, Inc.

Resource books

Froschl, M., & Sprung, B. (1988). *Resources for educational equity: A guide for grades pre-K–12.* New York: Garland.

Ramsey, P. G., Vold, E. B., & Williams, L. R. (1989). *Multicultural education: A source book.* New York: Garland.

Raising Adult Consciousness

Disabilities

Brightman, A. (1983). *Ordinary moments: The disabled experience.* Baltimore: University Park Press.

Browne, S. (Ed.). (1985). *With the power of each breath: Writings by disabled women.* New York: Norton.

Campling, J. (1981). *Images of ourselves: Women with disabilities talk.* Boston: Routledge & Kegan Paul.

Gliedman, J., & Roth, W. (1980). *The unexpected minority: Handicapped children in America.* New York: Harcourt Brace Jovanovich.

Orlansky, M., & Howard W. (1981). *Voices: Interviews with handicapped people.* Westerville, OH: Merrill.

Women and Disabilities Awareness Project. (1984). *Building a community: A manual exploring issues of women and disability.* New York: Educational Equity Concepts.

Gender

Barnett, M. (1986). Sex bias in the helping behavior presented in children's books. *Journal of Genetic Psychology, 147*(3), 343–352.

Belenky, M., Clinchy, B., Goldberger, N., & Tarule, J. (1986). *Women's ways of knowing: The development of self, voice. and mind*. New York: Basic.

Best, R. (1983). *We've all got scars: What little boys and little girls learn in elementary school*. Bloomington: Indiana University Press.

Carmichael, C. (1977). *Non-sexist childraising*. Boston: Beacon.

Condry, J. C., & Ross, D. F. (1985). Sex and aggression: The influence of gender label on the perception of aggression in children. *Child Development, 56*, 225–233.

David, D., & Brannon, R. (Eds). (1976). *The forty-nine percent majority: The male sex role*. New York: Random House.

Goodman, J. (1983). Out of the closet, but paying the price: Lesbian and gay characters in children's literature. *Interracial Books for Children Bulletin, 14*(3 & 4), 13–15.

Hull, G., Scott, P., & Smith, B. (Eds.). (1982). *But some of us are brave*. Old Westbury, NY: The Feminist Press.

Magdelina, M., & Del Castillo, A. (1980). *Mexican women in U.S. struggles: Past and present*. Los Angeles: Chicano Studies Research Center, University of California at Los Angeles.

Miller, C., & Swift, K. (1980). *The handbook of nonsexist writing*. New York: Barnes & Noble.

Pollack, S., & Vaughn, J.. (1987). *Politics of the heart: A lesbian parenting anthology*. Ithaca, NY: Firebrand Books.

Sadker, M., & Sadker, D. (1982). *Sex equity handbook for schools*. New York: Longman.

Scanzoni, L., & Mollenkott, V.R. (1978). *Is the homosexual my neighbor: Another Christian view*. New York: Harper & Row.

Seifer, N. (1976). *Nobody speaks for me: Self-portraits of American working class women*. New York: Simon & Schuster.

Sprung, B. (Ed.). (1978). *Perspectives on non-sexist early childhood education*. New York: Teachers College Press, Columbia University.

Tinney, J. (1983). Interconnections: Racism, sexism, heterosexism and homophobia. *Interracial Books for Children Bulletin, 12*(3 & 4), 4–6.

Twenty Questions About Homosexuality. (undated). New York: National Gay Task Force.

Race and ethnicity

Brandt, G. L. (1986). *The realization of anti-racist teaching*. London: The Falmer Press.

Chessler, M. (1981). Creating and maintaining interracial coalitions. In B. P. Bowser & R. G. Hunt (Eds.), *Impact of racism on White Americans* (pp. 217–244). Beverly Hills, CA: Sage Publications.

Cross, W., Jr. (1980). Models of psychological nigrescence: A literature review. In R. L. Jones (Ed.), *Black psychology* (pp. 82–98). New York: Harper & Row.

Dorris, M. (1978). Why I'm NOT thankful for Thanksgiving. *Interracial Books for Children Bulletin, 9*(7), 6–9.

Freire, P. (1970). *Pedagogy of the oppressed*. New York: Seabury.

Guthrie, R. (1976). *Even the rat was white: A historical view of psychology*. New York: Harper & Row.

Jones, J. (1981). The concept of racism and its changing reality. In B.P. Bowser & R.G. Hunt (Eds.), *Impact of racism on White Americans* (pp. 27–50). Beverly Hills, CA: Sage Publications.

Katz, J. (1979). *White awareness: A handbook for anti-racism training*. Norman: University of Oklahoma Press.

Phillips, C. B. (1988). Nurturing diversity for today's children and tomorrow's leaders. *Young Children, 43*(2), 42–27.

Pierce, C. (1980). Social trace contaminants: Subtle indicators of racism in TV. In S. They & R. Abelis (Eds.), *Television and social behavior* (pp. 249–257). Hillsdale, NJ: Erlbaum.

Ryan, W. (1976). *Blaming the victim*. New York: Random House.

Smith, L. (1961). *Killers of the dream*. New York: Norton.

Spencer, D. (1988). Transitional bilingual education and the socialization of immigrants. *Harvard Educational Review, 58*, 133–153.

Cultural issues

Chu-Chang, M. (Ed.). (1983). *Asian- and Pacific-American perspectives in bilingual education: Comparative research*. New York: Teachers College Press, Columbia University.

Escobedo, T. H. (Ed.). (1983). *Early childhood bilingual education*. New York: Teachers College Press, Columbia University.

Hale-Benson, J. (1986). *Black children: Their roots, culture and learning styles*. Baltimore: Johns Hopkins University Press.

Smitherman, G. (1977). *Talkin' and testifyin': The language of Black America*. Boston: Houghton Mifflin.

Multiple issues

Council on Interracial Books for Children. (1988). *Bias and today's research* (five pamphlets). New York: Author.

History of peoples' struggles for equality and justice

Acuna, R. (1972). *Occupied America: The Chicano's struggle toward liberation*. New York: Harper & Row.

Baxandall, R. (Ed.). (1976). *America's working women: A documentary history—1600 to the present*. New York: Random House.

Boyer, R. & Morais, H. (1970). *Labor's untold story* (3rd ed.). United Electric, Radio and Machine Workers of America, 11 E. 51st St., New York, NY 10022.

Chen, J. (1980). *The Chinese of America*. New York: Harper & Row.

Council on Interracial Books for Children. (1979). *Chronicles of American Indian protest*. New York: Author.

CIBC History Project. (1988). *Thinking and rethinking U.S. history*. New York: Council on Interracial Books for Children.

Hansen, A., & Mitson, B. (Eds.) (1974). Voices long silent: An oral inquiry into the Japanese-American evacuation. Fullerton, CA: CSUF Oral History Project.

Harding, V. (1981). *There is a river: The Black struggle for freedom in America.* New York: Harcourt Brace Jovanovich.

Jacobs, P., Landau, S., & Pell, E. (1971). *To serve the devil: A documentary analysis of America's racial history and why it has been kept hidden* (Vols. 1 & 2). New York: Vintage.

Kitano, H. (1969). *Japanese-Americans: The evolution of a subculture.* Englewood Cliffs, NJ: Prentice-Hall.

Weinberg, M. (1977). *A chance to learn: The history of race and education in the United States.* Cambridge, England: Cambridge University Press.

Zinn, H. (1980). *A people's history of the United States.* New York: Harper & Row.

Media

America's women of color [filmstrips]. Women's Educational Equity Act Publishing Center, Education Development Corporation, 55 Chapel St., Newton, MA 02610.

Anti-bias curriculum [videotape]. Pacific Oaks Extension Services, 714 W. California Blvd., Pasadena, CA 91105.

Black history: Lost, stolen or strayed [film]. Kit Parker Films, 1245 10th St., Monterey, CA 93940-3692.

Chinese Americans: Realities and myths [filmstrip]. Institute for Peace and Justice, 4144 Lindell, Room 122, St. Louis, MO 63108.

Council on Interracial Books for Children, 1841 Broadway, New York, NY 10023:
Understanding institutional racism [filmstrip].
Understanding institutional sexism [filmstrip].
Unlearning "Indian" stereotypes [filmstrip].
Unlearning Asian American stereotypes [filmstrip].
Unlearning Chicano and Puerto Rican stereotypes [filmstrip].
Identifying sexism and racism in children's books [filmstrip].
Childcare shapes the future: Anti-sexism [filmstrip].
Childcare shapes the future: Anti-racism [filmstrip].

Frontline: A class divided [videotape]. Public Broadcasting Service, 1320 Braddock Place, Alexandria, VA 22314.

Japanese-Americans: An inside look [filmstrip]. Japanese American Curriculum Project, 414 Third Ave., San Mateo, CA 94401.

National Public Radio, Customer Service, P.O. Box 55417, Madison, WI 53705:
Hispanic heritage [cassette; order number VW-79-09-09].
The Japanese-American: Four generations of adaptation [cassette; order number CR-79-08-17].
Native American youth: The new warriors [cassette; order number HO-80-11-26].
Proverbs: Wit and wisdom of Afro-Americans [cassette; order number HO-84-04-18].

Not all parents are straight [videotape]. Full Frame Production, 363 Brannan St., San Francisco, CA 94107.

Six Native American families [6 filmstrips]. Society for Visual Education, 1345 Diversey Parkway, Chicago, IL 60614.

Women and disability: The issues [videotape]. Educational Equity Concepts, 114 E. 32nd St., 3rd Floor, Room 306, New York, NY 10016.

Women on the march [film]. National Film Board of Canada, 1251 Avenue of the Americas, New York, NY 10020.

Women in American history [filmstrip]. Educational Activities, Inc., P.O. Box 392, Freeport, NY 11520.

STEREOTYPES WORKSHEET

GENDER STEREOTYPES

Male Stereotypes

Active
Brave
Strong
Rough
Competitive
Inventive
Intelligent, Logical
Quiet, Easygoing
Decisive, Problem-solving
Messy
Tall
Mechanical
Independent
Leader, Innovator
Expressing anger
Unemotional
Playing or working outdoors
Unconcerned about appearance
As parent, playing with children
Having innate need for adventure

Female Stereotypes

Passive
Frightened
Weak
Gentle
Giving up easily
Unoriginal
Silly, Illogical
Shrewish, Nagging
Confused
Neat
Short
Inept
Dependent
Follower, Conformer
Controlling anger
Emotional
Playing or working indoors
Concerned about appearance
As parent, nurturing children
Having innate need for marriage and motherhood

STEREOTYPES OF ASIAN-AMERICANS

Male Stereotypes

smiling, polite, and small
servile, bowing
bucktoothed and squinty-eyed
mystical, inscrutable, and wise
expert in martial arts
exotic foreigner
sinister, sly
places no value on human life
model minority who worked hard and "made it"
super-student

Female Stereotypes

sweet, well-behaved girl
sexy, sweet "China Doll"
sexy, evil "Dragon Lady"
overbearing, old-fashioned grandmother

STEREOTYPES OF AFRO-AMERICANS

Male Stereotypes

the shuffling, eye-rolling, fearful, superstitious comic
the gentle, self-sacrificing older man
the athletic super-jock
the smooth-talking con man
the super-stud
the stupid, but comical, little boy
the rough, dangerous criminal
the loudly-dressed, happy-go-lucky buffoon
the exotic primitive

Female Stereotypes

the big-bosomed "mammy," loyal to whites
the big, bossy mother or maid—commander of the household
the sexy temptress
the stupid, but sweet, little girl
the tragic mulatto

STEREOTYPES OF LATINOS

Male Stereotypes

sombrero-wearing, serape-clad, sandaled man or boy
man taking a siesta near a cactus or an overburdened burro
ignorant, cheerful, lazy peon
sneaky, knife-wielding, mustached bandit
humble, big-eyed, poor-but-honest boy
teenage gang member
macho boaster and supreme-commander of household

Occupational Stereotypes

impoverished migrant workers (most Latinos actually live in cities)
unemployed barrio dwellers

Female Stereotypes

hard working, poor, submissive, self-sacrificing religious mother of many
sweet, small, shy, gentle girl
sexy, loud, fiery, young woman (who often prefers a white man to Latino men)
undereducated, submissive, nice girl with marriage as a life goal

STEREOTYPES OF NATIVE AMERICANS

Male Stereotypes

savage, bloodthirsty "native"
stoic, loyal follower
drunken, mean thief
drunken comic
hunter, tracker
noble child of nature
wise old chief
evil medicine man
brave boy, endowed by nature with special "Indian" qualities

Occupational Stereotypes

hunters
cattle thieves
warriors
unemployed loafers
craftspeople

Female Stereotypes

heavyset, workhorse "squaw"
"Indian princess" (depicted with European features and often in love with a white man for whom she is willing to sacrifice her life)

STEREOTYPES OF DIFFERENTLY ABLED PEOPLE

Male Stereotypes

evil blind man with unnatural powers
village "idiot"
evil "peg-leg" or "hook-arm"
pitiful paraplegic
ugly "hunchback"
happy "moron"
deaf and "dumb" sad character
super-"cripple"
pitiful, little "cripple"
childlike dwarf
"insane" criminal
one-eyed pirate
"hard of hearing" crank

Female Stereotypes

"hunchbacked" old crone
blind witch
pitiful blind girl
pitiful, little "cripple"
sexless sad creature
victim of violence
evil witch with a cane
self-pitying whiner

TEN QUICK WAYS TO ANALYZE CHILDREN'S BOOKS FOR SEXISM AND RACISM

Both in school and out, young children are exposed to racist and sexist attitudes. These attitudes—expressed over and over in books and in other media—gradually distort their perceptions until stereotypes and myths about minorities and women are accepted as reality. It is difficult for a librarian or teacher to convince children to question society's attitudes. But if a child can be shown how to detect racism and sexism in a book, the child can proceed to transfer the perception to wider areas. The following ten guidelines are offered as a starting point in evaluation of children's books from this perspective.

1. Check the Illustrations

Look for Stereotypes. A stereotype is an over-simplified generalization about a particular group, race, or sex, which usually carries derogatory implications. Some infamous (overt) stereotypes of Blacks are the happy-go-lucky, watermelon-eating Sambo and the fat, eye-rolling "mammy"; of Chicanos, the sombrero-wearing peon, or the fiesta-loving, macho bandito; of Asian Americans, the inscrutable, slant-eyed "Oriental"; of Native Americans, the naked savage or "primitive" craftsperson and his "squaw"; of Puerto Ricans, the switch-blade-toting, teenage gang member; of women, the completely domesticated mother, the demure, doll-loving little girl or the wicked stepmother. While you may not always find stereotypes in the blatant forms described, look for variations which in any way demean or ridicule characters because of their race or sex.

Look for Tokenism. If there are minority characters in the illustrations, do they look just like whites except for being tinted or colored in? Do all minority faces look stereotypically alike, or are they depicted as genuine individuals with distinctive features?

Who's Doing What? Do the illustrations depict minorities in subservient and passive roles or in leadership and action roles? Are males the active "doers" and females the inactive observers?

2. Check the Story Line

The liberation movements have led publishers to weed out many insulting passages, particularly from stories with Black themes and from books depicting female characters; however, racist and sexist attitudes still find expression in less obvious ways. The following checklist suggests some of the subtle, covert forms of bias to watch for.

Standard for Success. Does it take "white" behavior standards for a minority person to "get ahead"? Is "making it" in the dominant white society projected as the only ideal? To gain acceptance and approval, do third world persons have to exhibit extraordinary qualities—excel in sports, get A's, etc.? In friendships between white and third world children, is it the third world child who does most of the understanding and forgiving?

Resolution of Problems. How are problems presented, conceived, and resolved in the story? Are minority people considered to be "the problem"? Are the oppressions faced by minorities and women represented as casually related to an unjust society? Are the reasons for poverty and oppression explained, or are they accepted as inevitable? Does the story line encourage passive acceptance or active resistance? Is a particular problem that is faced by a minority person resolved through the benevolent intervention of a white person?

Role of Women. Are the achievements of girls and women based on their own initiative and intelligence, or are they due to their good looks or to their relationship with boys? Are sex roles incidental or critical to characterization and plot? Could the same story be told if the sex roles were reversed?

3. Look at the Lifestyles

Are third world persons and their setting depicted in such a way that they contrast unfavorably with the unstated norm of white, middle-class suburbia? If the minority group in question is depicted as "different," are negative value judgments implied? Are minorities depicted exclusively in ghettos, barrios, or migrant camps? If the illustrations and text attempt to depict another culture, do they go beyond over-simplifications and offer genuine insights into another lifestyle? Look for inaccuracy and inappropriateness in the depiction of other cultures. Watch for instances of the "quaint-natives-in-costume" syndrome (most noticeable in areas like clothing and custom, but extending to behavior and personality traits as well).

4. Weigh the Relationships Between People

Do the whites in the story possess the power, take the leadership, and make the important decisions? Do minorities and females function in essentially supporting, subservient roles?

How are family relationships depicted? In Black families, is the mother always dominant? In Latino families, are there always lots of children? If the family is separated, are societal conditions—unemployment, poverty—cited among the reasons for the separation?

5. Note the Heros

For many years, books showed only "safe" minority heros—those who avoided serious conflict with the white establishment of their time. Minority groups today are insisting on the right to define their own heros (of both sexes) based on their own concepts and struggles for justice.

When minority heros do appear, are they admired for the same qualities that have made white heros famous or because what they have done has benefited white people? Ask this question: "Whose interests is a particular hero really serving?" The interests of the hero's own people? Or the interests of white people?

6. Consider the Effects on a Child's Self-Image

Are norms established which limit any child's aspirations and self-concepts? What effect can it have on third world children to be continuously bombarded with images of the color white as the ultimate in beauty, cleanliness, virtue, etc., and the color black as evil, dirty, menacing, etc.? Does the book reinforce or counteract positive associations with the color white and negative associations with the color black?

What happens to a girl's self-image when she reads that boys perform all of the brave and important deeds? What about a girl's self-esteem if she is not "fair" of skin and slim of body?

In a particular story, is there one or more persons with whom a minority child can readily identify to a positive and constructive end?

7. Consider the Author's or Illustrator's Background

Analyze the biographical material on the jacket flap or the back of the book. If a story deals with a minority theme, what qualifies the author or illustrator to deal with the subject? If the author and illustrator are not members of the minority being written about, is there anything in their background that would specifically recommend them as the creators of this book?

8. Check Out the Author's Perspective

No author can be entirely objective. All authors write from a cultural as well as from a personal context. Children's books in the past have traditionally come from authors who were white and who were members of the middle class, with one result being that a single ethnocentric perspective has dominated children's literature in the United States. With any book in question, read carefully to determine whether the direction of the author's perspective substantially weakens or strengthens the value of his/her written work. Is the perspective patriarchal or feminist? Is it solely Eurocentric or do third world perspectives also surface?

9. Watch for Loaded Words

A word is loaded when it has offensive overtones. Examples of loaded adjectives (usually racist) are "savage," "primitive," "conniving," "lazy," "superstitious," "treacherous," "wily," "crafty," "inscrutable," "docile," and "backward."

Look for sexist language and adjectives that exclude or in any way demean girls or women. Look for use of the male pronoun to refer to both males and females. While the generic use of the word "man" was accepted in the past, its use today is outmoded. The following examples show how sexist language can be avoided: ancestors instead of forefathers; chairperson instead of chairman; community instead of brotherhood; fire-fighters instead of firemen; manufactured instead of man-made; human family instead of family of man.

10. Look at the Copyright Date

Books on minority themes—usually hastily conceived—suddenly began appearing in the mid and late 1960's. There followed a growing number of "minority experience" books to meet the new market demand, but these books were still written by white authors, edited by white editors, and published by white publishers. They therefore reflected a white point of view. Not until the early 1970's did the children's book world begin to even remotely reflect the realities of a pluralistic society. The new direction resulted from the emergence of third world authors writing about their own experiences in an oppressive society. This promising direction has been reversing in the late 1970's. Non-sexist books, with rare exceptions, were not published before 1972 to 1974.

The copyright dates, therefore, can be a clue as to how likely the book is to be overtly racist or sexist, although a recent copyright date, of course, is no guarantee of a book's relevance or sensitivity. The copyright date only means the year the book was published. It usually takes two years—and often much more than that—from the time a manuscript is submitted to the publisher to the time it is actually printed and put on the market. This time lag meant very little in the past, but in a period of rapid change and new consciousness, when children's book publishing is attempting to be "relevant," it is becoming increasingly significant.

SAMPLE PERSONA DOLL STORY

This is an example of a persona doll story used by Kay Taus in her classroom. Make up your own stories about issues relevant to your class.

Additional persona doll stories are available from Kay Taus at Seeds University Elementary School, UCLA, 405 Hilgard Ave., Los Angeles, CA 90024. Write to find out what stories are available on the topics you're interested in and current copying charges.

— Marisela and the Lay-Off —

Background

I grew up, like most of us, with the idea that so-called "intellectual work" was much more valuable than physical labor. Everything in this society teaches us to devalue certain kinds of work and to devalue the people who do it as well. Since my father was a carpenter at one time and a T.V. repairman at another, I grew up with ambivalence. I saw his skilled hands at work yet sensed the prevailing attitudes of the society that negated his skill. I also went to a high school where the majority of other kids were wealthy. I deeply resented the class biases that existed.

Now, as a teacher, I have children of very many different class backgrounds. I want to develop a respect for different kinds of work and an understanding that families have a great variation in the style of life they can afford. Even very young children have already begun to make judgments about their classmates based on clothing or the number of trips to nearby Disneyland.

I tell this story about Marisela and her mother because it deals with two issues. It is respectful about the work Marisela's mother does and appreciates her sewing skill. It also talks about the hard times that result from the loss of a job.

The Story

"Hurry up, Marisela! Andole! I need to get to work!" said her mother, Lupe.

"What do you do at work, Mami?" Marisela asked as they quickly finished their breakfast.

"I make dresses, Marisela. I sew the pieces together on a sewing machine."

"You mean, like my dress?"

"Yes, and other dresses and shirts and skirts too. I work in a factory where lots of women sit at sewing machines and sew. Now we have to get going. I'll tell you more later."

Marisela's mami works very hard. She takes the bus to the factory, or la fábrica, after she walks Marisela to school. When she arrives at work, she goes to her sewing machine. Another worker brings her the pieces of material, already cut into pieces for sleeves, pieces for collars, pieces for fronts and backs, pieces for skirts, and so on. Lupe takes the pieces and begins to put them together on the sewing machine. She works quickly. It is amazing how beautiful the dress looks after she has sewn all the parts together. When the dress is completely finished, another worker comes and puts it, along with others, on big racks. The big racks get rolled outside to trucks, where they are loaded on and taken to department stores or dress stores to be sold. By the time the dress is hanging in a store, waiting to be bought, it has a price tag of $50.00 on it! But Lupe got only about $7.50 for the sewing work that she did on the dress. It doesn't seem fair to her that she does all the work of sewing the dress together and the boss of her factory and the store he sells it to get a lot more money. She likes to sew, but she wishes she got more money. It's hard to pay the rent and buy clothes and food for her and Marisela. Everything costs so much! She also wishes that la fábrica had air conditioning. There are very few windows and in the summertime it gets terribly hot inside when she is working. But she is meeting with some of the other workers to figure out ways to make the job better. Soon, they plan to talk to the boss about making some changes.

On this day Lupe is sewing the pieces together to make pairs of beautiful red overalls.

"Marisela would look so wonderful in these overalls. I wish I could afford to buy them for her!" she thought. Then she got a little angry. "Here I am sewing these overalls together and I can't even afford to buy them! It just doesn't seem fair!" But she kept on working all day until she had a stack of the overalls ready to be loaded and driven to a big, fancy store.

At the end of the day, as she gathered her things together to head for the bus stop, the boss came out and asked her to come into his office.

"Lupe," he said, "this is our slow season. The stores are not ordering as many clothes as they usually do. So we don't have enough work for everyone. I have to lay you off until business gets better. When we have more orders, I'll call you back to work again."

Lupe was stunned! She was getting laid off from work. That meant she wouldn't have a job. And she needed a job to be able to pay for all the things that she and Marisela needed. Sadly, she walked to the bus. She picked up Marisela at her friend's house and together they walked home.

Right away, Marisela knew something was bothering her mami.

"You look very sad, Mami. Que te pasa? What's wrong?"

"Today, I got laid off from my job, Marisela. That means there isn't enough work for everyone to do, so some of us can't go back to work there until there is more to do."

"You mean, you don't have a job anymore?"

"That's right. And I need a job, mija."

"Now you can stay home with me after school," said Marisela.

"That's a nice idea, mija, but we need to have the money from my job. I can't just stay home."

"I'll get a job and help you!"

"Thank you, Marisela. But your job is to go to school. I'll have to start looking right away."

After Marisela went to bed that night, Lupe figured out how much money she had. She knew that if she could find a new job right away she and Marisela would be OK.

The next morning, after Lupe walked Marisela to school, she got a newspaper and looked at the job advertisements. There were a few ads for people who could sew. So she called the places. They told her to come in and fill out an application. She wrote down the addresses and worked out the bus routes. Then she walked to the bus stop. She went to three different dress factories and filled out papers for jobs. She took the bus home. It was already time to pick up Marisela from her child care center. Lupe was exhausted!

The next day, she did exactly the same thing. The next day, she called other friends who worked in dress factories to see if they knew of any job openings. "It's a slow time everywhere, Lupe," one friend told her. "Most of las fábricas are not hiring people right now." Marisela knew that her mami was worried. Marisela started getting worried too. She wondered if they would have enough money to pay the rent for the apartment. When she asked her mami if she could get a kitten, Lupe said, "Marisela, we can't afford to feed a kitten right now. I don't have a job." Marisela really felt sad; she really wanted one of kittens that her friend Zoreisha was giving away.

That day when Lupe went to pick up Marisela she was very discouraged. One of Marisela's teachers saw her come into the center and began to talk to her. "Lupe, Marisela told me that you lost your job. That must be really hard."

"Yes, I've looked everywhere for a new job but all the fábricas are laying off workers and no one seems to be hiring them! I'm getting worried."

"I have an idea for you. There is a group of women who are carpenters. They are looking for two new women to join their group."

"But I'm not a carpintera," said Lupe, "I wouldn't know what to do."

"They want to train two women to work with them. You don't have to know the job to start with—you only need to be willing to work hard. Besides, I remember when you came to volunteer here at the center, you fixed the stairs on the playhouse for us. I think you know more carpentry than you think."

"Well, that's true. I did learn some things about carpentry back in Mexico."

The teacher gave Lupe the phone number to call. When she and Marisela got back home, Lupe called a woman named Janet, who explained about the women carpenters who were called Building Women.

"Come in tomorrow and see me," said Janet. "I think we can work something out."

So, the next morning, Lupe kissed Marisela good-bye at school and took the bus to Janet's workshop. There were big saws, piles of wood, and all kinds of other equipment. Lupe was excited! They talked for a while, and Janet showed her around. At the end of the morning, Lupe had a new job! She was going to be a carpintera! She knew she could learn the job. It would be hard work, but she could do it!

That night, Lupe and Marisela celebrated.

"Now," said Marisela, "you can teach me how to build things and how to sew!"

"And now," said Lupe, "you can have one of those kittens that Zoreisha wants to give you."

"Hooray!" shouted Marisela.

Follow-Up

"My dad's a carpenter," said Darren. "He shows me how to do things."

"Do they have enough money now?" asked Kira.

"Well, they're not rich, but they will be all right," I answered. "And Lupe, Marisela's mother, is happy because she's learning a new job."

"Did she get her kitten?"

"Oh, yes."

"Did her mother make this dress?" asked Anne.

"I don't know. There are lots of people who are sewing clothes all over Los Angeles. Marisela's mommy was just one of them. But she made lots of dresses. But now, she's a carpenter. She's sewing dresses now only for Marisela and for friends."

"That was a pretend factory, right?" asked Emily.

"Yes, because Marisela is a doll."

"This isn't a true story, is it?" Emily asked again.

"It's a pretend story, but the same kinds of things happen to people for real all the time."

The look on Emily's face was one of interest and puzzlement. I could just see the inner workings of her mind in process.

"Well, my mama didn't have a job for awhile. And she was scared! She was crying," said Kira.

"Were you worried about it, too?"

"Yes!"

As a follow-up to the story, I made sure we had lots of sewing things available including many different skill levels—all the way from making pillows to embroidering with yarn on burlap to lacing cards. I brought in my sewing machine and borrowed another so that we could set up a portion of the room like a garment factory. I also made sure we had lots of hammers, nails, and wood so we could do carpentry. We set up our blocks like a wood shop and we named it Lupe's Carpentry Workshop.

"I wonder who made these overalls?" Jessie said one day as we were sewing on the machine.

"I don't know—there are a lot of people who are making clothes here in Los Angeles," I answered.

"It's hard to make these!" she said.

"Yes, you have to know how to sew really well!"

"I just can't do this at all," added Emily. "I don't understand how a doll could do it."

"Real people do the sewing, Emily. And they learn how to sew really well."

"Wow," she added.

All of the boys tried sewing and all of the girls did carpentry. Even though the thrust of the story was about respecting different kinds of work, it was very important to me to include a piece about gender roles. One of the ways that jobs are devalued is if they are done by women.

Information about NAEYC

NAEYC is . . .

an organization of nearly 100,000 members, founded in 1926, that is committed to fostering the development and learning of children from birth through age 8. Membership is open to all who share a commitment to promote excellence in early childhood education and to act on behalf of the needs and rights of all children.

NAEYC provides . . .

• *Young Children,* the peer-reviewed journal for early childhood educators

• **Books, posters, brochures, and videos** to expand your knowledge and commitment and support your work with young children and families

• **A network of nearly 450 local, state, and regional Affiliates**

• **Research-based position statements and professional standards** on issues such as inclusion, diversity, literacy, assessment, developmentally appropriate practice, and teacher preparation

• **Professional development resources and programs,** including the annual National Institute for Early Childhood Professional Development, improving the quality and consistency of early childhood professional preparation and leadership

• **Public policy information** through NAEYC resources and the Children's Champions Action Center, for conducting effective advocacy in government and in the media

• **An Annual Conference,** the largest education conference in North America, that brings people together from across the United States and other countries to share their expertise and advocate on behalf of children and families

• **A national, voluntary, professionally sponsored accreditation system** for high-quality early education through the National Academy of Early Childhood Programs

• *Early Childhood Research Quarterly,* the field's leading scholarly publication; special rate for NAEYC members

• **Young Children International,** encouraging information exchange and networking among NAEYC's international colleagues

• **Week of the Young Child** celebrations planned annually by NAEYC Affiliate Groups in communities across the country to call public attention to the critical significance of the child's early years

• **Insurance plans** for members and programs

For information about membership, publications, or other NAEYC services, visit NAEYC online at www.naeyc.org.

National Association for the Education of Young Children
1509 16th Street, NW
Washington, DC 20036-1426
202-232-8777 or 800-424-2460

A companion brochure on anti-bias curriculum, *Teaching Young Children to Resist Bias: What Parents Can Do,* is available from NAEYC. Single copies of this brochure are 50¢ each; 100 copies are $12.00. Order #565 (Spanish edition #564).